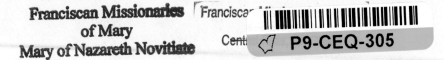

P9-CEQ-305

The Shroud of Turin, the True Cross, the blood of Januarius....
History, Mysticism, and the Catholic Church

RELICS

JOAN CARROLL CRUZ

author of The Incorruptibles

Our Sunday Visitor, Inc.
Huntington, Indiana 46750

Nihil Obstat:
Rev. John H. Miller, C.S.C.
Censor Librorum

Imprimatur: ☩Archbishop Philip M. Hannan, D.D.
Archbishop of New Orleans
July 4, 1983

The Nihil Obstat and Imprimatur are official declarations that a book or pamphlet is free of doctrinal or moral error. No implication is contained therein that those who have granted the Nihil Obstat or Imprimatur agree with the contents, opinions or statements expressed.

All scriptural quotations appearing in this work have been quoted or paraphrased from various editions of the Bible, including the Revised Standard Version and Douai-Rheims.

Library of Congress Catalogue No: 84-60744
ISBN 0-87973-701-8

Printed in the United States of America

Acknowledgements

ONCE again I am overwhelmingly indebted to Serena Bodellini Burke for assisting with the translation of Italian and French research material. I am likewise indebted to my brother, Daniel Carroll, for his help in editing this work. Gratitude is also extended to my husband and children for their help and patience during the five years I was occupied with this project.

As with a previous work, I relied heavily upon information gathered from European shrines, churches, monasteries and convents. The clergy and religious in 18 countries who kindly answered my queries are quite numerous. Their thoughtfulness and generosity in supplying books, pamphlets, magazines, papers and photographs proved invaluable to the research of this volume. Should I attempt to mention all my correspondents I would be afraid of unintentionally omitting a single name, therefore, I am taking this means to express to all of them my profound respect and deepest, heartfelt appreciation.

Joan Carroll Cruz

For my dear husband, Louis,
my children Tommy, Mike,
Jeannine, Carolyn, Louis
and his wife June,
for their patience, understanding,
helpfulness and love.

Table of Contents

Introduction

THE veneration of relics is practiced by Christians and non-Christians alike. It is in no way restricted to the Catholic religion, but is, to some extent, a primitive instinct with origins that predate Christianity.

It is known, for instance, that relics of Buddha, who died in 483 B.C., were distributed soon after his death. Although there remain only a limited number of authentic relics, parts of his body, including teeth and hairs, have been carefully preserved and enshrined in various domed, towerlike shrines that are found in cities and in the countryside throughout the Buddhist world. Known as stupas, or pagodas, these shrines are visited by both monks and laymen who walk around them in a practice known as circumambulation, making offerings of food and flowers while meditating on the doctrines taught by Buddha. Since there are only a few authentic relics, some of the millions of stupas in Asia contain only images, prayers or sacred writings as reminders of the prophet. The extreme development of relic worship among the Buddhists of every sect is a fact beyond dispute.

The relics of Confucius have been venerated every year by Chinese and Asian peoples since the year 195 B.C. when Emperor Kao Tsu of the Han Dynasty visited the tomb and offered sacrifices. Although Confucius laid no claim to being more than a man, his system of ethics gradually assumed the aspects of a religious cult. His *analects* are wise sayings similar to the Proverbs in the Bible. In accordance with tradition there are no statues or images of the sage, only tablets inscribed with his name. The followers of his teachings number more than 300 million, with many paying homage at his tomb.

Relics of Mohammed, who died in A.D. 632, are likewise revered, these being two hairs of the prophet which are kept in a reliquary resembling a domed temple that stands several feet high beside the huge rock in a building in Jerusalem called the Dome of the Rock. This limestone rock, measuring 58 feet by 44 feet, figures in Islamic, Jewish and Christian traditions and is something of a relic itself, being regarded by Moslems as the rock visited by an angel before the creation of Adam and Eve and the place where Mohammed ascended to heaven. Here Abraham is said to have nearly sacrificed his son, and it is claimed that

1

all the great prophets from Elijah onward prayed beside it. Many Christian churches profess the belief that Christ will descend on the spot at the Second Coming.

Since the early days of the Church the remains of a saint or holy person were called relics, from the Latin *Reliquiae* meaning remains. Relics are divided into three categories. First-class relics are parts of the bodies of saints and the instruments of Our Lord's Passion. Second-class relics are objects sanctified by close contact with saints, such as articles of clothing, objects used in life, or, in the case of a martyr, the instruments of his torture. Third-class relics are objects or cloths touched to either first- or second-class relics.

Material benefits obtained through relics of saints have often included miracles, as is witnessed not only by the history of the Church and the lives of the saints, but also by Sacred Scripture. In the Old Testament the relics of the prophet Elisha are mentioned. It is related that,

> "Elisha died and was buried. At the time bands of Moabites used to raid the land each year. Once some people were burying a man when suddenly they spied such a raiding band. They cast the dead man into the grave of the prophet Elisha, and everyone hurried off. But when the man came in contact with the bones of Elisha, he came back to life and rose to his feet" (2 Kings 13:20-21).

The New Testament mentions second-class relics of the Apostle Paul and the wonders the Lord worked through them. The Acts of the Apostles relate that,

> ". . . God worked extraordinary miracles at the hands of Paul. When handkerchiefs or cloths which had touched his skin were applied to the sick, their diseases were cured and evil spirits departed from them" (Acts 19:11-12).

Other cloths known as *brandea*, after lying for a time in contact with the remains of the holy apostles, were likewise treated as relics.

After the Apostolic times, the earliest record of honor paid relics of holy persons was written by the inhabitants of Smyrna about A.D. 156 which described the death of St. Polycarp. After the saint had been burned at the stake, we are told that his faithful disciple, after encountering delays by Roman officers,

> ". . . took up his bones which are more valuable than precious stones and finer than refined gold, and laid them in a suitable place where the Lord will permit us to gather ourselves together in gladness and joy

2

and to celebrate the birthday of his martyrdom."

The authenticity of this *passio* is beyond question, since it has been proven that it was written soon after Polycarp's martyrdom in the year 156 or 157.

We learn three times from St. Cyril of Jerusalem (d. 386) that relics of the wood of the cross, discovered about the year 318, were already distributed throughout the world. St. Gregory of Nyssa (d. about 400), in writing about the 40 martyrs, described how their bodies were burned by persecutors and recorded that,

> ". . . their ashes and all that the fire had spared have been distributed throughout the world so that almost every province has had its share of the blessing. I also myself have a portion of this gift and I have laid the bodies of my parents beside the relics of these warriors."

From the early Catholic standpoint there was no extravagance or abuse in honoring relics and, indeed, the practice was taken for granted by writers such as St. Augustine, St. Ambrose, St. Jerome, St. Gregory of Nyssa, St. Chrysostom, St. Gregory Nazianzen and by other great doctors without exception.

St. Jerome instructed that,

> "We do not worship, we do not adore for fear that we should bow down to the creature rather than to the Creator, but we venerate the relics of the martyrs in order the better to adore Him whose martyrs they are."

St. Cyril of Alexandria writes,

> "We by no means consider the holy martyrs to be gods, nor are we wont to bow down before them adoringly, but only relatively and reverentially."

Gregory the Great for a time expressed displeasure with the interference, dismemberment or the removal of the remains of the honored dead from one place to another, although he offered to send the Empress Constantina some filings from St. Peter's chains, a type of gift often mentioned in his writings. The saint is known to have enriched a little cross, destined to hang around the neck as an *encolpion*, with some filings both from St. Peter's chains and from the gridiron of St. Lawrence.

During the fourth century, St. Augustine wrote in *De Civitate Dei* (The City of God) about miracles wrought by soil from the Holy Land, flowers which had touched a reliquary or had been laid upon a particular altar, oil from lamps of the church of a martyr, or by other things no less remotely connected with the saints themselves.

The writings of St. Gregory of Tours abound in stories of the marvels wrought by relics, as well as of the practices used in their honor, while St. Theodore, archbishop of Canterbury, declared that, "The relics of the saints are to be venerated." He further adds that, ". . . if possible a candle is to burn there every night."

We learn from Kleinclausz, the contemporary biographer of Charlemagne (d. A.D. 814) that the emperor visited all the famous sanctuaries, St. Peter's of Rome being particularly dear to him and where he had been at least four times to pray. He likewise assisted at the transfer of sacred remains from one place to another and assisted at the dedication of churches where his favorite relics were enshrined. We learn further from Kleinclausz that "Charlemagne caused relics to be searched for at Rome, Constantinople and Jerusalem and, when found, shared them with his friends." Primary among the relics Charlemagne hoped to acquire were relics of Our Lord's Passion that had gone undiscovered by St. Helena (d. A.D. 330), who looked for and found the True Cross and many instruments used at the Crucifixion.

It would not be hard to imagine that the followers of Jesus Christ, being convinced that He was the Son of God, kept and honored all material objects that He had used during His life and those of His mother, and that they revered those objects that were used during His Passion. It would not be unreasonable to believe that these were faithfully guarded and passed with care from one generation to another. Nor would it seem improbable that honor would be given the remains of those who had upheld the Lord's honor, professed faith in Him in the face of persecution and torture, or those who willingly and heroically gave up their lives rather than denounce Him.

After the death of Jesus, the persecution of His followers brought about the death of countless martyrs. They were buried in the secrecy of the catacombs, which later became a veritable treasury of relics for worldwide distribution. Upon the tombs of these heroes of the Faith, religious services and Holy Mass were reverently offered. Soon the possession of these saintly remains became an obsession and a matter of jealous rivalry. In order that no one person or group should be privileged above any other, the remains were divided, the least part being as cherished and reverenced as the whole.

While many instinctively shrink from the very thought of disturbing the dead, these divisions of the remains were not acts of desecration, but acts of veneration. Since the number of Christians increased rapidly, and the apostles and disciples put into practice the Lord's injunction that they should go forth and share the Gospel with all nations,

4

it seemed reasonable that they should take with them all they held dear, including the relics of their honored dead.

After the year 313 when Constantine issued the Edict of Milan, putting an end to persecution of the Christians, the monuments built over the graves of the martyrs were transformed into magnificent sanctuaries and basilicas. When churches were erected apart from the tombs of martyrs, the remains of one or the other of the martyrs, or at least part of these, were transferred and enshrined often within the altars. This gave rise to the practice, down to modern times, of having relics of saints enclosed in a flat stone situated in the center of the altar directly beneath the spot where the Holy Sacrifice of the Mass is offered.

It is impossible to determine the time when the practice of venerating minute fragments of the bodies of saints first came into vogue, but it is known to have been widespread during the fourth century. These small pieces of bone or blood were, for those who possessed them, imbued with a spiritual force that could produce miracles through the intercession of the saint to whom they belonged. They were so greatly esteemed by their owners that every kind of priceless jewel, every manner of artistry and craftsmanship were expended upon the cases in which they were preserved, and excessive amounts of money were invested in the shrines that housed them. To these shrines, many of which are still the glory of the land, pilgrims traveled great distances to pray and make vows. When the cult of relics came to its full height during the Middle Ages, many great churches owed their sanctity and renown simply to the presence of important relics.

With the increase in pilgrimages and processions to the churches that possessed outstanding relics, a rival town could improve its fortunes by acquiring a precious relic, sometimes by bold theft, thus transforming itself into a place of honor that deserved respect and attention. Eventually monasteries and parishes sought to increase their prestige by possession of treasured relics. Since the supply was naturally limited this often led to unfortunate rivalries. Few saints were allowed to rest in peace. Tombs were ransacked, the remains quarreled over, translated from one church to another, and dismembered to be divided among numerous shrines. The securing and honoring of relics became so widespread that it was impossible to control avarice and competition or to prevent certain abuses, such as the distribution of fraudulent relics.

As early as the fourth century St. Augustine denounced certain impostors wandering about in the clothing of monks who were profiting from the sale of spurious relics. The writings of St. Gregory the Great (d. A.D. 604) and St. Gregory of Tours (d. A.D. 593) prove that many un-

5

principled persons found a means of enriching themselves by a trade in relics, the majority of which were fraudulent. Ecclesiastical authority did what it could to secure the faithful against deception, but the discovery and distribution of huge collections of relics made the task impossible to properly manage.

The Councils of Lyon (1245 and 1275) prohibited the veneration of recently found relics unless they were first approved by the Roman pontiff. This was echoed by Bishop Quivil of Exeter in 1287 when he wrote,

> "We command the prohibition to be carefully observed by all, and decree that no person shall expose relics for sale, and that neither stones, nor fountains, trees, wood, or garments shall in any way be venerated on account of dreams or on fictitious grounds."

The decrees of synods upon this subject are practical and sensible and prove that some check was exercised upon the excesses of the unscrupulous and the mercenary. The Council of Trent (1545-1563), which ranks with Vatican II as the greatest ecumenical council held in the West, ordered bishops to take special pains in this regard and established the norm that relics be subject to the control of the Vatican. It is unknown when it became customary for a relic to be accompanied by a special document of authentication.

At a later time it was maintained that those who made or knowingly sold, distributed or displayed false relics for veneration incurred *ipso facto* excommunication reserved to the bishops.

Before the 1983 revisions in the Church's Code of Canon Law, the rules regarding relics were outlined in a special section (Canons 1276-1289). At the present time first-, second- and third-class relics may be authenticated and distributed by religious orders on the approval of the local bishop. But the most formidable task of authenticating and historically approving first-class relics rests with the Relic Office in the Vatican which receives, keeps and distributes relics of saints and those holy persons declared *blessed* who are candidates for canonization.

In this matter we are presently instructed by the vicar general of the Diocese of Rome,

> "Relics should be handled intelligently, without abuses. They are signs which can be useful to spread devotion to holy men and women all over the world. When relics are requested for private and public veneration they must be accompanied by official papers warranting their validity and authenticity. In no way may they be sold. A contribution may be requested merely to cover expenses such as for the relic case and mailing charges."

No one is constrained to pay homage to a relic, and supposing it to be false, no dishonor is done to God by the continuance of an error which has been handed down in perfect good faith for many centuries. Nor can ecclesiastical authority be blamed for permitting the continuance of a cult which extends back into remote antiquity. The Council of Trent dealt with this matter and noted that while no Catholic is formally bound to the veneration of relics, he is, nevertheless, forbidden to say that such veneration ought not to be given authentic relics.

Devotion of ancient date, deeply rooted in the heart of people cannot be swept away without some measure of popular disturbance. To create this disquiet by forbidding honor paid to articles of doubtful authenticity might be injurious to the faith of many unless proof of falsity is so overwhelming as to amount to a certainty. There is justification, then, for the practice of the Holy See in allowing the cult of certain doubtful ancient relics to continue.

It can be reasonably assumed that some famous relics are almost certainly false, but there is no need to assume deliberate fraud. Some have come about by facsimiles and imitations being touched to a shrine or the contents, and having some sanctity achieved as a result. In the case of the holy nails, facsimiles which had touched the authentic ones were at first venerated as articles of a second-class nature that simply touched the original, but with the passage of time and the dimming of memories, or the misplacement of written histories, they were eventually regarded as the original itself.

In some ancient inventories the extravagance and utter improbability of many of the entries cannot escape the most uncritical, yet many of our cherished relics which the skeptic might label of doubtful origin or which have been looked upon by some with suspicion might well be authentic and worthy of our honor and attention.

It should be mentioned that the relics included in this work are presented with facts gathered from extensive research to which has been added data as supplied by the custodians of shrines under consideration. The genuineness of each is left to the judgment and discernment of the reader.

One historian has observed that the most suspicious circumstances about the crucifixion relics is the astounding fact that they were discovered by the Empress Helena about 300 years after the event. When a queen is known to be a searcher of relics, it can be anticipated that relics in any amount would be forthcoming. It was also noted that an enthusiast of 80 years is not exactly the person to discriminate between truth and fraud, especially when all her sympathies are one way. We pray and assume that the saint worked under divine inspiration and selected the articles with care.

Several saints and holy persons have been given the grace to distinguish true from false relics. The Venerable Ann Catherine Emmerick could not only distinguish false from true relics, but could identify their nature and origin. Several chapters are dedicated to this subject in her biography. During her ecstasies, the stigmatist Therese Neumann could likewise identify and describe true relics and distinguish these from false ones.

It should be noted that if a relic is false, the saint would still be honored since we pray not to a bit of bone, but to the saint to whom it is supposed to belong.

The veneration of relics is permitted and encouraged by the Church out of honor for the bodies of the saints — which were temples of the Holy Spirit, and which will be raised to eternal glory — and to satisfy the universal instinct of mankind to treat with affection and reverence the material souvenirs of those we love. To this the Council of Trent concurred and added long ago that relics could be honored, since through them many benefits are granted to men by God.

The Church has repeatedly warned, however, against the temptation to confuse sound spirituality with magic, blasphemous idolatry and superstitions.

Vatican II addressed the matter of relic veneration by noting that,

> "The saints have been traditionally honored in the church and their authentic relics and images held in veneration. For the feasts of the saints proclaim the wonderful works of Christ in His servants, and display to the faithful fitting examples for their imitation."

While the acquisition or honoring of relics is commendable, there are relics of a nonmaterialistic nature which are more deserving of our attention. St. Gertrude the Great learned the identity of these, and to this we should give careful consideration since Our Lord himself instructed her in the matter. It is recorded in her biography that the saint desired to have some relics of the wood of the cross. To this yearning Our Lord said to her,

> "If you desire to have some relics which will draw My Heart into yours, read My Passion, and meditate attentively on every word contained therein and it will be to you a true relic which will merit more graces for you than any other . . . thence you may know and be assured that the words which I uttered when on earth are the most precious relics which you can possess."

Relics
of
Jesus
Christ

These Miraculous Hosts have remained white, fresh and incorrupt since 1730, when they were stolen from the Church of St. Francis in Siena and later recovered.

Eucharistic Miracles

EUCHARISTIC miracles have authenticated the real presence of Christ in the sacrament of the altar since the earliest ages of the Church. In such miracles the host is transformed into flesh, sometimes it has bled, or was preserved for long periods of time. As early as the third century St. Cyprian mentioned a eucharistic miracle while Sozomen, a fifth-century historian, relates another. In the eighth century the most complete, the most carefully recorded, the best preserved, and certainly the most scientifically studied of such miracles occurred in Lanciano, Italy.

During the 700th year of Our Lord, in a monastery then named for St. Longinus, the Roman centurion who pierced the side of Christ with a lance, a monk of the Order of St. Basil was celebrating Holy Mass according to the Latin Rite. Although his name is unknown, it is reported in an ancient document that he was "... versed in the sciences of the world, but ignorant in that of God." Having suffered from recurrent doubts regarding transsubstantiation, the turning of the bread and wine into the invisible body and blood of Christ, he had spoken the solemn words of consecration when the host was suddenly changed into a circle of flesh while the wine was transformed into blood. Bewildered at first by what he had witnessed he eventually regained his composure and though weeping joyously he announced to the congregation, "O fortunate witnesses to whom the Blessed God, to confound my unbelief has wished to reveal Himself visible to our eyes. Come brethren and marvel at our God so close to us. Behold the flesh and blood of our Most Beloved Christ."[1]

The congregation rushed to the altar, wondered at the sight, and went forth to spread the news to townspeople, who in turn came to witness the miracle for themselves.

The flesh remained intact, but the blood in the chalice soon divided itself into five pellets of unequal sizes and irregular shapes. It has been

[1]*The Eucharistic Miracle of Lanciano, Italy*, Bruno Sammaciccia, Sanctuary of the Eucharistic Miracle, Lanciano, Italy, 1977, p. 18.

10

conjectured that Divine Providence prompted the monks to undertake the weighing of the nuggets. On a scale obtained from the archbishop it was discovered that one nugget weighed the same as all five together, two as much as any three, and the smallest as much as the largest.[2]

The host and the five pellets were placed in a reliquary of artistic ivory and were safeguarded in turn by three religious orders. At the time of the miracle the Church of St. Longinus was staffed by Basilian monks, but was abandoned by them at the close of the 12th century, the property passing quickly to the Benedictines and then to the Franciscans, who had to demolish the old church because of damage incurred by earthquakes. The new church that was built on the site was dedicated to their founding father.

History records that after the miracle was certified, a document was written on parchment in both Greek and Latin and was safeguarded by the monks between two tablets. We are told that in the first years of the 16th century, when the monastery was then in the possession of the Franciscans, the document was shown to two visiting monks of the Order of St. Basil. Wishing perhaps to save their order the disgrace of having the weakness of one of their members persist throughout history, they left during the night with the document, and despite many investigations, the Franciscans "... have never been able to find out whither the two fugitives had fled."

The ivory reliquary was replaced in 1713 by the one which now exhibits the relics. The ostensorium is of finely sculptured silver, the flesh of the host being held between two round crystals, the nuggets of blood being enclosed in a chalice of artistically etched crystal which some believe might be the actual chalice in which the miraculous change occurred.

On a February day in 1514 Monsignor Rodrigues verified in the presence of reputable witnesses that the total weight of the five pellets of congealed blood was equal to the weight of either of them, a fact that was later chiseled on a marble tablet dated 1636 that is still located in the church. During subsequent authentications, however, the prodigy was not repeated.[3] A number of these authentications have been performed throughout the ages, but the last verification in 1970 is the most scientifically complete and it is the examination that we will now consider.

Performed under strict scientific criteria, the task was assigned to Professor Doctor Odoardo Linoli, university professor at large in anatomy and pathological histology, and in chemistry and clinical mi-

[2]*Ibid.* p. 18.
[3]*Ibid.* pp. 38-39

11

croscopy, head physician of the united hospitals of Arezzo. Professor Linoli also availed himself of the services of Doctor Ruggero Bertelli, a professor emeritus of normal human anatomy at the University of Siena, who concurred with all of Professor Linoli's conclusions and who additionally presented an official document to that effect.[4]

Assembled in the sacristy of the Church of St. Francis on November 18, 1970, were the archbishop of Lanciano, the bishop of Ortona, the provincial to the Friars Minor Conventual, the chancellor of the archdiocese, the reverend secretary of the archbishop and the entire community of the monastery together with Professor Linoli.

On examining the ostensorium it was observed that the lunette containing the flesh was not hermetically sealed and that the particles of the unleavened bread that had remained for many years had by then entirely disappeared. The flesh was described as being yellow-brown in color, irregular and roundish in shape, thicker and wrinkled along the periphery, becoming gradually thinner as it reached the central area where the tissue was frayed with small extensions protruding toward the empty space in the middle. A small sample was taken from a thicker part for examination in the laboratory of the hospital in Arezzo.[5]

On examining the five pellets of blood it was noted that the prodigy of identical weight of one pellet as against the other four was not effected as it was for the last time in 1574. The five pellets were found to be quite irregular in form, finely wrinkled, compact, homogeneous and hard in consistency, being a yellow-chestnut color and having the appearance of chalk. A small sample was taken from the central part of one pellet for microscopic examination and scientific study.[6] Later, after all the studies were completed, the fragments of both relics were returned to the church for safekeeping.

The conclusions reached by Professor Linoli were presented on March 4, 1971, in detailed medical and scientific terminology to a prestigious assembly including ecclesiastical officials, the provincials and superiors of the Friars Minor Conventual, representatives of religious houses in the city, as well as civil, judicial, political and military authorities, representatives of the medical staffs of the city hospitals, various Religious of the city and a number of the city's residents.

The conclusions that were presented were later discussed by the Very Rev. Father Bruno Luciani and Professor Urbano, the chief analyst of the city hospital of Lanciano and a professor at the University of Flor-

[4]*Ibid.* p. 72.
[5]*Ibid.* pp. 44-48.
[6]*Ibid.* pp. 44-50.

ence. A copy of the scientific report and the minutes of the meeting and discussions are kept in the archives of the monastery. True copies were sent to various Church officials and superiors of the order, while another was delivered in a private audience to His Holiness Pope Paul VI.

As a result of the histological studies the following facts were compiled: The flesh was identified as striated muscular tissue of the myocardium (heart wall) having no trace whatsoever of any materials or agents used for the preservation of flesh.[7] Both the flesh and the sample of blood were found to be of human origin, empathically excluding the possibility that it was from an animal species.[8] The blood as well as the flesh were found to belong to the same blood type, AB.[9] The blood of the Eucharistic Miracle was found to contain the following minerals: chloride, phosphorus, magnesium, potassium, sodium in a lesser degree, but calcium in a greater quantity.[10] Proteins in the clotted blood were found to be normally fractionated with the same percentage ratio as those found in fresh and normal blood.[11]

Professor Linoli further stated that the blood, had it been taken from a cadaver, would have been rapidly altered through spoilage and decay and that his studies conclusively reject the possibility of a fraud perpetrated centuries ago. In fact, he maintained that only a hand experienced in anatomic dissection could have obtained from a hollow internal organ, the heart, such an expert cut made tangentially. That is, a round cut, thick on the outer edges and lessening uniformly in a gradual degree into nothingness in the central area.[12] The doctor ended his report by stating that while the natural condition of the flesh and blood were conserved in receptacles not hermetically sealed, they were not damaged, although they were exposed to the influences of physical, atmospheric and biological agents.[13]

The ostensorium containing the relics was previously kept to the side of the altar in the Church of St. Francis, but it is now situated in an open tabernacle atop the main tabernacle of the high altar. A stairway at the back of the altar enables the visitor to climb closer, where he can view the reliquary containing the flesh and blood through an opening that has been conveniently provided.

The visitor will notice that the host appears rosy in color when it is backlighted, and as he gazes he must undoubtedly reflect upon the

[7]*Ibid.* p. 54.
[8]*Ibid.* pp. 60-62.
[9]*Ibid.* pp. 63-65.
[10]*Ibid.* p. 70.
[11]*Ibid.* p. 70.
[12]*Ibid.* pp. 70-71.
[13]*Ibid.* p. 71

countless numbers of others who have looked upon this Eucharistic Miracle during its 1200 years of existence.[14]

The Eucharistic Miracle that occurred at Bolsena, Italy, is noteworthy because an investigation was immediately initiated by Pope Urban IV who, on being satisfied with the results, commissioned St. Thomas Aquinas to write the Mass and Office of the Body of Christ, a feast initiated one year following the miracle and now celebrated throughout the world as the Feast of Corpus Christi.

The year was 1263 when Peter of Prague, a Bohemian priest, paused at Bolsena on his journey to Rome. Bolsena was then famous for the shrine of St. Christiana and it was over this saint's tomb that the priest celebrated Holy Mass that eventful morning. Although a devout priest, he nevertheless doubted the real presence of Christ and was astonished, on breaking the host after the Consecration, to see blood flowing from it onto the corporal, the square piece of linen placed under the chalice and host during Mass. An effort was made to conceal the bloody miracle, but realizing that such an occurrence could not be kept secret the priest interrupted the Mass and asked to be taken to neighboring Orvieto where the pope had sought refuge. After listening to the account, Pope Urban IV absolved the emotional priest of his doubts and ordered an immediate investigation. The facts were speedily compiled. The pope ordered the bishop of the diocese to bring the miraculous host, together with the linen that bore the splotches of blood, to Orvieto in solemn procession. The corporal was enshrined in the cathedral of the city where it is still venerated.

In 1964, on the 700th anniversary of the institution of the Feast of Corpus Christi, Pope Paul VI attended ceremonies in the cathedral after flying from the Vatican to Orvieto by helicopter, the first pope ever to use such a means of transportation.

The Eucharistic Miracle of Santarem is unique in that it did not occur in a church, but nearby, and was not occasioned by a doubting priest as mentioned previously, but by a woman who was fullyl aware of the sacrilege involved.

The miracle originated in the parish of St. Stephen, located in Santarem, Portugal, 35 miles south of Fatima. A woman of the parish, unhappy with the activities of an unfaithful husband, had consulted a sorceress who promised a deliverance from her trials for the price of a consecrated host. After many hesitations the woman consented, re-

[14]The foregoing has been summarized from the book published by the Church of the Eucharistic Miracle in which all the tests made on the samples are more thoroughly detailed, together with photographs of the microscopic studies.

14

ceived Holy Communion, but removed the Host from her mouth and wrapped it in her veil with the intention of conveying it to the sorceress. Within moments blood issued from the Host and increased in volume until it dripped from the cloth, thereby attracting the attention of bystanders. On seeing blood on the woman's hand and arm, and thinking her injured, the witnesses rushed forward to help. The woman avoided their concern and ran to her home, leaving a trail of blood behind her. Hoping to hide the bloody veil and its contents, she placed them in a chest; but during the night she was obliged to reveal her sin to her husband when a mysterious light penetrated the trunk and illuminated the house.

Both knelt in adoration for the remaining hours until dawn, when the priest was summoned. News of the mysterious happenings spread quickly, attracting countless people who wished to contemplate the miracle. Because of the furor, an episcopal investigation was promptly initiated.

The Host was soon taken in procession to the Church of St. Stephen where it was encased in wax and secured in the tabernacle. Sometime later, when the tabernacle was opened, another miracle was discovered. The wax that had encased the Host was found broken in pieces with the Host now enclosed in a crystal pyx. The Host was later placed in the gold and silver monstrance in which it is still contained.

After receiving the approbation of ecclesiastical authorities, who saw no reason to condemn or suppress the miracle, the Church of St. Stephen was renamed the Church of the Miracle. It is here that the Host is still preserved and willingly displayed for the admiration and veneration of pilgrims.

The Host, as seen by visitors, appears to be a thin piece of flesh with delicate streaks of blood running from top to bottom, where a quantity of blood is collected. In the opinion of a physician who recently examined the miracle, the blood that is coagulated at the bottom appears to be fresh blood of recent clotting.

This miracle, occurring as it did in the early part of the 13th century, has endured for over 700 years.

Siena, Italy, is known worldwide as the home of St. Catherine, the Dominican mystic and the second woman installed as a doctor of the Church, and also as the home of St. Bernardine, the Franciscan reformer and preacher. The city is, regrettably, little known outside the region for the sustaining miracle that is guarded in the Church of St. Francis.

To introduce the miracle we must first look back through history to the 13th century when the people of the city first began the traditional vigil services in honor of the Feast of the Assumption. On August 14, 1730, while most of the Sienese population were attending the services in the cathedral, together with all the priests of the city, thieves entered the deserted Church of St. Francis. Taking advantage of the friars' absence, they made for the chapel where the Blessed Sacrament was kept, picked the lock to the tabernacle and carried away the golden ciborium that contained consecrated Hosts.

The theft went undiscovered until the next morning when the priest opened the tabernacle at the Communion of the Mass. Later, when a parishioner found the lid of the ciborium lying in the street, the suspicion of a sacrilege was confirmed. The resultant anxiety of the parishioners forced a cancellation of the festivities planned for the feast. The archbishop ordered public prayers of reparation, while the civil authorities began a search for the consecrated Hosts and the culprits who had taken them.

A few days later, on August 17, while a priest was praying in the Church of St. Mary in Provenzano, his attention was directed toward a whiteness protruding from the offering box attached to his prie-dieu. Recognizing the substance as a Host, the cleric informed the other priests of the church, who in turn notified the archbishop and the friars of the Church of St. Francis.

When the offering box was opened in the presence of local priests and the representative of the archbishop, a large number of Hosts were found, some of which were suspended by cobwebs. The Hosts were compared with the unconsecrated ones used in the Church of St. Francis, and these proved to be exactly the same shape and had on them the same stamp that was impressed by the irons upon which they were baked. The number of Hosts corresponded exactly to the amount the Franciscan friar had estimated he had placed in the ciborium before they were consecrated. These numbered 348 whole Hosts and six halves.

Since the offering box was opened but once a year, the Hosts were covered with dust and debris that had collected in it. After being carefully cleaned by the priests the Hosts were enclosed in a ciborium that was placed inside the tabernacle of the main altar of the Church of St. Mary. The following day Archbishop Alessandro Zondadari, in the company of a great gathering of townspeople, carried the Sacred Hosts in solemn procession back to the Church of St. Francis.

It has been wondered through the two centuries that followed why the Hosts were not consumed by a priest during Mass, which would have been the ordinary procedure in such a case. While there is no definite answer, there are two theories. One explanation is that crowds of people from both Siena and neighboring cities gathered in the church to offer prayers of reparation before the Sacred Particles, forcing the priests to conserve them for a time. The other reason the priests did not consume them is perhaps because of their soiled condition. While they were superficially cleaned after their discovery, they still retained a great deal of dirt. In such cases it is not necessary to consume consecrated Hosts but to permit them to deteriorate naturally, at which time the Real Presence would no longer exist.

To the amazement of the clergy, the Hosts did not deteriorate, but remained fresh and pleasant smelling. With the passage of time the Conventual Franciscans were convinced of a continuing miracle of preservation.

Fifty years after the recovery of the stolen Hosts an official investigation was conducted to determine the validity of the miracle. The minister general of the order, Father Carlo Vipera, examined the hosts on April 14, 1780, and upon tasting one of them found it fresh and incorrupt. Since a number of the Hosts had been distributed during the preceeding years, the minister general ordered that the remaining 230 particles be placed in a new ciborium and additionally forbade further distributions.

A more detailed investigation took place in 1789 by Archbishop Tiberio Borghese of Siena with a number of theologians and other dignitaries. After an examination of the hosts under a microscope, the commission declared that they were perfectly intact with no trace of deterioration. The three Franciscans who had been present at the previous investigation of 1780 were questioned under oath by the archbishop. It was then established that the Hosts under examination were the same ones stolen in 1730.

As a test to strengthen the authenticity of the miracle, the archbishop, during this 1789 examination, had unconsecrated hosts placed in a sealed box that was kept under lock in the chancery office. Ten years later these were examined and were found to be not only disfigured, but also withered. In 1850, 61 years after they were placed in a sealed box, three unconsecrated hosts were found reduced to particles of a dark yellow color while the consecrated Hosts retained their original freshness.

Other examinations were made at intervals throughout the years, the most significant one taking place in 1914 on the authority of Pope Saint Pius X. At this time the archbishop selected a distinguished panel of investigators, including various scientists and professors from Siena and Pisa, as well as theologians and Church officials.

The results of acid and starch tests performed with one of the frag-

17

ments indicated a normal starch content. The conclusion reached from microscopic tests indicated that the Hosts had been made of roughly sifted wheat flour that was well preserved.

The commission agreed that unleavened bread, if prepared under sterile conditions and if kept in an airtight antiseptically cleaned container could be kept for an extremely long time; unleavened bread prepared in a normal fashion and kept exposed to air and the activity of microorganisms could be kept intact for no more than a few years. It was concluded that the stolen Hosts were both prepared without scientific precautions and were kept under ordinary conditions that should have caused their decay more than a century before.[15] The commission concluded that the preservation was extraordinary, "... e la scienza stessa che proclama qui lo straordinario."[16]

Another investigation was conducted in 1922, this one in the presence of Cardinal Giovanni Tacci, who was accompanied by the archbishop of Siena and by the bishops of Montepulciano, Foligno and Grosseto. Again the results were the same: the Hosts tasted like unleavened bread, were starchy in composition and were completely preserved with no explanation being given for their conservation.

In 1950 the Miraculous Hosts were taken from the old container and placed in a more elaborate and costly one that caught the eye and the fancy of another thief.

Despite the precautions of the priests, another sacrilegious theft took place during the night of August 5, 1951. This time the thief was considerate enough to take only the container and left the Hosts in a corner of the tabernacle. Placed temporarily in a silver ciborium which the archbishop himself sealed, the Hosts were counted and were found to be 223 in number. After being photographed they were placed in an elaborate container that replaced the one that was stolen.

The miraculously preserved Hosts are displayed publicly on various occasions, but especially on the 17th of each month, which commemorates the day the Hosts were found after the first theft. On the Feast of Corpus Christi the sacred particles are placed in their processional monstrance and are triumphantly carried in procession from the church through the streets of the town, an observance in which the whole population participates.

Of the many distinguished visitors who have worshiped the Hosts are St. John Bosco and Pope John XXIII, who signed the album of vis-

---

[15]*Una Delle Piu Grandi Meraviglie*, Felice M. Rossetti, Edizioni Periccioli, Siena, Italy, 1965. pp. 159-160.
[16]*Ibid.*, p. 161.

18

itors on May 29, 1954, when he was still the patriarch of Venice. Although unable to visit the Miraculous Hosts, Pope Pius X, Benedict XV, Pius XI and Pius XII issued statements of interest and admiration.

With a unanimous voice the faithful, priests, bishops, cardinals and popes themselves marvel and worship the Holy Hosts as a permanent miracle, both complete and perfect, that has endured for 250 years — a miracle that has kept the Hosts shiny, whole and maintaining the characteristic scent of unleavened bread. Since the particles are in such a perfect state of conservation, theology assures that the Hosts consecrated in 1730 are still in reality the Body of Christ.[17]

The late Professor Doctor Siro Grimaldi, professor of chemistry of the University of Siena, director of the Municipal Chemical Laboratory, and the holder of several other distinguished positions in the field of chemistry, was the chief chemical examiner of the Holy Particles in 1914. Thereafter he gave numerous and elaborate statements concerning the miraculous nature of the Hosts and in addition wrote a book about the miracle entitled *Uno Scienziato Adora* (A Scientific Adorer). In 1914 he declared: "The Holy Particles of unleavened bread represent an example of perfect preservation . . . a singular phenomenon that inverts the natural law of the conservation of organic material. It is a unique fact in the annals of science."[18]

The eucharistic miracle of Faverney, France, involved not a Host turned to flesh nor one that bled, but consisted of a holy, yet a flagrant, disregard for the laws of gravity.

The abbey in whose church the miracle occurred was established by St. Gudwal as far back as the eighth century. Under the Rule of St. Benedict it was named *Notre Dame de la Blanche*, Our Lady of the White, for a small statue that is now situated in the chapel to the right of the choir. Construction of the church was begun in the 11th century with men Religious replacing the nuns in 1132. Various architectural enlargements and improvements were made throughout the centuries before the year 1608 when the grand miracle took place.

The religious life of the abbey at that time was not fervent, with the community numbering only six monks and two novices, of which one, Friar Hudelot, was only 15 years of age. In order to maintain the people's faith then weakened by the Protestant cynicism of the time, the monks organized every year certain ceremonies, including adoration of the Blessed Sacrament, in honor of Whitsunday (Pentecost) and the

[17]*Il Miracolo Eucaristico Permanente Di Siena.* A cura dei Frati Minori Conventuali del Santuario Eucaristico di Siena, Siena, Italy, 1962, p. 71.
[18]*Ibid.* p. 71.

Monday following the feast. In preparation for the ceremonies an altar of repose was arranged before a decorative grille near the entrance gate of their choir. The services on Whitsunday were attended by a great number of people, and at nightfall, when the doors to the church were shut and the monks were preparing to retire, two oil lamps were left burning before the Sacrament left exposed on the altar.

The following day, Monday, May 26, when the sacristan, Don Garnier, opened the doors he found the church filled with smoke and flames rising on all sides of the altar. He at once rushed to the monastery to warn the monks, who lost no time in joining his efforts to save the church. While the flames were being extinguished, it was the young monk, Hudelot, who discovered the monstrance suspended in the air, slightly inclined toward, but not touching, the grille at the back of the altar.[19]

News of the miracle spread quickly, with villagers and priests from surrounding areas soon filling the church. Many knelt in awe before the suspended monstrance while a great many of the skeptics approached the altar to examine the miracle for themselves. Throughout the rest of the day and during the night no restrictions were made and the curious were permitted to move freely about the altar.

The Host that defied gravity at Faverney, France

During the early morning hours of Tuesday, May 27, priests came from surrounding neighborhoods and took turns in unbroken sequence in offering Holy Mass during the time of the miracle. At about 10 o'clock, during the Consecration of the Mass celebrated by the priest — Nicolas Aubry, Curé of Menoux — the congregation saw the monstrance move its angle to a vertical position and slowly descend to the altar below it that had been constructed for that eventuality. The suspension of the monstrance had lasted 33 hours.[20]

As early as May 31 an inquiry was ordered by His Grace, Archbishop Ferdinand de Rye. Fifty-four depositions were collected from monks, priests, peasants and villagers. Two months later, on July 30, 1608, after studying the depositions and the material collected during his investigation, the archbishop concluded in favor of the miracle.

[19]*Le Miracle de Faverney.* M. Lescuyer & Fils. Imprimeurs a Lyon. 1957. pp. 19-22.
[20]*Ibid.* pp. 30-31

We should study in some detail certain pertinent aspects of this miraculous happening.

Burned in the fire were the altar table, which was reduced to a heap of ashes with the exception of the four legs; all the altar linens and certain ornaments were destroyed. One of the two chandeliers placed as decoration on either side of the altar was found melted from the force of the heat, yet despite this heat the ostensorium was preserved from harm. The two Hosts in this vessel were intact and suffered only a slight scorching. Four articles inside the crystal tube attached to the ostensorium were also spared injury. These included a relic of St. Agatha, a small piece of protective silk, a papal proclamation of indulgences, and an episcopal letter whose wax seal melted and ran over the parchment without altering the text.

Concerning the suspension of the ostensorium, 54 witnesses, including many priests, affirmed that while the vessel seemed to incline toward the grille, the little cross atop the monstrance was not in contact with it and that the monstrance remained without support for 33 hours. These witnesses who gave sworn statements also signed a document that is still preserved in the church. They also swore that the suspension of the vessel was not affected by the vibrations of the people who moved around it, nor from people constantly moving in and out of the church, by those standing and whispering beside the burned altar, by those who touched the nearby grille, nor by the activities of the monks in removing the effects of the fire and assembling a temporary altar in the same location.[21]

In December 1608, the year of the miracle, one of the two Hosts that was in the monstrance at the time of the miracle was solemnly transferred to the city of Dole, which was then the capital of the county.

During the time of the French Revolution of 1790, the ostensorium was unfortunately destroyed, but the Host was preserved from harm by members of the municipal council of Faverney who kept it hidden until the danger passed. In time a monstrance was reproduced from paintings dating before the Revolution. The Host kept within this new monstrance is the same one that survived the fire of 1608.

The wonder of this miracle, in addition, of course, to the suspension of 33 hours, is how and why the Hosts were preserved together with the crystal tube containing perishable articles, while the force of the heat was such that a nearby chandelier was reduced to a melted ruin.[22]

[21]*Ibid.*, pp. 26-31
[22]Eucharistic miracles are numerous and have occurred in all ages of the Church. Because their histories are so varied and interesting, they will be the subject of the author's next work.

21

The Holy Manger

TO catalogue the relics of Jesus Christ, these being articles He touched or used during His lifetime, we should perhaps start at the very
beginning with His holy birth. The first relic to be considered would be
the manger at Bethlehem. The remains of this consist of boards, black-
ened with age, that are kept in a sumptuous reliquary. These five boards
are of special interest to visitors and those who report on the holy relics
kept in the Basilica of St. Mary Major in Rome. The boards are believed
to have been brought to the basilica from the Holy Land during the pontificate of Pope Theodore (640-649), who was himself a native of
Palestine. Four of the boards are considered to be boards from the Holy
Manger. One board is different than the others. On its surface are Greek
characters which are understood to be a note etched by an artist as a re-
minder of religious figures still to be sculptured. The remaining four
boards were examined in 1893 and were found to be of sycamore wood,
of which there are several varieties in the Holy Land.

The crib or manger in which the Child Jesus was placed after His
birth is thought to have been the place in the stable where food for
domestic animals was placed, and is believed to have been hewn from
the limestone of the cave walls. One theory is that the four boards were
used as supports for the limestone manger, two on each end in the form
of an X. Another theory is that the shape of the wood suggests that
when fitted together with certain additional parts, they would have
formed a proper bottom for a crib.

The gold and silver reliquary in which the relics of the crib are kept
is topped by a figure of the Christ Child in a reclining position with one
hand raised in blessing. Beneath him is a container in the shape of a bowl
having several crystal windows through which the boards may be seen.
The five pieces of wood are secured to one another by two metal strips
which suggest an ancient assembly.

Of the many relics kept by the Basilica of St. Mary Major, the two
most greatly prized are the portrait of Our Lady, Salus Populi Romani,
mentioned elsewhere in this volume, and the relics of the manger.[1]

---

[1] The preceding was summarized from a paper supplied by the Basilica of St. Mary Major, entitled
La Sacra Culla.

The Swaddling Cloth

A CLOTH believed to have served as the Baby Jesus' swaddling garment is kept in a unique reliquary in the shrine that Charlemagne built called Aix La Chapelle in Aachen, Germany.

The city of Aachen was made the capital of the empire by Charlemagne and it remained the capital of the Holy Roman Empire until the middle of the 16th century. Thirty-seven German emperors were crowned there. When Charlemagne built the cathedral, he took pride in securing for it many important relics from the Holy Land and Rome. One of the most valued of these was the cloth believed to have been worn by the Infant Jesus.

The golden reliquary, whose hollow encloses the relic, depicts the Presentation in the Temple. Called the Reliquary Shrine for the Arm of St. Simeon, the shrine was built to house the bone of the saint, but actually enshrines the Holy Cloth. On one side of the small short-legged, gem-studded table is a golden figure of the Blessed Mother with her outstretched hands holding the two doves of the temple offering. On the opposite end is the golden figure of Simeon with his outstretched arms holding a figure of the Infant Jesus.

The relics in the cathedral are carefully guarded and were seldom exposed to public veneration before the 14th century. Since then they have been shown on an average of once every seven years, when great pilgrimages flock to Aachen to venerate them.

The Seamless Garments

THE Basilique Saint-Denys of Argenteuil, France, and the Cathedral of Trier, Germany, have the distinction of owning garments recognized as having once belonged to Our Lord. The garments are different in fibers, shapes and functions — that of Argenteuil being identified as a tunic, the one in Trier recognized as a coat. Each garment is regarded as authentic and each has its venerable tradition.

The oldest document relating to the relic of Argenteuil is dated 1156 and is entitled *Charta Hugonis*, although the relic's tradition takes us further back to the time of Charlemagne. In time it was entrusted to a relative of Charlemagne, the Abbess Theodorade of the Benedictine Monastery of Argenteuil to which the *Charta Hugonis* refers. In this document Archbishop Hugh of Rouen testified that in the treasury of the Church of the Benedictines of Argenteuil there was preserved a garment of Christ from *temporibus antiquis*, from ancient times, that he himself had inspected in the company of various ecclesiastical witnesses. All agreed that the garment was genuine before presenting it amid great pageantry to the examination of King Louis VII and his court. At the same time the archbishop granted an indulgence to all the faithful who would honor it.

When the Normans began to invade and pillage the surrounding areas, the tunic, together with other revered relics, was hidden for safekeeping. While the guardians considered it fortunate that the relic escaped its time of ordeal completely unharmed, it was not so fortunate during the French Revolution when it was damaged — not through violence, but because of the well-meaning intentions of a parish priest who apparently acted without the proper authorization.

Before the Benedictine convent was despoiled in 1791, the Holy Tunic was transferred to the parish church for safekeeping. But in 1793, when situations proved even more hazardous, the parish priest cut from the main body of the relic several small pieces that he concealed in various places, in the hope that at least some of the pieces, thus scattered, might survive. In 1795 those portions that could be found were brought back to the church. They numbered four in all, the main part of the tunic and three small pieces.

As to the nature of the garment, four features are presented.

The first is that the garment is seamless and is regarded as an undergarment, an inner vestment. There are no tailoring marks and no connecting stitches either in its length or width.

The color of the relic has been described as a mixture of brown, red and purple, while some have indicated that it is the color of wine.

The fiber was once analyzed by Gobelins of Paris, whose firm was expert in the identification of materials as well as manufacturers of fine fabrics. They identified the cloth as having animal origins — that is, wool. It was noted that the Holy Coat of Trier is of vegetable origins — flax or cotton. The tunic, they declared, was of a supple and light tissue, indicating that it was woven by a delicate hand, although in a manner that was primitive. According to experts, the nature of the tissue and its fabrication made it identical and equal to the materials used in the Christian era of the first and second centuries.

Undoubtedly the most unexpected feature of the relic is the presence of spots in the region of the shoulders and in the area of the kidneys. Having been submitted to scientific analysis the conclusion reached was that the spots were undoubtedly those of human blood.

The records of the church indicate that beginning with the death of Charlemagne and for many centuries thereafter, a Mass was offered each month for the repose of his soul in gratitude for his gift of the Holy Tunic. It remains a practice even to this day that the bells of the church are rung one hour after noon to commemorate the hour in which the relic was first brought to the city.

While the foregoing has been summarized from papers published by the Basilique Saint-Denys of Argenteuil entitled *La Ste Tunique de A. A. En L'Eglise D'Argenteuil*, mention must be made of the many disputes that have been made and published elsewhere concerning the function and correct title of each relic. Both the Cathedral of Trier and the Basilica of Argenteuil readily acknowledge the authenticity of each garment, yet arguments against one or the other continue to be made by various writers who, according to one knowledgeable observer, have expressed, ". . . merely their own opinions . . . furnishing no substantial proof of their contention."

The difficulty seems to arise from the fact that both garments are seamless, with factions arguing over which is the *Tunice inconsutilis*, the seamless garment of Scripture that was worn by the Savior during His Passion. The presence of blood on the Tunic of Argenteuil would seem to indicate that it was the garment worn at that time. As for the garment of Trier, so many miracles and manifestations were recorded during various expositions that Bishop Korum himself published an accounting of them in 1894.

The Holy Coat of Trier is first depicted in art on an ivory tablet that dates from the fifth or sixth century. On its artistic surface is shown a translation of relics to Trier with the cooperation of St. Helena.

Why should Trier have the honor of guarding such a precious relic? Since the second century Christians are known to have inhabited the city in great numbers. With the increase in their population the first episcopal See in Germany was established in Trier. Additionally, as the capital city of Belgica Prima, the chief city of Gaul, it was the frequent residence of emperors. Here it is believed Constantine built a castle for his mother, St. Helena, that she might oversee this portion of his empire.

In the 11th-century biography of the first administrator of the See of

Trier, Bishop Agricius, it is reported that the Holy Coat was given to him by St. Helena to enrich the cathedral with which she had been so closely connected.

In this cathedral, portions of which date from Roman times, the Holy Coat was solemnly transferred in 1196 from the St. Nicholas Chapel to the high altar. Here it remained concealed and undisturbed for almost 350 years.

On the occasion of a great Parliament held in Trier in 1512 it was suggested that the occasion should be distinguished by a special event. The gesture decided upon was the exposition of the Holy Coat.

Having received the consent of the pope for this display, the archbishop of Trier caused prayers to be offered in all the monasteries of the town and vicinity in preparation for the event.

While indisputable documents of ancient age prove the former residents of Trier firmly believed the relic was the garment of Christ, still, since no one had seen the relic within living memory, some of the people of the 16th century doubted the existence of the relic, while others declared it a mere legend.

When the solemn day arrived for doubts to be rested and curiosities satisfied, the clergy accompanied the archbishop to the high altar. On opening the small repository a closed chest was found bearing an episcopal seal and the words, "This is the Seamless Garment of our Lord and Saviour Jesus Christ." Believed to be the first public display of the relic, the exposition lasted 23 days with about 100,000 pilgrims traveling from all parts to venerate it — this in consideration of the bad roads and the uncertainty of travel in those days.

During times of war the relic was several times taken to fortified places for safekeeping. In 1810 it was brought back to its original home amid great rejoicing. In celebration of this return, the robe was exposed for 17 days with no fewer than 227,000 pilgrims paying homage.

Another exposition of the Holy Coat occurred in 1844 that led to the rise of a sect called the German Catholics. During the exposition of 1891 over two million pilgrims are said to have viewed it. Again over two million visitors were counted during the three-week exposition of the relic in 1933. The last display of the relic was in 1959 when it was shown from July 19 until September 20.

There is nothing to dispute the genuiness of the relic as determined by the archeological examination of 1890-1891. Inspection of the garment at the present time reveals that it is plain, brownish in color, with the appearance of being linen or cotton. No trace of a seam can be detected.

While it is true that no official records have been found concerning the authenticity of the garments of Trier and Argenteuil from the time of the Crucifixion until the time of St. Helena, still their revered traditions and their documented histories from ancient times go far to confirm the probability of their genuiness.

The Holy Coat of Trier might be the very one touched by the woman in the Gospels who thought: " 'If I just touch his clothing, I shall get well.' Immediately her flow of blood stopped. Jesus was conscious at once that healing power had gone out from him and turning to the crowd, he asked, 'Who touched my clothing?' " (Mark 5:28-30).

The Holy Tunic of Argenteuil is believed to be the one mentioned in Scripture: "The soldiers, therefore, when they had crucified him took his garments and made of them four parts, to each soldier a part, and also the tunic. Now the tunic was without seam, woven in one piece from the top. They, therefore, said to one another, 'Let us not tear it, but let us cast lots for it, to see whose it shall be.' That scripture might be fulfilled which said, 'They divided my garments among them, and for my vesture they cast lots' " (John 19:23-24, *Douai-Rheims* version).

The Holy Grail

T HE cup used by Jesus at the Last Supper has been memorialized in prose, poetry and music, having been the subject of the King Arthur legends and Sir Thomas Malory's *A Le Morte d' Arthur*. In poetry it has been immortalized as the Holy Grail in Alfred Lord Tennyson's poem *Idylls of the King*, and in music it has been celebrated in two of Richard Wagner's operas, *Parsifal* and *Lohengrin*. Numerous other works in several languages have contributed to the endurance of the legends that have cost the lives of countless knights who quested after the Holy Grail.

The meaning of the word *Grail* has been variously explained. The generally accepted meaning is that given by the Cistercian chronicler Helinandus, who mentions a vision manifested to a hermit in the year 717 during which the cup of the Last Supper was mentioned. The hermit subsequently wrote a Latin book called *Gradale*. The Medieval Latin *Gradale* became in old French, Graal, Greal or Greel, and in English it became Grail.

The early history of the grail is intimately connected with the story of Joseph of Arimathea, with two versions of its acquisition being recorded. In one, the vessel was simply passed into his possession and he used it to gather the blood of Jesus during the Crucifixion; in the other, he received it from the hands of Jesus during a vision. After a time it arrived in England, carried there by Joseph or one of his kin, and was there subsequently lost.

Other legends of the grail are numerous, fanciful and often at variance with historical truth. For this reason the Church ignores the subject completely, and with the exception of Helinandus, clerical writers do not mention it. Nevertheless, at least four vessels seeking authentication have emerged. Of these we will mention two whose claims seem more probable. One cup is located in the United States, the other is reverently kept in Valencia, Spain. Each seems satisfied and secure with its claim and each seems content with the care and attention given it.

The cup in the New York Metropolitan Museum of Art is in a position to boast that eminent archeological and scientific authorities believe in its genuineness. Its discovery occurred in the year 1910 when Syria was experiencing a severe drought. The starving had to resort to digging for roots or anything that was edible. During these struggles surprising discoveries of ancient dry wells yielded all manner of treasures which were offered for sale to antique dealers. One such dry well yielded a treasury of altar vessels probably hidden for safekeeping during a time of invasion. Among the articles was a chalice which immediately caught the fancy of a wealthy dealer, Kouchakji Freres. This in turn attracted the attention of historians and scientists who called it the Chalice of Antioch for the city near its place of discovery.

Examiners and viewers of the cup immediately recognized its unusual and rare qualities. The vessel is in two parts, the inner cup being composed of plain silver of great age, which has a capacity of two and a half quarts. The outer chalice is of intricately carved silver. Dr. William Newbold who is associated with the University of Pennsylvania suggests that the cup is older than the holder since the holder was apparently made to preserve and exhibit it. The sacredness of the inner cup seems confirmed, since it was thought worthy and deserving of the costly and magnificent holder. Concurring with the opinion is Professor Gustavus Eisen, an authority on early Christian art and the former curator of the California Academy of Science. Professor Eisen wrote two books concerning the cup after studying it for nine years. His learned opinion is that the inner cup is the Holy Grail used by Jesus at the Last Supper.

The ornately carved outer cup is resplendent with more than 240 designs, including animal and botanical items, two figures of Christ, one on either side, with additional figures gathered in two groups of five each. It is regarded as significant that there are 10 figures instead of 12 which would symbolize the apostles. Professor Newbold explained that one group represents the Church of the East and the other represents the Church of the West. Only one period in Church history would justify placing two groups of five men in a position of authority and prestige, this being the time immediately following A.D. 50 when two Christian churches existed: the Church of Jerusalem, the mother church of the Jewish Christians, and the Church of Antioch, the mother church of the Gentile Christians. Each church had been governed by five men. It is, therefore, calculated that the outer cup was crafted during the first century.

How did the cup arrive at Antioch from Jerusalem and the site of the Last Supper? The Acts of the Apostles inform us that Barnabas and Saul journeyed to Antioch. It is speculated that the cup was brought there by them and was eventually entrusted to the care of the faithful. The Acts record that for a whole year Barnabas and Saul labored in Antioch and that it was in Antioch that the disciples were called Christians for the first time (Acts 11:26).

The Holy Grail on display

Kouchakji Freres, the fortunate antique dealer who acquired the cup shortly after its discovery in 1910, placed his treasure on display in Paris at the Louvre 20 years later and showed it again in Chicago in 1933-34 during the World's Fair, where it was honored with its own hall at the Century of Progress exhibition. After visits to other museums in the United States, the Kouchakji family relinquished responsibility for its safety to the New York Metropolitan Museum of Art. Here it is occasionally displayed in the Cloisters.[1]

---

[1]The information about the Chalice of Antioch has been taken for the most part from the article, Chalice of Art and Mystery, by Anne Tansey in *Messenger of St. Anthony*, Basilica of the Saint, Padua, February 1981, pp. 26-27.

The grail at the Cathedral of Valencia also claims recognition as the cup used by Christ at the Last Supper. Composed of a dark red oriental cornelian, it is undoubtedly of Roman date. Its shape is that of a chalice with a bowl, stem and base, but the stem and knop have been covered with golden designs. Handles of gold were added and the base was circled in gold that is studded with gems and pearls. It has been estimated that the golden additions were crafted in the 9th century.

Tradition relates that the cup was used by popes down to Sixtus II. During the persecution of Valerian the cup was entrusted to St. Lawrence, a deacon, and was taken by him in 258 to Huesca, his birthplace. Here it remained in safety until a threat of Moorish invasion forced its removal elsewhere. It was then moved to the Monastery of San Juan de la Pena in 713.

Recorded history confirms that the cup was at the Monastery of San Juan de la Pena in the 13th century and was removed to Saragossa in 1399 by King Martin. It was taken in 1424 to Valencia by Alfonso V and was given to the cathedral in 1437. At the start of the Spanish Civil War in 1936 the cup was again moved to safety. It escaped possible destruction only three hours before the cathedral was sacked by a mob. It remained hidden until the end of the war in 1939 after the victory of the Nationalist forces.

The history of the grail, together with its composition and style, have been subjected to archeological scrutiny for centuries. Scientific judgments of more recent date have been consistent in declaring the possibility of the cup's validity.[2]

The Cathedral of Valencia has always held the cup in high regard and built a splendid chapel for it in the former chapter-house. The cup is beautifully displayed in a recess that is topped with carved spires. It is situated on a small pedestal before a panel of gold, all of which is surrounded by sheets of glass. The walls on either side have been enriched with 12 panels of bas-relief that are framed with artistic carvings.

It is certain that during the cup's sojourn at the Monastery of San Juan de la Peña it contributed greatly to the grail legends of the Middle Ages.

---

[2]*El Santo Caliz*, Antonio Beltran, Cathedral of Valencia, Valencia, Spain, 1960, p. 125.

Relics of the Passion

Reliquary of the Holy Crown of Thorns is kept at Notre Dame Cathedral in Paris.

The Holy Stairs

NEAR the Lateran Basilica is the sanctuary which was originally the papal chapel of the palace where popes lived from the time of Constantine until the papacy was exiled to Avignon in 1313. Here is located the Scala Sancta, the Holy Stairs and the chapel called the Sancta Sanctorum.

The Holy Stairs were taken from Pilate's palace and consist of 28 steps of white marble. Tradition states that these were climbed by Our Lord during the night of His Passion. Believed to have been brought to Rome by St. Helena, they have been given the utmost consideration for 1500 years.

At all times of the day pilgrims are seen ascending the steps on their knees and reverently kissing the glass panes marking the places touched by the Savior's bleeding feet. Many popes have likewise climbed these stairs, including Gelasius I, Gregory the Great, Sergius I, Stephen III, Leo IV, Gregory VII and St. Leo III, who often went there to meditate on the Sacred Passion. On the eve of the invasion of Rome by the troops of Victor Emmanuel, Pope Pius IX climbed the stairs on his knees in spite of his 78 years.

To aid in the descent, two flights of steps, one on either side of the Holy Stairs, have been constructed so that the pilgrim may walk away without disturbing those still ascending.

Another flight of steps climbed by Our Lord, these of monumental proportions, were excavated in Jerusalem between 1968 and 1975. They consist of 33 stone steps that served as the principal entrance to the temple in the lifetime of Jesus. According to archeologists these are unquestionably the ones Jesus climbed, as mentioned in St. Matthew's Gospel,

> "And Jesus went into the temple of God, and cast out all them that sold and bought in the temple, and overthrew the tables of the money changers and the chairs of them that sold doves: And he saith to them: 'It is written, *My house shall be called a house of prayer; but you have made it a den of thieves*' " (Matthew 21:12-13 *Douai-Rheims*).

At the top of the steps is the temple wall with a double gate now bricked shut. This gate gave access to a 60-meter-long tunnel which led to the open-air Outer Court where stalls had been set up by the money changers and dove venders catering to pilgrims with foreign currency, and to worshippers offering sacrifices.

During excavation of the steps some 22,000 coins were found bearing effigies of emperors, emperors' wives, gods and goddesses. Other small articles were found, including dice made of bone, perhaps like those used by Roman soldiers when casting lots for the garments of Christ.

The Scourging Post

THE post at which Christ was scourged was shown on Mount Sion in the Holy Land, according to St. Gregory Nazianzen (d. 389). A portion of it is now kept in Rome in a small chapel in the Church of St. Praxedes (Santa Prassede). Visitors to this chapel are informed by an inscription above the entrance that Cardinal John Colonna brought the relic from Constantinople to Rome in 1223. No documentary evidence exists on the column's prior history, but it bears a striking similarity to the stone column in the "Ecce Homo" chapel in Jerusalem. Here research has established beyond reasonable doubt that the subterranean flooring in the Convent of the Sisters of Notre Dame de Sion is the actual courtyard of Pilate's palace in Jerusalem.

We are told by Anne Catherine Emmerich (1774-1798), a German Augustinian nun whose visions of the life of Jesus and Mary were recorded, that,

> "This pillar, placed in the center of the court, stood alone, and did not serve to sustain any part of the building. It was not very high, for a tall man could touch the summit by stretching out his arm; there was a large iron ring at the top, and both rings and hooks a little lower down.[1]

The very base of the column, a portion called the socle, is said to be kept in St. Mark's Cathedral in Venice.

The relic at St. Praxedes is made of oriental jasper and is protected by a glass case. It stands near the chapel of St. Zeno where visiting priests are permitted to offer the Holy Sacrifice. The column can be viewed from the main body of the church through an iron grille.

[1] *The Dolorous Passion of Our Lord Jesus Christ*, Anne Catherine Emmerich, Burns & Oates, London, 1955, p. 206.

The church was built over the original house of St. Praxedes and now enshrines her relics and those of her sister, St. Pudentiana, both early martyrs whose relics were removed by Pope Pascal I from the Catacombs of Priscilla.

Other relics in the church include those of St. Zeno, an early martyr, a small piece of the seamless garment of Our Lord, a small portion of the Crown of Thorns, all of which have been honored for centuries.

St. Charles Borromeo favored this church and celebrated Holy Mass every morning in the Chapel of the Column when he visited Rome, and sometimes spent the night in prayer in the chapel, which is situated beneath the main altar.

The Crown of Thorns

THREE evangelists speak in their Gospels of the Crown of Thorns, but, unfortunately, give no description of it. It is principally in the western world that we think of the crown as a circular band similar to a wreath, but in the Orient, crowns took the shape of a cap or helmet, that is, one that covered the whole top of the head. This theory that the crown was really in the shape of a cap is supported by sindonologists who have studied the Holy Shroud, including the scientists of the Shroud of Turin Research Project, who studied the cloth in 1978.

St. Bridget described a similar crown based on one of her revelations in which she maintained that the crown tore the whole head of Jesus.

This design of the crown is likewise supported by St. Vincent of Lerins (d. 445), a priest described as "preeminent in eloquence and learning." The saint wrote, "They placed on His head a crown of thorns. It was in fact, in the shape of a pileus, so that it touched and covered His head in every part."

The crown as it is now kept consists only of a circlet devoid of thorns. It is believed that the upper part and all the thorns were distributed as relics.

The earliest writers of the Church have written about the crown. St. Paulinus of Nola (354-431) wrote that, "The thorns with which Our Saviour was crowned was held in honor together with the Holy Cross and the pillar of the scourging."

The crown is mentioned as having been found in the Holy Sepulchre. Cassiodorus (c. 570) spoke of the crown being at Jerusalem: "There we may behold the thorny crown, which was set upon the head of the Redeemer." St. Gregory of Tours (d. 593) asserts that the thorns of the crown still looked green, a freshness he said that was ". . . miraculously renewed each day." Antoninus of Piacenza in the 6th century clearly states that the Crown of Thorns was at the time shown in the church on Mount Sion. Moreover the monk Bernard, in the *Pilgrimage*, states that the relic was still at Mount Sion in 870. It is certain that what was purported to be the Crown of Our Lord was venerated at Jerusalem for several hundred years.

The crown was transferred to Constantinople during the reign of French emperors about 1063, but in 1238 Baldwin II, the Latin emperor of Constantinople, anxious to obtain support for his unsteady empire, offered the crown to King Louis of France. It was then actually in the hands of the Venetians as security for a large loan once made by Baldwin. The loan was satisfied by Louis, who claimed the relic. The crown was carried in 1239 by two Dominicans to France. King Louis, with many prelates and his entire court, met it five leagues beyond the Sens. The pious king and his brother, both dressed humbly and barefoot, carried the crown into the city to the Cathedral of St. Stephen. Two years later it was taken to Paris, where it was placed in the Sainte Chapelle which the saint had built for its reception. Every year on August 11 the transfer of the relic from Venice to Paris was celebrated in the Holy Chapel.

During the Revolution the crown was kept in the Bibliothèque Nationale, but was eventually restored to the Sainte Chapelle in 1806 through the efforts of Archbishop Jean-Baptiste Belloy of Paris, who was then in his 90s. Napoleon was so pleased with the successful transfer that he obtained the cardinal's hat for the archbishop, which Pope Pius VII placed on the prelate's venerable head in a consistory held in Paris.

The crown is now kept in a magnificent reliquary in Notre Dame Cathedral in Paris and is shown once a year during services in commemoration of Good Friday.

Studies have shown that the crown is from the bush botanically known as Zizyphus Spine Christi. This grows to heights of 15 to 20 feet and is found in abundance along the waysides around Jerusalem. It is interesting that a separate study of some of the thorn relics was made by Professor Edoardo Prilleux and Professor Pietro Savi of the University of Pisa. The thorns included those at the Parochial Church of

Weverlghem in Belgium, one given by St. Helena to Treviri and the large piece consisting of a branch connected to a thorn in the chapel of Spedali Riuniti di S. Chiara in Pisa. In 1933 Professor Ugolino Martelli of the Botanical Department of the same university, after a careful study of these same relics stated that, "These relics belong to the botanical plant Zizyphus Bulgaris Lam." This plant was later renamed in honor of the Redeemer, Zizyphus Spine Christi, the same plant to which the crown in Notre Dame belongs. The crooked branches of this shrub are armed with thorns growing in pairs.

St. Vincent of Lerins affirms that the Savior's head received 70 wounds. It is curious that M. de Mély, who did considerable research on the crown and published articles about it at the turn of the century, agrees with this number and asserts that from 60 to 70 thorns had been separated from the crown and were kept in different reliquaries until St. Louis and his successors distributed them.

Of the thorns that were once part of the crown, we know that some were given to Eastern emperors at an early date and that Justinian, who died in 565, is known to have given a thorn to St. Germanus, bishop of Paris, which was long preserved at Saint-Germain-des-Pres. Empress Irene in 798 or 802 sent Charlemagne several thorns that were deposited by him at Aachen. Eight of these are known to have been at Aachen for the consecration of the basilica by Pope Leo III. Four were given to Saint-Corneille at Compiegne in 877 by Charles the Bald. One was sent by Hugh the Great to the Anglo-Saxon King Athelstan in 927, which eventually found its way to Malmesbury Abbey. Another was presented to a Spanish princess about 1160 and another taken to Germany in 1200.

The Holy Thorn at Stonyhurst College and one at St. Michael's Church, Ghent, both profess, upon what seems like quite satisfactory evidence, to be the thorns given by Mary Queen of Scots to Thomas Percy, Earl of Northumberland. In Oviedo Cathedral eight thorns were claimed until the revolution of 1934 when the Holy Chamber was dynamited. Only five are still retained. Thorns are likewise claimed by Santa Croce in Jerusalem (Rome), the Cathedral of Barcelona and Stanbrook Abbey, England.

M. de Mély is said to have made a survey of the thorns kept as sacred relics and to have counted more than 70. It is theorized that these extra thorns were those thorns plucked from bushes and simply touched to the crown, to be kept as souvenirs. In time they were accepted as genuine relics of the crown when their true origins were lost. This situation is similar to that concerning the strange multiplication of the Holy Nails.

The largest pieces of the crown outside Paris are those pieces given to Trier and the Capella della Spina at Pisa, whose history is well told and whose deposit is of some interest. Located in the same city as the famous leaning tower, the chapel resembles an oversized reliquary because of its miniature scale and its innumerable outdoor statues and pinnacles. The church was built during Crusader times, in the year 1230, beside a new bridge. The prevailing belief of the time was that a chapel built close to a bridge would draw down God's protection upon it.

The story of this church takes on added interest about 30 years after its dedication when a wealthy merchant of Pisa journeyed to the Holy Land to receive from a friend a fragment of the Crown of Thorns. The treasure was conveyed to Pisa where its owners placed it in an urn. Unfortunately, in 1266, when the merchant experienced a drastic alteration in his fortune and was subject to imprisonment on the complaint of his creditors, he fled Pisa leaving the sacred thorn in the custody of the Longhi family. Offers were continually made to purchase the relic, religious orders pleaded for it, while at times even threats were made by those who wished to own it. In spite of the pressures the relic remained securely in the possession of the Longhi family until the year 1333. It was during this year that Benedetto Longhi became seriously ill and donated the relic to the little oratory of the bridge where it was brought in a grand procession and placed in a silver tabernacle.

During the time that the little chapel was being repaired, the thorn was entrusted to the Capuchin Fathers of the Hospital of St. Chiara as a precaution against possible damage and to protect it from those who might take advantage of the situation to steal or defile it. It is in the chapel of the Spedali Riuniti di S. Chiara, a hospital to which the little church was associated for many years, that the relic is still enshrined.

The relic consists of a small, slightly curved branch, shiny and dark in color, measuring eight centimeters long. One of its four thorns had been broken off, as can be easily noted. There is only one other relic that consists of more than a thorn and that one is enshrined in the Parochial Church of Weverlghem in Belgium.

Thorns from
the Holy Crown
displayed at the
Cathedral of Oviedo

The Holy Cross

WHEN Emperor Constantine the Great was in danger of being defeated by the tyrant Maxentius, whose army greatly outnumbered his own, a vision of a brilliant cross appeared in the sky with the words, "In this sign conquer." With his warriors carrying Christ's monogram on their shields and atop their banners, Constantine went boldly to the Milvian Bridge that crossed the Tiber River to meet Mazentius and the pagan oppressors of the Holy City of Rome. Constantine was victorious, Maxentius' hold on Roman life was broken, official paganism was eclipsed and Christian freedom was won. Constantine was subsequently instructed in the Faith and was baptized by Pope Eusebius. Some years later he dispatched his mother, St. Helena, to Jerusalem to recover the True Cross and the relics of the Passion. In this he displayed a considerable measure of faith in the health and stamina of his mother, who had to undergo an arduous journey from Rome to Jerusalem since she was then, in the year 326, almost 80 years of age.

It had been rumored that the True Cross was hidden in the Holy Sepulchre, which had been covered with a mound of dirt and further concealed by the Jews by the placement of various pagan buildings in an effort to discourage Christian worship. Slightly different versions of the findings have come down to us. One maintains that only a few chosen Jews knew the exact location and that one of these, named Judas, having been touched by Divine inspiration, revealed the site to St. Helena.

Excavations revealed the tomb and within it the title that had been nailed to the cross proclaiming Christ as King of the Jews. Here also were found three crosses. Since the title was not attached, the identity of the true cross was revealed when a dead man was restored to life by contact with it. After witnessing this event, Judas was thereupon converted, assumed the name of Cyriacus and was later consecrated by Pope Eusebius himself.

Another report claims that Bishop Macarius, the patriarch of Jerusalem, who himself was seeking to locate all the holy places, was present at the excavation site and had the three crosses brought to the bedside of a prominent woman who was then grievously ill. The patient was unaffected when touched by two crosses, but contact with the third caused a complete restoration of health.

Still another legend tells us that St. Helena indicated the place of concealment by divine inspiration. St. Paulinus of Nola tells us that the empress engaged in an extensive investigation, then called both Jews and Christians for consultations.

Whichever is the correct version, it is known that St. Helena found the True Cross and that she and her son Constantine erected a magnificent basilica over the Holy Sepulchre with the exact place of discovery situated beneath the atrium.

A portion of the True Cross was retained here and enclosed in a silver reliquary. According to Socrates the historian, a piece was given to Constantine, who had it enclosed in a statue of himself. Placed on a porphyry column in the Forum of Constantinople, the statue with the relic was thought to render the city impregnable.

A considerable portion was brought to Rome by St. Helena and for this she erected the basilica named the Holy Cross in Jerusalem, so named because it was built wholly or partially on a bed of earth brought by St. Helena from Jerusalem — a claim that is inscribed on the pavement of the floor. This was reason enough for early pilgrims to break the flooring and claim pieces of the soil. The relics of the cross retained in the reliquary chapel are three in number, each measuring approximately six inches in length and are kept in a cross-shaped reliquary.

St. Cyril, in his catechetical lectures before the year 350, assures the candidates for baptism that the Cross of Christ was in the possession of the Church and that "It has been distributed fragment by fragment from this spot and has already nearly filled the world." St. Cyril spoke the words on the site of the Crucifixion some 20 years after the discovery. St. Cyril's words were echoed by St. Ambrose, St. Paulinus of Nola, Sulpicius Severus, Rufinus, Socrates, Sozomen and Theodoret. What is certain is that as early as the second half of the fourth century pieces of the cross were known to be scattered throughout the empire.

St. Paulinus of Nola (353-431) in one of his letters refers to the fact that no matter how many pieces were removed from the cross, it grew no smaller in size. This has been likened to the miraculous multiplication of the loaves and fishes at the feeding of the five thousand.

St. Paulinus once sent to Sulpicius Severus a fragment of the cross with the words, "Receive a great gift in a little case and take this segment as an armament against the perils of the present and a pledge of everlasting safety." Whether or not St. Paulinus began the practice or not, it seems that distribution of small relics led to the making of reliquary crosses to be hung about the neck. St. John Chrysostom recorded that both men and women had relics of the cross enclosed in gold and wore them around the neck. Specimens of these ancient crosses have come down to us, many being kept in museums or in the treasuries of European churches.

Before the end of the fourth century it is indicated by dated inscriptions that the stem of the cross and the title were both intensely venerated in Jerusalem. Of the portion reserved there, great care was exercised to ensure that slivers were not taken indiscriminately. Reports of the earliest date have consistently referred to the Jerusalem relic as being in three pieces.

The cult of the cross and its relics during the fifth and succeeding centuries was so great that even the iconoclast emperors of the East, in their suppression of the cult of images, nevertheless, respected that of the cross. The devotion of the cross likewise gave rise to the building of many churches and oratories as a worthy treasury of their relics. Of these, the Church of S. Croce at Ravenna was built before the year 450. Pope Hilarius, between 461-468, built an oratory in the Lateran where he placed a relic, while Pope Symmachus (498-514) built an oratory of the Holy Cross behind the baptistry at St. Peter's wherein he placed a jeweled golden cross containing a relic.

The section of the cross at Jerusalem, so carefully guarded against unscrupulous relic-seekers was, nevertheless, seized by the Persian King Chosroes II when he stormed and captured Jerusalem in 614. Thousands of Christians were butchered, many were taken into slavery, and over 300 churches, monasteries and church buildings were burned or destroyed. Harmed in this attack was the Church of the Holy Sepulchre. From here were taken many valuables together with the True Cross in its jeweled case. Emperor Heraclius vainly tried to negotiate peace, then gathered his forces for an attack. Chosroes was soundly defeated, and after being 15 years in his charge, the relic was reclaimed in the year 629. Heraclius triumphantly carried the relic with him to Constantinople and the following year completed the journey to Jerusalem. The relic had been retained in its costly case during captivity, the patriarch and clergy finding the seals intact. The return of the relic occurred in the month of September on or about the 14th of the month.

This recovery of the cross is liturgically commemorated each year on the date of its return to Jerusalem, September 14, with a feast called the Triumph of the Cross. In Paris a notable observance of this feast was observed on September 14, 1241, by King Louis of France, who divested himself of his royal robes and, walking barefoot, carried a fragment of the Holy Cross in procession. The relic escaped destruction during the Revolution and is still preserved in Paris.

A September feast in honor of the cross was initiated in 335 when

40

the church Constantine built over the Holy Sepulchre was solemnly dedicated. At present, though, the feast seems to commemorate, or to have included, the celebrated rescue of the Jerusalem relic from the hands of infidels.

The feast known as the "Invention" or Finding of the Holy Cross by St. Helena was kept from the earliest times on May 3 until it was suppressed by Pope John XXIII in 1960.

A microscopic examination of the fragments of the cross reveals that the cross of the Crucifixion was made of pine. According to an ancient, but dubious tradition, the measurements of the cross were said to be nearly 189 inches in length with the crossbar being between 90-1/2 to 102-1/2 inches.[1] The cross is known to be *immissa* in style, which means that the vertical trunk extended a certain height above the transverse beam. It was, therefore, higher than the crosses of the two thieves, Our Lord's crime being judged a graver one, according to St. John Chrysostom.

Relics of the cross of a notable size are claimed by the Cathedral of Trier, Notre Dame in Paris, the Cathedral of Ghent in Brussels, Oviedo Cathedral and the Monastery of St. Toribio of Liebana.

A sizable piece of the relic is in the Vatican and is enclosed in one of the four huge piers that face the high altar. The pier is readily identified by a monumental statue of St. Helena that stands before it.

The Holy Nails

ALBAN Butler (1710-1763), whose *Lives of the Saints* occupied 30 years of research, tells us that before the discovery of the cross, St. Helena was credibly informed that if she could find the sepulchre she would likewise find the instruments of the punishment. We are told that the custom among the Jews was to dig a hole near the place where the body of a criminal was buried, and to throw into it whatever belonged to his execution.

If this was indeed the practice then we need not be surprised that the nails used to attach Jesus to the cross were also found in or near the Holy

[1]*The Catholic Encyclopedia*, The Encyclopedia Press, Inc., New York, 1908, p. 520.

Sepulchre. This is supported by St. Ambrose, who recorded that St. Helena found the nails together with the cross and the title.

Of these holy nails history tells us that one was sent along with a portion of the cross and a part of the title to the Roman Church of Santa Croce in Jerusalem where it is still kept in a precious reliquary. The other two nails were believed sent by St. Helena to Constantine, one of which was attached to his helmet. The other was attached to his horse's bridle, although St. Gregory of Tours tells us that this nail was used to make a bit for the emperor's horse. This is thought to fulfill what was written by the Prophet Zacharias: "In that day that which is upon the bridle of the horse shall be holy to the Lord" (Zacharias 14:20).

If the nail of Constantine's crown or the one upon the horse's bridle had been removed, it would account for the report that one of the holy nails was set into the famous "Iron Crown of Lombardy" that was used in the coronation of Charlemagne. The crown is preserved in the Cathedral of Monza.

Of the great cathedrals that boast possession of holy nails are counted Notre Dame Cathedral in Paris, where a relic of the cross and the crown of thorns are also kept. The Cathedral of Florence likewise has a relic, as does the Cathedral of Trier in Germany where Constantine maintained a residence. St. Helena forwarded to Trier not only a relic of the cross, but also a seamless garment supposedly worn by Our Lord.

Some of these nails might very well be authentic, but what of the almost 30 nails claimed by churches throughout Europe? It would seem reasonable that filings or portions of the true nails were removed and given to prominent persons or churches. Alban Butler also tells us that nails made to resemble the holy nails were forged so that they included filings from the original. Others were made to resemble the holy nails and were simply touched to the original and given as mementos. He further claims that St. Charles Borromeo had many such nails at Milan that he distributed after touching them to the original.

We can only suppose that these nails, originally identified as imitations that touched the true nails, later lost their true identity with the passage of time until both clergy and faithful, in good faith, accepted them as authentic.

Of these nails, the one that has the greatest claim to authenticity is that of Santa Croce, which was built specifically by Constantine to house the holy relics. This church remains the most important shrine containing relics of the Passion and is the prototype of several later European shrines.

The Title

DISCOVERED with the three crosses was the title, which seems to have been divided by St. Helena into three pieces. One portion was given to Constantine, another was either sent or carried by the saint to Santa Croce in Jerusalem, the church she built in Rome as a fitting reliquary for a large portion of the true cross. The third portion of the title remained in Jerusalem.

Of this Jerusalem relic, we are told by the pilgrim Aetheria how in 385 she witnessed an exposition of the cross and the inscription and the methods used by the bishop and his deacons to safeguard it from relic seekers. The title, she has told us, was touched to the foreheads and eyes of pilgrims.

Another pilgrim, Antoninus of Piacenza, two centuries later tells us that:

> "In the basilica of Constantine which adjoins the tomb in the atrium of the church itself, there is a chamber where wood of the Holy Cross is kept, which we adored and kissed, and I also saw and held in my hand the Title which was placed over the head of Jesus."

The history of the title at Santa Croce is unique. When confronted by Visigoth attacks, the clergy (c. 455) hid the title above the main arch behind a red slab inscribed, "Hic est titulus Crucis." Whether the clergymen who placed it there were killed in the attack and the location was unknown to others, or whether they meant to ensure its safety by keeping it at its height for a longer time and then forgot its location, we do not know. On February 1, 1492, during work on the roof, workmen from their high perch saw the red slab with the words "Titulus Crucis." Behind the slab they found a lead coffer that bore the seal of Cardinal Gerardus, later Pope Lucius II. The box contained the title with words in Hebrew, Greek and Latin written in red letters on a measure of white wood. In 1492 the color was not at all faded, but when Bosio saw it some 60 or 70 years afterwards, the color was greatly faded and the wood so worm-eaten that the words Jesus and Judaeorum were both gone. Lipsius (1547-1606) in his *De Cruce* claims that the board, when he saw it, measured nine inches in length, but must originally have been three feet long, according to his estimation.

Of the Jerusalem portion of the title, the monk Antonine

(1389-1459) asserts that he held in his own hands the wood bearing the accusation when he visited the Holy Sepulchre.

The Holy Sponge

T HE sponge that was filled with vinegar and offered to Christ on the cross, and the reed to which it was attached, were objects of veneration in Jerusalem during the lifetime of St. Gregory of Tours (544-595). They were brought for safekeeping to Constantinople in 614 when Jersualem was taken by the Persians, but were apparently returned since the Venerable Bede (672-735) assures us that he himself saw the holy sponge in a silver tankard in Jerusalem. A part of the sponge is kept in France with other relics obtained by St. Louis. Fragments are also in the possession of St. John Lateran, St. Mary Major, St. Mary in Transtevere, St. Mary in Campitelli, all of which are in Rome, and St. Jacques de Compiegne in France and Aachen, Germany.

The reed was divided into parts that are now in Florence, Lunegarde, Bavaria and Greece.

The Holy Lance

T HE lance that was used by the Roman soldier Longinus to pierce the side of Jesus on the cross was supposedly found with the other relics in the Holy Sepulchre. Nothing is recorded about it, however, until the pilgrim St. Antoninus of Piacenza in about the year 570, in describing the holy places of Jerusalem, tells us that he saw in the Basilica of Mount Sion ". . . the crown of thorns with which Our Lord was crowned and the lance with which He was struck in the side." We know that the lance was venerated at Jerusalem during the 6th century with its presence confirmed there by both Cassiodorus and St. Gregory of Tours.

When Jerusalem was captured in 614 by the Persian King Chosroes, the holy relics of the Passion fell into the hands of pagans, as previously mentioned. In the same year the point of the blade was removed and deposited in Constantinople in the Church of St. Sophia. The relics, with the exception of the blade's point, were restored by Heraclius with the other relics of the Passion, since in 670 it was again seen in Jerusalem in the Church of the Holy Sepulchre.

The point of the blade that had been left in Constantinople was given in 1241 by Baldwin to St. Louis, who enshrined it with the Crown of Thorns in the Sainte Chapelle. During the French Revolution these relics were removed to the Bibliothèque Nationale for safety. The crown was happily restored when danger had passed, but the point was unfortunately lost.

There is some reason to believe that the shaft and the blade of the lance were again conveyed to Constantinople before the 10th century together with other relics. Their presence there was clearly confirmed by various Russian pilgrims and though they were enshrined in various churches in succession, it is possible to trace them at this time and to distinguish them from the companion relic of the point.

Sir John Mandeville declared in 1357 that he had seen the blade of the holy lance in Constantinople. While it was at Constantinople it fell into the hands of the Turks, who sent it to Innocent VIII in 1492 as ransom for the sultan's brother who was the pope's prisoner. The relic of the lance and its blade remained in Rome since that time and is kept under the dome of St. Peter's in one of the four huge piers facing the main altar, and is opposite the pier containing the piece of the holy cross. The statue of St. Longinus stands before the pier containing the lance.

Pope Benedict XIV between 1740 and 1758 satisfied his curiosity about the missing tip of the blade by obtaining from Paris an exact drawing of this section. In comparing it with the blade kept in St. Peter's, the pontiff was satisfied that the two had originally formed one blade.

Since 1492 when the relic was sent by the Turks to Innocent VIII, other lances have vied with one another for recognition as the Holy Lance of the Crucifixion. One such lance is kept at Nuremberg, others are found at Paris, Antioch and Krakow. Another claiming recognition is preserved among the imperial insignia at Vienna and is known as the lance of St. Maurice. This weapon was used as early as 1273 in a coronation ceremony. It is claimed, in a weak fashion, to be that of Emperor Constantine which enshrined some portion of the nail of the Crucifixion.

None of these lances withstands historical scrutiny. If any staff seems the most valid it would undoubtedly be that which has been honored at St. Peter's Basilica.

The Holy Shroud

A MONG the many relics of the Church the one that is the most mysterious, controversial and scientifically challenging is undoubtedly the Holy Shroud of Turin, which is marked with the full length image of a crucified man. Since the 14th century it has been regarded as the burial shroud of Jesus Christ. Its existence before then is not definitely recorded, but its history has been connected to that of a cloth called the Edessan Image, or the Mandylion, which was revered from the earliest times.

It is believed that one of the cloths which Luke and John record in the Gospels as having been seen in the tomb shortly after Jesus' resurrection was taken by Thaddaeus, "one of the seventy" (Luke 10:1) to Edessa, now Urfa in eastern Turkey, which was evangelized soon after the dispersion of the Twelve Apostles. During the persecution of Christians by Man'nu VI, it was hidden for safekeeping in a niche above Edessa's west gate, where it remained in a hermetically sealed condition until its rediscovery in 525 during the rebuilding of the wall following a flood. Without dispute it was identified as the original Image of Edessa and was confirmed as a holy cloth by Emperor Justinian, who built the magnificent Hagia Sophia Cathedral in Constantinople for its safekeeping.

From this time on the cloth known as the Image of Edessa also became known as the Holy Mandylion, an Arabic word meaning veil or handkerchief. How could a cloth approximately 14 feet long and three and a half feet wide be considered a veil or handkerchief? During Apostolic times it is believed the burial linen was folded so that only the face was exposed, this to disguise the shroud, which was an unclean thing to be avoided according to Jewish law. It was apparently folded and framed. A system of eight folds appears in recent photos which supports this theory, according to a team of researchers who reconstructed the pattern.

Since the year 525, paintings of Christ were based on the image. Researchers have conducted exhaustive comparisons of the shroud face with ancient images, particularly Byzantine icons. They have developed evidence that the shroud was known as early as the 6th century, since they have found 20 similarities in Byzantine frescoes, paintings and mosaics which resemble peculiarities of the shroud image.

In 944 the Mandylion left for various travels. Now for the first time since its transfer from Jerusalem, the Mandylion was unfolded to reveal the complete image. Once again art was influenced by the Mandylion since lamentation scenes of the dead Christ, previously depicted as wrapped mummy style, now show Christ reclining in death in the attitude consistent with that on the shroud.

Various journeys for devotional exhibitions were conducted until the year 1204 when the image disappeared. Historians have established that this resulted during a shameful episode of Church history by members of the Fourth Crusade who, for reasons unknown, but unquestionably prompted by misdirected zeal, turned their attention from combating infidels to aiming fury on Constantinople. Buildings were destroyed and Church treasures stolen, including the Mandylion. Its disappearance lasted 150 years.

It has been theorized that it eventually came into the possession of the Knights Templar, a group of righteous knights which was founded eight years before the sack of Constantinople. Its noble purpose was to defend crusader territories. During their initiation rites it is known that a mysterious image of a head was honored. Members took vows of poverty, chastity and absolute obedience. Their honesty was unquestioned and they were often entrusted with valuables, including relics. As pious knights they would have honored the Mandylion and cared for it.

One of these knights, Geoffrey de Charny, emerged in the 1350s as owner of the Mandylion. To alleviate financial difficulties following his death, his widow exhibited the relic for financial gain. Although the exhibition in 1357 in the small French village of Lirey, a place 100 miles southeast of Paris, was discontinued at the request of the bishop, it nevertheless brought the Mandylion into prominence. Evidence indicates that the relic was an ancient object at the time it emerged during this exhibition in 1357.

Geoffrey de Charny II inherited the relic after his mother's death, but he, too, left his widow in financial difficulty. After searching for a suitable family to properly care for it the widow deeded it in 1453 to Louis of Savoy. The House of Savoy owned it until 1983 when Italy's last king, exiled Umberto II of the House of Savoy, bequeathed it to the Vatican.

Pope Sixtus IV in 1464 let it be known that he regarded the shroud as authentic.

The shroud was conveyed to Turin, Italy, in 1578. On October 10 of that year St. Charles Borromeo journeyed on foot from Milan to view it. During an exposition in 1613 St. Francis de Sales was one of the assistant bishops who held the cloth before the people. His helper in the founding of the Order of the Visitation, St. Jane Frances de Chantal, venerated the shroud during another exposition in 1639.

A permanent home was finally established in the Royal Chapel of the Turin Cathedral in 1694, where the Holy Shroud remains today.

The cloth is made of linen, a textile derived from flax. Threads from the shroud were studied in 1973 by Gilbert Raes, a professor at Ghent Institute of Textile Technology in Belgium. He observed traces of cotton among the linen fibers, an indication that the cloth had been woven on a loom also used for cotton. The presence of cotton supports its Middle East origins since cotton was grown in the Middle East, but was not grown in Europe. He also determined that the weave of the cloth, a herringbone pattern, was a type common in the Middle East in the first century. His findings are in accord with the opinion of Silvio Curto, associate professor of Egyptology at the University of Turin, who declared that the fabric could indeed date to the time of Christ.

In 1973 Max Frei, a Swiss criminologist, was asked to authenticate photographs of the shroud. A botanist by training, he noticed pollen spores on the cloth and was permitted to take samples for examination and classification. These were photographed and identified as 49 different plants. Thirty-three of these were grown only in Palestine, the southern steppes of Turkey and the area of Istanbul. Sixteen of the plants had European origins and probably attached themselves during open air exhibitions in France and subsequent showings in Italy. It is known that the shroud never left Europe since its display in Lirey in 1357. Max Frei's findings are said to support the Mandylion-shroud theory.

A recent examination of the shroud was made by the Shroud of Turin Research Project in 1978. Participating scientists were permitted to handle the cloth and were surprised to find it light and silky to the touch, ivory colored with age, clean looking, and having a damask-like surface sheen. They found that the cloth measured 14'3" in length by 3'7" in width. It was woven in a single piece except for a strip approximately three and a half inches wide running the length on the left side, which is joined by a single seam.

The image appears as a sepia monochrome tint that is consistent throughout the shroud. Pale and subtle, it clearly shows the frontal and back view of a powerfully built man in an attitude of death. A curiosity exists in that the closer one tries to examine it, the more it dissolves like a mist. It is difficult to distinguish, except at a distance, while photographs seem to enhance its details.

Recent examinations reveal that the image does not penetrate the cloth, but affects only the topmost fibers of each thread with the yellow discoloration extending only two or three fibers into the thread structure. The darker areas are not a deeper yellow, but only appear darker because they contain more discolored fibers than the lighter areas.

Prominent on the shroud are 14 large triangular-shaped patches and eight smaller ones that were sewn on the cloth by Poor Clare nuns who repaired holes burned into the relic during a fire in the chapel at Chambery, France, on December 4, 1532. Intense heat melted parts of the silver chest in which it was kept, causing molten silver to drip, scorch and burn its way through. Two Franciscan priests saved the relic when they carried its casket to safety and doused it with water. The image was not altered and only slightly touched, although the cloth bears scorch marks, water stains and small holes caused by the molten silver that were not repaired. The scorch marks proved to be advantageous since they provided scientists in recent times with opportunities to test various theories of how the image was formed.

A deliberate attempt to destroy the relic by fire was made on October 1, 1972, by an unknown person who broke into the chapel. The shroud thankfully survived, due to the asbestos in the interior of the shrine.

The most dramatic event in the shroud's history is unquestionably that which took place during the exhibition of 1898 when it was photographed for the first time. With photography only 30 years old, its science and techniques still in an experimental state, the holy relic was photographed by Secondo Pia, then a 43-year-old counselor and attorney, and winner of several awards as an amateur photographer. Although the use of electric lighting was then new and uncertain, Pia used this illumination to photograph the shroud at night as it was kept under a glass covering. A first exposure of 14 minutes was followed by another of 20 minutes. Towards midnight Pia retired to his darkroom to develop the plates. All his life Pia would recount the emotions he experienced when the image formed under his gaze. In Pia's own words he recorded,

"Shut up in my darkroom, all intent on my work, I experienced a very strong emotion when, during the development, I saw for the first time the Holy Face appear on the plate with such clarity that I was dumbfounded by it."

With the positive image in his hands, Pia's historic discovery revealed for the first time that the image on the ancient cloth was a negative, a photographic representation that was unknown until the late 19th century.

Pia's cumbersome, wooden, boxlike camera that was used for these first photographs is kept in the Holy Shroud Museum in Turin.

The shroud was next photographed during an exhibition in 1931. In the presence of septuagenarian Secondo Pia, Commander Giuseppe Enrie took a dozen photos of the shroud. These prints, of superb quality, are still reproduced today from the glass plates that he used.

In attendance at this 1931 exhibition was a young priest, the future Pope Paul VI. Many years later, during a televised exposition of the shroud in 1973, the pontiff recalled his emotions when he saw the shroud at that time. "It appears so true, so profound, so human and so divine, such as we have been unable to admire and venerate in any other image."

It has been determined from these and more recent photos that the man of the shroud was between 30 and 35 years of age, measured at approximately 5'11" in height and weighed about 175 pounds.

A former Harvard professor, an ethnologist, observed that the height of the victim is consistent with Jewish grave findings of the first century, the average male measuring approximately 5'10".

According to the Smithsonian Museum of Natural Sciences, the man's beard, hair and facial features are consistent with a Jewish or Semitic facial grouping, the facial features matching those of modern-day Arabs of noble rank or sephardic Jews.

The body is clearly naked and unwashed. The Gospels tell us that Christ died on the eve of the Passover Sabbath, a day of special solemnity. After His death at three o'clock, various delays followed that caused a postponement of the body's anointing. Joseph of Arimathea had to gain an audience with Pilate to ask permission for the body, documents had to be drawn, death had to be confirmed, a burial linen had to be purchased, the body removed from the cross and carried to the tomb. Since a body had to be removed by sundown, and all work terminated at six o'clock, the body of Christ had to be consigned to the tomb hurriedly, with its washing and anointing delayed for another time. As we learn from Scripture, the anointing was never accomplished since the women who arrived at the tomb on Easter morning found the tomb empty.

The shroud has been an object of scientific curiosity and study for many distinguished men of learning, among them Dr. Pierre Barbet, an eminent French surgeon who, in his book *A Doctor at Calvary*, has given us a detailed study of the wounds. Another medical man, Yves Delage, a professor of anatomy at the Sorbonne and an acknowledged agnostic, gave a detailed study in 1902 in which he concluded that the man of the shroud was none other than Jesus Christ. Both physicians declared that the body was of a man accustomed to hard labor, well built and muscular. All the wounds proved to be anatomically correct, and while the body showed clear signs of rigor mortis, there was no evidence of decay. In the Middle East during Jesus' time and under conditions with which He was buried, severe bodily decomposition would normally occur within three to four days.

These and other men of science have noted that the face upon which the photographer Secondo Pia first gazed is covered with bruises. Swellings are about both eyes, both cheeks and chin. A fracture of the nose is possible. The wounds around and atop the head indicate that the Crown of Thorns was really in the shape of a cap.

The wound of the lance which pierced the heart was measured at one and three quarters of an inch by seven sixteenths of an inch and was made after death, since the flow dribbled down instead of spurting out as it would have if the victim had been alive at the time.

The two flows of blood from the left wrist are an important feature since they are measured at approximately 10 degrees apart, indicating that the victim assumed two positions on the cross. With the body hanging full weight against the nails in the wrists, causing the muscles of the chest to be stretched to the extreme, the victim had the double pain in the wrists combined with difficulty in breathing. He was, therefore, forced to exchange this difficulty repeatedly for yet another problem, since the victim had to stand on the nail that pierced both feet to relieve the pressure for breathing.

The distended abdomen indicates asphyxiation, the essential aspect of crucifixion, since the muscles of the chest become paralyzed from the position of the body in the hanging attitude.

The knees are bruised and cut, particularly the left one, while the bruises and abrasions on the upper back indicate that a heavy object was carried — this after the scourging, since the marks of the scourging in that area were altered by this larger wound.

The scourging wounds have been numbered by one examiner as being between 90 and 120. Another has counted 220. Both, however, agree that they were inflicted by a dumbbell-shaped instrument identical in size and shape to the Roman flagrum. Two men inflicted the wounds, the one on the right being taller, more aggressive and sadistic than his companion on the left.

The most thorough and scientifically probing examination of the shroud was made by a group of 20 highly qualified scientists from the

51

United States. In October 1978 the team arrived in Italy with the neutral tools of modern science amounting to 72 crates of instruments for the most extensive study of an ancient artifact ever conducted.

Represented among the scientists were a pathologist, a medical school professor, image-enhancement specialists, physicists, physical chemists, spectroscopy experts, archeologists, thermography and micro-analysts and X-ray specialists. Only two of the scientists had studied the shroud previously. Most of the others expected that the tests would expose the shroud as a forgery. The tests performed over a five-day period only deepened the mystery of the shroud so much so that it took three years for numerous scientists in the United States and Europe to draw conclusions.

For the first time in 400 years the back of the cloth was examined. No trace of the image could be seen, confirming the fact that the image penetrates only the topmost fibers of the threads.

Tests revealed that the image is that of a real corpse. Using a process called isodensity, it was revealed that the unnatural bulges on the eyes were actually coins having 24 coincidences with a coin issued by Pontius Pilate between A.D. 29 and 32 known as a lepton. This process also revealed the three-dimensional properties of the shroud to such perfection that a model of the body was fashioned from it.

The theory that the image was an impression made by contact with a statue or an actual body was considered and explored, but all the contact impressions made by the scientists proved to be improperly shaded and distorted. None were superficial or three-dimensional. The theory was dispelled since the man of the shroud was lying on his back with the body pressing against the cloth whereas only the weight of the cloth came in contact with the top of the body, thus producing unequal pressures that made it impossible to duplicate. It was also found that the cloth had to be removed other than by natural means, since blood clots would have smeared or broken, especially at the back area where maximum pressure existed. The scientists claimed that the body was not moved, unwrapped or rewrapped.

The suggestion that the image was formed by vapors from the body, such as from sweat, blood, burial spices, ammonia or urea was likewise discounted. It was explained that vapors diffusing from a body through space cannot be that exact, since they do not necessarily travel upward in an orderly manner, but diffuse randomly into the air.

The team, however, did confirm the scorch theory. With the scorch areas caused by the fire of 1532 so close to the image, a resemblance was noted. Using fluorescence, infrared spectroscopy and spectrometry tests, it was concluded that the image was caused by heat or light applied in a slow manner.

The blood marks were also examined thoroughly and were found to contain iron oxide, protein and porphryin, all components of human blood.

The supposition that the image was a painting was emphatically dismissed. Paul Vignon, a professor of biology at the Institut Catholique in Paris claimed that, "No painter, in his most elaborate work, has ever risen to such exactitude." The markings on the shroud have proven to be anatomically and pathologically accurate, exhibiting medical expertise unknown in the 14th century. Since the image can barely be seen up close, and can only be discerned at a distance of from 15 to 20 feet, the artist would have had extreme difficulty in checking the progress of his work. Moreover the shroud can be traced to the Middle Ages when the concept of negativity in photography was unknown. It has been questioned why a 14th-century forger, if he could have painted the image in negative form, would have done so when his work would not have been appreciated for 500 years when the principles of photography were discovered.

Employing a battery of elaborate tests, the Shroud of Turin Research Project discovered that not only is the image three-dimensional and superficial, but it is also non-directional. There were no signs of any medium that a medieval artist could have used, including no trace of pigments, stains, oils, powders, dyes, inks, painting media or liquids. Nor were there signs of brush strokes or a directional pattern as would have been produced by hand. The only direction found was the pattern of the cloth itself. It was concluded that the image unquestionably was not produced by an artist.

In addition to these conclusions, it was also found that the image was not affected by the dousing with water during the 1532 fire and that the yellow coloration of the image is chemically stable and cannot be changed by chemical agents, nor can it be dissolved, or bleached.

Valiant efforts were made to duplicate the image using modern technology, but all attempts proved futile, leading one authority to declare that, "The image is a mystery."

While many popes and ecclesiastics have voiced the opinion that the image of the shroud is that of Jesus Christ, the Roman Catholic Church has never advanced this opinion in an official manner.

Although the research team avoided identifying the image as that of Jesus, a number of its members have independently and publicly voiced this belief. They have also claimed that the physical, historical and chemical facts advance strong evidence for the victim's resurrection. They have also pointed out various aspects recorded in Scripture that are present on the shroud but which are not present in a normal crucifixion. These included the scourging, the crowning with thorns, the absence of broken leg bones, the postmortem wound of the lance and the presence of blood and water in the area of the heart. The team as a whole supported the conclusion that the shroud does not contradict the Gospels on any fact. They were also of the opinion that the shroud was an authentic archeological artifact with many believing that it was the actual burial garment of Jesus Christ. The scientists were in agreement that the accumulated evidence has shifted the burden of proof to those who believe that the shroud is a forgery.

The Grave Cloth

WHEN mention is made of the Holy Shroud, the cloth of Turin immediately comes to mind, but the Cathedral of Oviedo in Spain has a cloth also known as a Holy Shroud, but its function in the tomb was quite different.

Of the sacred relics in the possession of the Cathedral of Oviedo, the most venerated is this cloth measuring 83 centimeters high by 52-1/2 centimeters wide. This is enclosed in a wooden frame that was sheathed in silver during the 17th or 18th centuries. Handles were affixed on either side of the frame for the convenience of the clergy who hold them when the cloth is used for the blessings given on Good Friday and the Feast of the Triumph of the Holy Cross.

The cloth is the color of bone, with its weave described as being fine and tight. It appears to have been folded for a long time with creases that are both horizontal and vertical. Stains are clearly seen on the cloth and these are said to be composed of water and blood. The stains diminish in intensity from the middle of the cloth until they disappear entirely as they progress toward the edges. The arrangement of the stains form a rough square measuring about 30 centimeters on each side.

Some have surmised that the cloth was applied to Our Lord's face after He was already covered with the shroud.

The authorities who have investigated the matter suggest the possibility of this being a cloth similiar in texture and composition to the Holy

Shroud of Turin and believe it was used to support the jaw of Jesus. This seems a possibility since scientists of the Holy Shroud of Turin Research Project indicated that a distinct gap between the frontal and dorsal images of the head was caused by the presence of a chin band tied around the face. The binding of the head, hands and feet are compatible with Jewish custom.

Just as some relics of the Passion have had a tendency to multiply, so have the grave cloths used about the body of Our Lord. These might well be genuine cloths, or portions of them, since it seems reasonable that cloths could have been placed on either side of the body or atop the Holy Shroud that has been adjudged closest to the body.

At least four churches in France and three in Italy claim portions of Our Lord's grave cloths, but none has commanded as much attention as the Shroud of Turin, which has intrigued its admirers for almost two thousand years.

The Veil of Veronica

THE cloth used by the pious matron, Seraphia, to wipe the face of Jesus as He made His way to Calvary has maintained the same aura of mystery that has intrigued the viewers of the Holy Shroud of Turin. It has been as carefully and reverently guarded, but it has not yet attracted the same amount of scientific interest as has the better known, full-length image of the crucified Christ, this probably due in part to the veil's faded and delicate condition.

The image that was impressed on the cloth as a symbol of Jesus' gratitude for Seraphia's courageous and compassionate act of mercy was known from the beginning as *vera icon*, Latin for true image. The two words were gradually appropriated as the proper name of the person instead of the relic, thus transforming the name Seraphia to Veronica.

We are told that Veronica was a woman of position, being the wife of Sirach, one of the councillors belonging to the temple, and that she was approximately 50 years of age at the time of the incident. Various reports have her living on or near the Via Dolorosa and it is popularly believed that she stepped into history during the pause when Simon of Cyrene was recruited to help in the carrying of the cross.

Just as Mary Magdalene anointed the head of Jesus and was honored with the words, "Wherever in the world this gospel is preached, this also that she has done shall be told in memory of her," so, too, has Veronica's kindly act been memorialized. Although not mentioned in Scripture, Veronica is recognized worldwide in the sixth Station of the Cross.

Tradition relates how the ailing Tiberius Caesar, on learning about this memorial, invited Veronica to Rome and sent a messenger to collect all that could be learned about the death, resurrection and ascension of Jesus. Veronica showed the cloth to the emperor, who was immediately cured of his grievance. It is believed she remained in Rome, living there at the time of Saints Peter and Paul.

Veronica is said to have bequeathed the veil to Clement I, the third successor of St. Peter. During the three centuries of persecution the relic was kept in the depths of the catacombs, but was afterwards placed in the church constructed over the tomb of St. Peter. It is in this church, that developed into the Basilica of St. Peter, that the Holy Face has been kept from the earliest times. It is now preserved in the chapel constructed in one of the four enormous pillars that sustain the cupola of St. Peter's. Adorned by Bernini with balustrades and niches and surrounded by twisted columns from the ancient church, the pier is fronted by an enormous statue of Veronica that stands 16 feet tall. It seems one of movement captured in stone. With her extended arm producing a sweep of the veil, Veronica seems to have been halted between the excitement of her discovery and her eagerness to exhibit the holy treasure of the Lord's likeness. A door arranged at the base of the statue gives access to two corridors, one leading to the Vatican grottoes where the relics of St. Peter repose, the other ascending to the interior niche where the Holy Icon is kept. The keys to the three locks affixed to the vault have been confided to the Canons of St. Peter's who are entrusted with the guardianship of the holy treasure. The veil is kept in a reliquary formed of a magnificent frame of crystal and silver gilt.

Early writers maintain that there cannot be the slightest doubt regarding the icon's genuineness. Father John van Bolland (1596-1665), whose name was adopted by the Bollandists, the Jesuit editor of the *Acta Sanctorum*, informs us that, "It is the unanimous opinion of all sacred historians and the firm belief of all true Christians that the Veronica seu Vultus Domini, now at Rome, is the identical and veritable cloth offered to the Redeemer on His way to Calvary." We are likewise told that St. Bridget, the visionary mystic, reproved anyone who doubted its authenticity. Confirmations were also made by various popes who permitted its mention in ancient ceremonials, bulls and correspondence, and its celebration in festivals and processions.

It has been conjectured that the length of the veil was originally three times its width. This seems to agree with the claim of the Cathedral of Jaen, Spain, that Veronica folded the cloth in three parts with the impression being miraculously transferred to the two contacting sections. A cloth at Jaen is reported to have retained a likeness of the Savior. A third portion is in Milan.

Scheduled expositions of the relic have varied throughout its history, at times being shown 13 times a year, at other times only during jubilees or seasons of public calamities. One such exhibition deserves mention.

When Pius IX fled to Gaeto in 1849 during a revolution, he endeavored to appease heaven and obtain an end to the evils that devastated the Church by permitting the Holy Veil to be publicly exposed between the feasts of Christmas and the Epiphany. On the third day of the showing the veil became engulfed with a soft light while the face assumed a tinge of color and shone forth as though it were alive. It appeared to be more distinctly in relief, its eyes deeply sunken while it wore an expression of profound severity. The canons of the basilica immediately ordered the bells to be rung, attracting crowds of people who witnessed the three-hour manifestation. An apostolic notary subsequently composed the document that testified to the fact.

The same evening that this event occurred, etchings and representations of the effigy were applied to the Holy Face and were then sent to France. It was in consequence of this that the custom was introduced of sending copies of the veil to Rome to be touched to the original, thus making the copies objects of special devotion. These copies were affixed with stamps and authenticating seals.

Although devotion to the Holy Face was always in existence in one form or another, it was greatly encouraged and promoted by the visions and writings of Sister Saint-Pierre (d. 1848), a Discalced Carmelite nun of Tours, France. As a result of her revelations the Archconfraternity of the Holy Face was established and approved by Leo XIII, who applauded its goals of reparation against blasphemy and the profanation of Sunday. It was in consequence of this nun's writings that St. Thérèse of the Child Jesus developed a love for the devotion and received permission to affix to her name that of the Holy Face.

In some localities Holy Mass and the Office were celebrated in honor of Veronica with the title of Saint being affixed to her name, but St. Charles Borromeo suppressed these liturgical honors. None of the early martyrologies mentions her name, nor does it appear in the present Roman Martyrology.

Relics of the
Blessed Mother

Our Lady of Czestochowa

The Cincture of the Blessed Mother

F OR over 800 years the Cathedral of Prato, Italy, has kept in a crystal and gold reliquary a strip of green ribbon believed to have been worn by the Blessed Mother as a belt. Consisting of either goat or camel hair with thin golden threads stretched along its borders, the ribbon measures 1.27 meters in length and has small buttons in the shape of olives for hooking.

The origin of the belt is not detailed by history before 1141, but tradition tells us that a gentleman of Prato named Michele, a tanner by profession, received the relic as a dowry upon his marriage to Maria of Jerusalem. A document written in Latin and kept by the cathedral tells us how Michele pilgrimaged to Jerusalem in the year 1141 and while there met and married Maria, who was thought to have been related to St. Thomas the Apostle. When Michele was preparing to return to Prato with his new wife, Maria's mother gave him what she valued most, the green cincture which she had kept with all care in a straw box. Michele was told how the belt had come into her possession, but these details are now unknown. Michele, himself, kept the relic with due respect. While upon his deathbed he summoned the priests to the church and bequeathed the relic to them. His marriage, his acquisition of the relic, his return journey to Prato with the relic, and the scene at his deathbed are all depicted in aged paintings within the cathedral.

Until the 16th century the relic was kept folded in a silver box and was carefully shown by priests who wore silk gloves. During the 16th century the Medici family thought it best to safeguard the relic by placing it in a special case and acquired for it the double reliquary in which it is still kept. The relic is stretched lengthwise in its golden case fronted with crystal, the whole of which is kept in a larger reliquary also fronted with crystal and framed in gold.

Among the numerous persons of distinction and renown who have visited the relic is counted St. Francis of Assisi, who visited Prato in 1212.

The Lady's Chair

CATHERINE Laboure was a postulant in the religious order of the Daughters of Charity when she was visited during the night of July 18, 1830, by a child of about five whom she immediately recognized as an angel. The vision said: "Come to the chapel. The Blessed Virgin awaits you."

Although unafraid, the postulant was concerned that her nocturnal walk through the halls would be discovered. Reading her thoughts, the angel responded: "Do not be uneasy. It is half past 11. Everyone is asleep. Come, I am waiting for you."

After dressing hurriedly, Catherine joined the angel, who led the way to the door, into the hallway, and down the stairs. To Catherine's amazement all the hall lights were brightly lit. On reaching the chapel the door swung open at the child's gentle touch. Again Catherine was surprised since the chapel was ablaze with light as though for a midnight Mass.

The child moved into the sanctuary and stopped by the chair that the director used when he gave conferences to the sisters. With Catherine kneeling beside him, they both waited several minutes. The angel then announced: "Here is the Blessed Virgin."

At that instant Catherine heard a sound like the rustling of a silk dress, and looking toward the sound saw a lady descend the altar steps and seat herself in the director's chair. As Catherine gazed at the vision she thought the lady resembled St. Anne in the picture that hung over the sacristy door. Once again the angel knew her thoughts and assured her in a voice deeper in its reverential tone, "This is the Blessed Virgin."

Catherine knelt beside the lady, placed her folded hands on her lap and looked into her eyes. During this vision the Blessed Virgin advised Catherine to confide everything to her spiritual director, foretold sorrows for France, and instructed Catherine to ". . . come to the foot of the altar. There graces will be shed upon all, great and little, who ask for them. Graces will be especially shed upon those who ask for them." After speaking of her love for the Vincentian Fathers and the Sisters of Charity, the Blessed Virgin warned that they should guard against ". . . useless reading, loss of time and visits." The Virgin reassured the visionary, "There will be an abundance of sorrows and the danger will be great. Yet do not be afraid; tell them not to be afraid. The protection

61

of God shall be ever present. . . . Always I have my eye upon you. . . ." While Mary spoke of these sorrows, Catherine noticed that she was burdened with sorrow, so much so that her eyes filled with tears and she spoke in broken sentences. The Blessed Mother repeated her messages, then faded from sight. With the child once again at her side Catherine returned to the dormitory. When they reached the side of Catherine's bed the angel vanished. The clock struck two. The vision had lasted over two hours.

Catherine experienced two other visions that resulted in the striking of the Miraculous Medal. These two subsequent visions were different in that they came upon Catherine suddenly while she was already at prayer in the chapel. These were concerned primarily with the designs on the medal and the graces that would be granted by its wearing.

The visions were reported only to Catherine's superiors and while the sisters all knew that the visionary of the Miraculous Medal was a member of their community, her identity was not revealed until Catherine was on her deathbed. Having often predicted that she would never see the year 1877, she died on December 31, 1876.

The body of the visionary was found miraculously incorrupt 56 years after burial. However, the body has since been maintained by artificial means. The body can be seen in a glass-sided reliquary beneath a side altar in the chapel of the apparitions. Here also can be found other interesting relics: the incorrupt heart of St. Vincent de Paul, founder of the order, and the relics of St. Louise de Marillac, the co-foundress of the order. Two statues of the Virgin are also found here. The one over the body of Catherine is positioned in the exact spot where the Blessed Mother appeared during the second vision and is a representation of her exactly as she appeared. The statue above the main altar represents the Blessed Mother as she appeared during the third vision and this is likewise situated in the exact place where the Virgin stood.

Also kept here in the chapel of the Motherhouse in Paris, France, is the blue velvet chair, pictured above, on which Our Lady sat during the first vision. Visitors are allowed to touch the chair and to leave papers with their written requests.

The Veil of Our Lady

FOR over a thousand years the Cathedral of Chartres has owned a length of fine material known throughout its history by three different names: the *Sainte Chemisa* (the saint's shirt), the *Voile de la Vierge* (The Veil of the Virgin), and *S. Tunica B.V.M.* (The Holy Tunic Blessed Virgin Mary).

The exact date of its arrival in Chartres is unknown, but tradition informs us that it was owned by the emperor of Constantinople, who presented it to Charlemagne. In the year 876 Charlemagne's grandson, Emperor Charles le Chauve, donated the cloth to Chartres to enrich its treasury of relics. The cloth emerged in a glorious way in the year 911 on the occasion of the siege of Chartres by the Normans. History repeats that when the veil was shown from a rampart, the wearied soldiers experienced a redoubling of energy and a renewal of courage. Trusting in the protection of the Holy Virgin, they fought determinedly until the city was delivered from the enemy, a victory that caused the citizens to regard the tunic as a protection, and acquired for the relic a permanent position in the glorious history of France.

A pious controversy over the description of the garment began as early as the 9th century when it was called a shirt, while pictures and representations of the 11th and 12th centuries actually represent it in drawings as a shirt-type garment with short sleeves. Throughout the ages it has been known variously as a *camisia ou tunica*, (chemise or tunic), and *tunique intérieure* (interior tunic), while 13th-century documents often repeat the words *camisia* (chemise), and *interula* (interior). Because of its silklike quality it has been described as a tissue "propre a la confection des pièces de lingerie. . . ."[1]

The reasons why it should be described as various garments, all of which require certain constructive seams, are unknown since the relic consists of a long piece of cloth, originally a little more than five meters in length, with no seam whatsoever. Its fine silklike texture and length lends itself more to being a scarf or veil, yet most statements in ancient documents insist that it was an undergarment. Could it have been that the women in the early days of Chartres promptly recognized it as an undergarment, and perhaps one that wrapped about the upper part of

[1] *Le Voile De Notre Dame*, Yves Delaports, Maison Des Clercs Dix-Huit, Cloître Notre-Dame, Chartres, 1927, pp. 7-8.

the female body in such a way that it resembled a chemise? Whatever its true function, the delicate fabric has always been venerated as having once belonged to the Mère de Dieu.

When Chartres took possession of the relic it was placed together with other articles in a wooden box that was embellished with gold and was examined at intervals. An official inspection of the cloth was made in 1712, but the bishop, anticipating a sad state of conservation, and wishing to safeguard the people from disappointment, had the ancient box opened in secret. To the surprise and joy of the bishop and the five priests who witnessed the event, they found a fine tissue of Oriental origin that was decorated with pictures of birds, fish and animals embroidered with golden threads. This piece of material was used as an enveloping wrap for the protection of the relic venerated for centuries.

When the veil of the Virgin was unfolded it was found to be plain, with no ornaments or embroidery, but with spots in some places caused by humidity. Other objects were found at the bottom of the box: a belt of leather with a buckle made of ivory, a manuscript in Latin of the Gospel of John and small items that belonged to Saint Lubin, bishop of Chartres who died in the 6th century. The veil was again wrapped in the decorated Oriental cloth and it, together with the other relics, was placed in a silver box that had been prepared in advance.[2]

During the revolution, when shrines were denuded of precious ornaments and altars and relics were profaned, the shirt was savagely mutilated on September 24, 1793, when it was divided into two parts with smaller divisions being given to all present. The cathedral was successful, however, in retaining the largest piece. Eventually the cathedral was able to reclaim another piece and this together with the original section were placed in the 19th-century reliquary that was positioned in a private chapel. The whereabouts of the small pieces are uncertain.

The 1,000th year of ownership of the valued treasure was celebrated by Chartres in 1876. In honor of this celebration the principal piece was placed in a new reliquary between two panels of glass — the same reliquary found in the chapel of Saint-Piat where it is on "habituelle exposition." During a meticulous examination of the fabric the pieces were found to measure 12 centimeters in length by 46 centimeters in width (approximately 4-1/2 inches by 18 inches), and 26 centimeters by 18 centimeters (approximately 10 inches by seven inches). Following this study the principal part of the veil was again entrusted to the monstrance of 1876.

[2]*Ibid.*, pp. 13-14.

Another inspection of the fabric was made in 1927 by M. Henri d'Hennezel, conservateur of the Historical Museum of Lyon and a recognized authority in the identification of ancient materials. In his learned decision he identified the material as silk of an ancient origin that was made in the East following simple and archaic (rudimental) procedures at a time when silk was not produced or worked in western Europe.[3] The opinion of this expert in no way contradicts the tradition of its origins, but seems instead to reinforce it.

It should be brought to the attention of the reader that many other European churches possess bits of cloth that are described as pieces from a veil of Our Lady. Whether or not these are pieces distributed at the time of the mutilation in 1793 is unknown, nor has it been determined if the pieces are the same in color or texture. Many of these might well be authentic, but it is certain that the veil of Chartres has received the most attention.

In its golden reliquary, the veil of Chartres is carried in a grand procession through the streets of Chartres each year on the Feast of the Assumption.

Shroud of Our Lady

THE golden shrine containing the shroud of Our Lady is kept in the Cathedral of Aachen, Germany. The cathedral, also called the *Shrine That Charlemagne Built* and the *Aix La Chapelle*, also houses other precious relics, including the swaddling cloth of the Infant Jesus and the loincloth worn by Our Lord on the cross. Seldom seen before the 14th century, the shroud of Our Lady is shown once every seven years when great pilgrimages flock to Aachen to view the relic and its costly reliquary.

[3]*Notre-Dame de Chartres*, Jean Villette, Revue Trimestrielle, Cloître Notre-Dame, Chartres, September 1976, p. 5.

Miraculous Pictures and Statues of the BVM

Our Lady of Kazan

Our Lady of Czestochowa

POLAND's beloved image of Our Lady of Czestochowa is kept in the Jasna Gora Monastery where pilgrims constantly stream despite communist occupation of the country and their rejection of all things religious.

The origin of the miraculous image rests entirely on legend before the year 1382. Likewise the exact location where the picture was painted is unknown although both Nazareth and Ephesus have been named. Nevertheless, the portrait was eventually located by St. Helena in the fourth century and together with other sacred relics was transported to Constantinople where her son, Emperor Constantine the Great, erected a church for its enthronement.

When Saracen tribes besieged the city, the portrait received special recognition when the devout, together with distinguished citizens and senators, carried the painting through the city and around the dikes. The Saracens, seeing this, became frightened and fled in dismay.[1]

During the dreadful reign of Emperor Izauryn, who was embittered against holy objects and destroyed many by fire, the image was secretly saved by his wife, the Empress Irene, who hid the portrait in the very palace of the Emperor.

The image remained in Constantinople for 500 years until the Faith spread from there into Bulgaria, Rumania and Russia. Since intermarriages took place between the nobilities of these countries, it is believed the portrait became a part of several dowries and in this way eventually found its way to Russia and that region of Russia that became Poland.

During the early part of the 14th century the portrait came into the possession of Ladislaus, a Polish prince who had it installed in a special chamber in the castle of Belz. Not long after its placement the castle was besieged by the Tartars. During the heat of battle an enemy arrow entered the chapel through a window and struck the painting, inflicting a scar on the throat of the Virgin, a mark that remains to this day despite several attempts through the years at repairing it.

[1]*The Glories of Czestochowa and Jasna Gora*, Our Lady of Czestochowa Foundation, Worcester, Mass., 1966, p. 61.

To save the image from the repeated invasions of the Tartars, Ladislaus decided to transport it for safekeeping to Opala, his birthplace. This journey took him through Czestochowa where he rested for the night. During this pause, the image was placed in a small wooden church named for the Assumption. The following morning the painting was replaced in its wagon to be taken away, but to the surprise of everyone, the horses could not move from the place. In a dream the prince received a special revelation that he should permanently deposit the portrait on Jasna Gora (meaning "bright hill"). Convinced that this was the will of God, especially since all were speculating about the peculiar behavior of the animals, he had the portrait solemnly installed in the Church of the Assumption. This occurred on August 26, 1382, a day still observed as the feast day of the painting. Also on this day the prince ordered the erection of a church, convent and cloister as a fitting location for the portrait, and financed the construction of these buildings himself. Wanting to have the portrait guarded by the saintliest of men, he brought to the shrine the Pauline Fathers from the Convent of Nosztre, Hungary, whose reputation for sanctity was well known. Since then, for almost six centuries, the white-habited Pauline Fathers have devoutly ensured the security of their charge.

A few years after the erection of the new monastery, a group of Hussites, who embraced extravagant heresies, invaded the monastery in 1430 with the intention of plundering the sanctuary that was richly decorated. Among other articles they took with them the image, placed it in a wagon and proceeded only a short distance when the horses refused to move. Recalling, perhaps, that a similar incident occurred to Prince Ladislaus some 50 years before, and realizing that the portrait was to blame, the heretics threw the portrait to the ground where it broke into three pieces. A report mentions that one of the robbers drew his sword, struck the image and inflicted two deep gashes. While preparing to inflict a third, he fell to the ground and died in agony. The two marks on the cheek of the Virgin, together with the previous injury to the throat made by a Tartar's arrow, have resisted repeated attempts at reconstruction. Regardless of what combinations of paint are used or the techniques employed, the scars have always reappeared.

The monastery was again threatened by treasure hunters, this time by Swedish troops. The year was 1655 when 12,000 Swedes confronted 300 men who were guarding the sanctuary. Our Lady's defenders, though vastly outnumbered, were successful in bitterly defeating the enemy.

The history of Poland and that of the image have been closely entwined since the painting's residence in that country. Closer to our own time, in 1920, the feast of Our Lady of Sorrows, the Russian army stood at the Vistula River ready to invade Warsaw. While the Polish people had recourse to Our Lady, her image appeared over Warsaw, causing the Russians to withdraw.[2] Our Lady has always supported her people during political invasions and suppressions. During the Nazi occupation when Hitler forbade pilgrimages, a half million Poles visited the sanctuary. The following year, 1945, more than a million and a half expressed their love for the Madonna by praying before her image. In 1948 when the Russian army occupied Poland, more than 800,000 came in a mass demonstration of faith on the Feast of the Assumption even while Communist soldiers patrolled the streets. Even today, as mentioned previously, the faithful continue to converge on the shrine in defiance of the wishes of the Communists.

Visitors to the portrait rarely see it without one of its two dresses. The more costly one is composed of precious jewels contributed by the citizens of Poland; the other, embroidered with beads of a golden texture, is less expensive, but is treasured in that it was assembled by peasant women. An ancient dress decorated with rare pearls was torn from the image in 1909 by a thief, and has never been recovered. Every Holy Thursday the two decorative dresses are interchanged during elaborate ceremonies. The priests remove the image from the altar and carry it into the treasure chamber where they strip it of its jeweled crown and decoration, clean the jewels, then affix the other dress to the painting. Amid solemn chants and prayers the image is carried in procession and restored to its place of honor. Since a restoration of the painting in 1925, the dresses no longer rest against the wood of the painting. A special shield was constructed which left a small air space, and it is against this shield that the dresses are attached.

The crown of gold is encrusted with jewels and was a gift of Pope Pius X who sent it as a token of love and sympathy for the suffering nation. A former crown, a gift of Pope Clement XI in 1717, was unfortunately stolen in 1909 together with the dress of pearls. It was the crown donated by Pope Clement XI that was used in the first official coronation of the painting. Another coronation, which has been described as the most solemn of all the ceremonies ever to be observed at Jasna Gora, took place in 1910.

Because of the dark coloration of the face and hands, the image has been affectionately called the Black Madonna, a phrase reminiscent of

[2]*Shrines of Our Lady*, Sr. Mary Jean Dorcy, O.P., Sheed & Ward, New York, 1956, pp. 84-85.

the Canticle of Canticles, "I am black but beautiful." The darkness is ascribed to various conditions, of which its age is primary. During its existence it was hidden for safekeeping in various places which were far from ideal for the storage of works of art; furthermore, countless candles burned before it, causing it to be almost constantly embraced by smoke which was not beneficial to its delicate and aged texture. Additionally it was handled innumerable times, resulting in unintentional abuse.

In addition to the restoration made in 1925, a number of others were made, the first occurring in 1430 after it was abused by the Hussites who threw it from the wagon. The second took place in 1682 during the reign of King John Sobieski. Unfortunately this renovation consisted of a partial repainting. It was found that the original paint had a resin base and that the cape and dress of the Virgin had a grayish-blue color decorated with golden designs in the shape of lilies. The lining of the cape was found to be of a carmine color with a golden border. The Child Jesus is dressed in shades of carmine decorated with lilies, rosettes and clusters of leaves all of a dull gilt. The face and hands of the Madonna have a bronze shade, the eyes are narrow, the nose elongated and the mouth is small. The Child is portrayed with curly black hair while his face and hands are the same color as those of His Mother.

Without the frame the painting is approximately 19 inches high by about 13 inches wide. It is almost a half inch in thickness. Scenes and designs representing the history of the painting and some of the miracles performed through the intercession of the Madonna are depicted on a piece of cloth stretched across the back of the painting.

The image of Our Lady of Czestochowa has three feast days, the main feast being that of the Assumption. May 3 was designated by Pope Pius XI as the feast of Mary under the title of Queen of Poland. This title was given to Mary in 1656 in the Cathedral of Lwow when Jan Casimir, the exiled king of Poland, returned to his homeland, laid down his crown at the foot of the Virgin's altar and vowed, "I, Jan Casimir, King of Poland, take thee as Queen and Patroness of my kingdom; I put my people and my army under thy protection. . . ." This vow was confirmed and ratified by both Houses of Parliament. In addition to these two feast days, that of the portrait is observed on August 26, the day reserved for its celebration since the time of Prince Ladislaus in the early 14th century. During the month of August, pilgrims come from all parts of Poland to plead with the Madonna for personal favors and to beg for the liberation of their country from Communist suppression.

The most distinguished of all the portrait's visitors in modern times was undoubtedly Pope John Paul II, a native son, who returned to Poland and prayed before the Madonna during his historic visit in 1979, several months after his election to the Chair of Peter. A second visit was made to this beloved portrait during the pope's second visit to Poland in 1983.

Our Lady of Einsiedeln

WHEN St. Meinrad left the monastic life at Reichenau in 840 to become a hermit, he took with him a wonder-working statue of the Virgin Mary that had been given him by the Abbess Hildegarde of Zurich. For more than 20 years he lived an austere life on the slopes of Mount Etzel in Switzerland until about the year 863. A rumor that valuables were kept in the shrine of the miraculous statue attracted the attention of two robbers, who entered the cell. Not finding any treasure they killed the hermit. We are told that two crows flew about the robbers' heads until they were identified as the murderers.

Meinrad's mountain retreat soon became a place of popular devotion. Spiritual favors and healings were attributed to the Blessed Virgin whom Meinrad had venerated with such filial devotion. In 940 a company of hermits established a Benedictine monastery on the mountain and fashioned the saint's cell into a small chapel. Known from ancient times as the Lady Chapel, the cell is enclosed in marble and precious woodwork and stands within the monastery church much the same as the Portiuncula in Assisi and the Holy House in Loreto.

The miracle-working statue of the Virgin is kept within the Lady Chapel against a golden background.

The monastery church was scheduled for consecration on September 14, 940 by Bishop Conrad of Constance, but the day before the ceremony, the bishop had a vision in which he saw the church suddenly fill with a brilliant light as our Lord appeared near the altar. The next day, while preparing to enter the church for the consecration, he heard a clear voice saying that there was no need to perform the service since it had already been consecrated by God. The deposition of Bishop Conrad regarding the vision, dated 948, is still intact and preserved at the abbey. The event was investigated and confirmed by Pope Leo VIII.

In 1854 a group of religious from Einsiedeln were sent to the United

72

States to work among Indian tribes, the first settlement established by them was St. Meinrad's Abbey in southern Indiana.

Meinrad was canonized in the 13th century. His statue of the miracle-working Madonna continues to attract pilgrims as it has since its origins over a thousand years ago.

Our Lady of Good Counsel

VISITORS to the Santuario Madonna del Buon Consiglio are alerted to the church's treasure by way of a Latin inscription above the main entrance which translates:

> In the year of the Incarnation, 1467, on the feast of St. Mark, at the hour of Vespers, the image of the Mother of God, which you venerate in the marble chapel of this church, appeared from on high.

The history of the portrait is closely aligned with that of Genazzano, a small town located about 30 miles southeast of Rome. As early as the fifth century Genazzano donated a large part of its revenues to Pope Sixtus III for the rebuilding of the basilica of Our Lady of the Snows, also known as St. Mary Major. As a gesture of appreciation, that portion of the town that had contributed the most was endowed with a church dedicated to Our Lady of Good Counsel. In 1356 the church was entrusted to the care of the Augustinians, who had been in Genazzano since 1278. With the passage of time the church fell into disrepair. During the year of the miracle, 1467, an Augustinian tertiary named Petruccia, widow of Giovanni da Nocera, pledged to assist the order in the restoration of the little church. After spending all her funds on this endeavor the restoration was halted due to the increased cost of both materials and labor. She was subsequently ridiculed by the parishioners who had considered her plans presumptuous. Her efforts were, nevertheless, rewarded in a marvelous manner.

On St. Mark's Day, April 25, 1467, while the entire population participated in a public festival, a cloud descended from an otherwise clear sky and obscured the unfinished church. Before thousands of witnesses the cloud dissipated, revealing a painting of Our Lady and the Christ Child, a portrait that had not been there moments before. News of the mysterious image spread rapidly. The provincial of the Augustinan order, Ambrogio da Cori, recorded that "all of Italy came to visit the blessed image; cities and towns came in pilgrimage. Many wonders occurred, many favors granted. . . ."[1] He likewise recorded that "the very beautiful image of Mary appeared on the wall without human intervention."[2]

The number of miracles worked in the three months and 17 days following the miraculous appearance was numbered by a notary as 159. Because of these miracles and the attention given the image, an investigation was initiated by Pope Paul II who sent a French bishop and a Dalmation bishop to ascertain the facts. The results of their inquiries are said to be preserved.

The widow who humbly set in motion the restoration of the church that was to occasion such wonders lived to see the church restored and a splendid monastery erected. After her death she was buried in the Chapel of the Madonna.

The portrait was first called the "Madonna of Paradise," but was soon changed as a result of information secured from two refugees who arrived in Genazzano from Albania, a country that was then being terrorized by the Turks. The men testified before the papal delegation that they had seen the very same image in a church in the Albanian town of Scutari only a few weeks before. The commission of inquiry established that a portrait of the Madonna that had been venerated in the church at Scutari was indeed missing. Where the picture had previously been located, there remained an empty space the exact size of the portrait. With the origin of the picture confirmed, the portrait was renamed "Our Lady of Good Counsel," after the church where it had been miraculously relocated. Even today, when the Albanians visit the portrait they refer to it as "their" Madonna and call her Our Lady of Scutari or the Madonna of the Albanians.[3] They maintain to the present that the portrait spontaneously left their church when Albania was invaded by the Turks.

Measuring 40 by 45 centimeters (approximately 15-1/2 inches by 17-1/2 inches), the painting is a fresco executed on a thin layer of porcelain no thicker than an eggshell. It has been ascertained that the removal of such a fragile material from the wall of the Scutari Church could not have been successfully accomplished by human hands.

The portrait is a charming and delicate rendition of the Madonna and Child. With their cheeks touching, the Child embraces His Mother's neck with the right hand, and with the left hand holds the edge of her

[1]*Sanctuary of Our Mother of Good Counsel*, The Sanctuary, Genazzano, Italy, p. 5.
[2]*Ibid.*, p. 8
[3]*Ibid.*, pp. 8-9.

dress. The tunic of the Child is red; the Mother's tunic is green. The ivory-colored mantle that covers the head and shoulders of the Madonna is also draped on the shoulder of the Child. Mary's chestnut hair is said to be arranged in a Roman style. The aureole of the Madonna is golden while that of the Child is red, in the same shade as His tunic. The Madonna seems half turned toward her Son and half turned toward the faithful in what is suggested as a double interest. A curiosity exists in that the face of the Madonna appears sad when viewed from an angle, but she appears to smile and look at the spectator who stands before her.[4]

Church authorities have noted that the redness of the Virgin's cheeks seem to grow deeper and lighter as if to awaken the emotions of the viewer. It is a recognized fact that the color acquires various tones in different periods of the year although the painting is protected by a sheet of glass.

When the church was restored and enlarged between 1621 and 1629 a proposal was made to strengthen the wall on which the holy image was attached to make it free for removal to a more conspicuous place in the church. The conventual chapter at first rejected the plan, wishing to leave the image in the place that heaven had selected, but they eventually relented. The image was then placed atop a splendid piece of marble within its own chapel.

The shrine of Our Lady has been visited by countless pilgrims throughout the centuries, with the church and the portrait remaining secure for 500 years. During World War II, however, a bomb fell on the basilica, crashed through the roof and exploded on the floor of the sanctuary. The main altar and several others were literally obliterated. The nearby altar of the Madonna remained intact with the fragile image being entirely unaffected.

Our Lady of the Two Guadalupes

THE statue of Our Lady of Guadalupe, given by Pope Gregory the Great to the noted churchman, Bishop Leander of Seville, was lost to the soil of northern Spain for 600 years, to be restored not by persons

[4]*Ibid.*, pp. 9-10

high in ecclesiastical ranks but by a humble cowherd who acted under heavenly direction.

Treasured by the people of Spain since its presention in 580, it was during the frightful time of the Moorish invasion in 711 that the statue was hidden for safekeeping. One report tells that it was hidden in a cave under a churchbell; another that it was buried in an iron casket. Whichever the case, it was hidden in the province of Estremadura with pertinent papers that documented its history. Those who had secured the statue died in the confrontation of the conquest, and it was thus lost for centuries.

During the 400-year occupation of the Moors, Christianity suffered hardships, but the devotion to the Mother of God was maintained, and it flourished after the liberation. Great emotion was experienced by the populace in 1326 when a cowherd named Gil Cordero related that while searching for a lost cow a radiant lady emerged from a nearby forest and, after indicating a place where he should dig to unearth a treasure, requested that a chapel be built on the spot.

When ecclesiastical authorities were summoned to the place, they found the entrance to an underground cave and the statue with its documents. Though hidden for 600 years, the statue of Oriental, unstained wood was examined and pronounced to be in perfect condition. The chapel that was later built by order of King Alfonso XI and the statue that was enthroned therein, was named Guadalupe for the village located near the place of discovery.

With great pomp and majesty the king of Spain visited the chapel in 1340, 14 years after the statue's discovery, as did many noblewomen through the years who regarded the statue as a symbol of the Virgin's royal maternity, since the statue holds in its left hand the Child Jesus while the right hand wields a scepter. Members of royalty presented the Virgin Mary with jeweled mantles which now constitute a costly and extensive wardrobe.

With the Franciscan Fathers serving as custodians of the shrine, it became one of the most important places of pilgrimage — with its popularity at its height during the time of the great discoveries of Columbus, who reportedly carried a replica of the statue with him as did the conquistadores. Furthermore, it is said that Christopher Columbus prayed at the shrine of Guadalupe before making his historic voyage, and upon discovering the West Indies Island of Karukera on November 4, 1493, he renamed it Guadalupe in honor of the Virgin. Interestingly, the visions of Our Lady of Guadalupe in Mexico, during which she left the miraculous image on the cloak of a humble Indian, occurred 39 years after Columbus discovered the New World. Some believe that the famous Mexican shrine of Our Lady of Guadalupe that was built following the apparitions of Our Lady to Juan Diego was named for the Guadalupe shrine of Estremadura, Spain. It is strongly maintained, however, that the name of the Mexican shrine came about because of various interpretations of the language used by the vision. An explanation of this will be presented later. Although the matter of the name is debated, it is factual that the first apparition occurred on the ninth day of September 1531 to a 55-year-old Indian, Juan Diego, as he was hurrying down Tepeyac Hill to attend Mass at a Franciscan mission. Suddenly he heard a woman's voice above celestial melodies calling him, not Juan Diego, but the affectionate diminutive, "Juanito, Juan Dieguito." After a tender dialogue she requested that he visit the bishop, tell his Excellency about the apparition and ask that a shrine be built in her honor.

The visions occurred five times, four to Juan Diego and once to his ailing uncle when the lady effected his cure. The last apparition to Juan Diego occurred on Tuesday, December 12. To provide the bishop with the sign he requested that would identify the apparition and confirm the supernatural aspect of what Juan had alleged, the lady asked Juan to walk higher up the hill and to collect the roses found there — this in spite of the rocky nature of the place and its unsuitability for the growth of any type of vegetation. Nevertheless, Juan picked the roses that he found there. The lady arranged the flowers inside the scoop of the tilma, a cloak worn by the Indians, and cautioned him against disturbing or revealing his burden except in the presence of the bishop.

When Juan opened the cloak for the prelate, he found not the skepticism he had received before, but the bishop kneeling among the flowers looking in reverential awe at a picture miraculously applied to the cloak — an exact likeness that Juan Diego identified as the lady he had seen four times on Tepeyac Hill.

News of the miracle spread rapidly. Crowds continually gathered at the bishop's house forcing the ecclesiastic, who had kept the tilma in his private chapel, to remove the tilma to the cathedral of the city where it was placed above the altar for all to see. When the Spaniards and Indians completed the building of the church where the lady had requested it, the image was transferred there and was placed atop the altar to the satisfaction and rejoicing of the people.

The tilma itself is cactus cloth made from the maguey plant. It is a fabric similar to sacking that usually disintegrates within 20 years — a fabric wholly unsuited to the application of paint. The garment is made of three strips, each one measuring 21 inches in width by 78 inches in length with the image imprinted on two lengths. In its golden frame the third panel which hung on Juan's back is folded behind the two front panels.[1] Another source states that the tilma was made of only two straight pieces sewn together.[2] Regardless, it is certain that two pieces are seen and these measure 78 inches in length by 42 inches in width. They are joined with the original loose stitching that can be seen running the length of the panel along the left ear of the figure, down the left wrist to the knee and passing to the side of the angel's head. The figure of our Lady measures four feet, eight inches in height.[3]

The fabric has been examined repeatedly by experts in painting media who have declared the fabric's loose weave and texture both unsuitable and unprepared for the application of paint. The fabric is so thin and of such a loose weave that if one stands behind it the features of the basilica can be seen as clearly as through a trellis.

Artists have reported that the portrait was painted without brush strokes, but like a wash in four different media: oil, tempera, water color and fresco. The head and hands of the image were executed in oils; the rose-colored tunic, the angel and clouds were painted in tempera; the blue-green mantle in water color; the background in fresco — a successful combination unexpected on such a flimsy cloth.[4] Moreover, the application was so permanent that compared to manmade paintings dating from 1531, the image has required no restoration and remains to this day an artistic marvel.

One hundred thirty-five years after the apparition, in 1666, a "Painters Commission" was formed to study the miraculous picture. Their conclusion was that:

> "No other but God, Our Lord, could effect so beautiful a production; and that we hold without doubt and affirm without scruple that the imprinting of the said picture of our Lady of Guadalupe on the tilma of said Juan Diego, was, and must be understood and declared to have been, a supernatural work and a secret reserved to the Divine Majesty."[5]

In the same year, 1666, "The Scientific Board" affirmed that:

> "The continuance through so many years of the holy picture's freshness of form and color, in the presence of such opposing elements of time

[1]*Am I Not Here*, Harold J. Rahm, S.J., Ave Maria Institute, Washington, New Jersey, 1962, p. 50.
[2]*A Handbook on Guadalupe, Our Lady Patroness of the Americas*, Franciscan Friars, Franciscan Marytown Press, Kenosha, Wisconsin, 1974, p. 65.
[3]*Ibid*. p. 65.
[4]Rahm. *Op. cit.* p. 32.
[5]*That Motherly Mother of Guadalupe*, Rev. L.M. Dooley, S.V.D., St. Paul Editions, Boston, Massachusetts, 1962, p. 45.

and decay, cannot have a natural cause. Its sole principle is He Who alone is able to produce miraculous effects above all the forces of nature."[6]

Of more recent date a similar opinion was reached by Dr. Philip Callahan, a University of Florida biophysicist who analyzed the painting in February of 1979. After studying infrared radiation photographs he found that the painting has no sketch underneath, a prerequisite for almost all paintings, and that the original blue and pink pigments had not faded, although later touch-up work showed signs of age. Moreover, he discovered that the fabric had not been sized, a process that prevents rot, and that pollution from votive candles should normally have darkened and damaged the fabric during the 116 years it was left unprotected. The scientist was especially impressed by the manner in which the rough cloth caused light diffraction, that is, an optical effect that causes the face of the image to appear white up close and olive at a distance. This same effect is found in nature when colors change under different angles, such as the smooth surface of bird feathers or butterfly scales. In his words, ". . . the original painting is miraculous."[7]

For more than a century this self-portrait of the Virgin Mary remained uncovered atop the altar and was exposed to the enthusiasm of the people and to the effects of the atmosphere during several solemn processions. The devout and the sick were never prohibited from kissing or touching it with devout objects during these processions — contacts that would have damaged it had it not been miraculously guarded. Finally placed under glass in 1647, the pane was often removed for long periods of time at the request of the faithful who wished to have an unobstructed contact with it. One observer in 1753 counted more than 500 articles that were pressed to the image.

The picture painted by supernatural means was not exempt from human interference. Just as treasured statues and images are adorned with jewels and golden trinkets, so also the devotees of Our Lady of Guadalupe wished to express their love and gratitude by the application of various trimmings. Several additions were painted on the cloth, including angels in the clouds that soon faded and fell away; the rays of the sun were gilded and these can be seen flaking away; the white moon was sheathed in silver which turned black and is still chipping off; and a crown that was painted on the head is now scarcely noticeable. It is believed by the custodians of the shrine that other embellishments were added — namely the gold border of the Virgin's mantle, the stars and the

[6]*Ibid.* p. 45.

[7]*Our Sunday Visitor*, Our Sunday Visitor, Inc., Huntington, Indiana, Vol. 68, No. 22, September 30, 1979.

embroidery design on the gown. These are thought to have been added during the 16th century. This theory is questioned, however, since unlike those that are known for certain were added by human hand, these three additions have shown little inclination to flake away.

The image escaped serious injury and possible destruction on two occasions: once when a goldsmith who was cleaning the frame accidentally spilled nitric acid that ran along the left side of the tilma miraculously leaving only a faint streak, and a second time on November 14, 1921, when a powerful bomb hidden in a bouquet of flowers was placed on the altar during the Calles persecution. The metal altar crucifix directly beneath the image was twisted in the blast and marble decorations and stained-glass windows were shattered, yet the tilma and the protective glass remained miraculously unharmed. The curved crucifix that attests to the strength of the explosion is in a decorative case for all to see.

Certain contradictions intrigue the thousands who view the image each day. While a century of touching and devout kissing wore away some of the paint, especially of the hands, yet when seen from a distance or when photographed, all are perfectly colored and formed. Moreover, the details are sharpest when viewed from a distance, unlike those of other paintings in which details are sharper when one draws nearer. The intensity of the coloring is likewise of interest since it pales when one is close to it and darkens at a distance. Another reversal exists in the shrinking and expanding of the image, that is, the painting seems large in its position atop the altar, but seems reduced in size when one draws near.

Many who have closely examined the face of the portrait have reported seeing the image of a man reflected in the lady's eyes. A bearded face is seen, a shoulder, and a part of a halo in a three-quarter image. This likeness matches exactly the contemporary portraits of Juan Diego. First discovered in 1929 by Alfonso Marcué Gonzáles while examining photographic negatives, Carlos Salinas made a similar discovery in 1951, although the findings were not immediately made known. Only after the conclusions of a commission were presented to him did the archbishop give permission for the discovery to be made public by a radio broadcast on December 11, 1955, the eve of the Feast of Our Lady of Guadalupe.[8] Confirmations of this discovery were made in 1956 by Doctor Javier Torroello Bueno, an oculist, and by Dr. Rafael Torija Lavoignet.[9] Optometrists who examined the eyes more recently have observed that in

[8]Handbook, Op. cit., p. 73.
[9]Ibid., pp. 73-74.

addition to the image of the man, the eyes reflect light rays the same as human eyes when examined optometrically.[10]

The natives who first studied the image read messages that were not apparent to others. Since the lady stood in front of the sun they understood that she was greater than their sun god Huitzilopochtli. Their moon god, Tezcatlipoca likewise lost stature, since the lady stood upon the moon's crescent. The broach at her throat with its small black cross reminded the Indians of the crucifixes of the Spanish friars and the symbol on the banner of Captain Hernando Cortes. They understood by this cross that the lady was bringing the true religion to the Mexicans. That she was held aloft by a child with wings singled her as a heavenly being, yet her hands joined in prayer meant that there was one who was greater than she.[11] The white fur at the neck and sleeves was taken as a mark of royalty, as were the 46 golden stars and the border of gold. The bluish-green of the mantle was taken as a color reserved to divinity. It was the reading of the picture that converted whole tribes to the Faith.[12]

The origin of the name *Guadalupe* has always been a matter of conjecture. While many strongly believed that the portrait was named for the statue of Our Lady of Guadalupe in Estremadura, Spain, it is nevertheless believed that the name came about because of the interpretation of the words used by the Virgin during the apparition to the ailing uncle of Juan Diego. An account of the apparition written by Don Antonio Valeriano three years after it occurred is translated:

> "... Here is (told) how he (Juan Bernardino) had seen his nephew and he said to him how she (the Blessed Virgin) had asked him to explain to the bishop, to set before him and to relate what he had seen and the manner in which marvelously she cured him and will thus be known, or named, or called, *Entirely Perfect Virgin Holy Mary of Guadalupe*, her precious image. ..."[13]

Since *Guadalupe* is Spanish, and the lady spoke in the Indian dialect, the word was taken to be the Aztec Nahuatl word *coatalocpia*, which is translated: coatl for serpent, tlaloc for goddess and tlalpia for watching over.[14] Another version is the Aztec word *te coatlaxopeuh* which is pronounced 'te quatlasupe': te meaning stone, coa meaning serpent, tla being the noun ending which can be interpreted as 'the,' while

[10]Rahm., *Op. cit.*, pp. 75-76.
[11]Rahm., *Ibid.*, p. 56.
[12]Handbook, Op. cit., p. 66.
[13]*Ibid.*, pp. 17-18.
[14]*The Grace of Guadalupe*, Frances Parkinson Keyes, Jullian Messner, Inc., New York, 1941, pp. 61-62.

xopeuh means to crush or stamp out.[15] Both words when pronounced rapidly sound remarkably like Guadalupe. Whichever is the valid Aztec word, both, nevertheless, refer to the feathered serpent god Quetzalcoatl, whose images are still found on many Aztec ruins. To this fierce serpent god the Indians annually offered 20,000 men, women and children in bloody sacrifice. The significance of the name *Guadalupe* was understood by the Indians to mean that the Virgin would crush their fearsome serpent god. This went far in converting eight million Indians in the seven years following the apparitions.[16]

The stone serpent, taken to represent Satan, reminds us of the biblical passage in Genesis, "I will establish a feud between thee and the woman, between thy offspring and hers; she is to crush thy head while thou dost lie in ambush at her heels. (Gen. 3:14-15)

Bishop Zumarraga to whom the portrait was first revealed, emphatically sealed the confusion regarding the name when he understood the Indian word to mean *Guadalupe*, since he and his staff were familiar with the shrine of Our Lady of Guadalupe at Estremadura, Spain. Many believe, however, that the bishop's understanding of the name and his pronouncement in the matter were made in error.

Of the 45 popes who have reigned since the creation of the miraculous portrait, 25 have issued decrees concerning it. The earliest recorded is that of Pope Gregory XIII in 1575 that *extended* the indulgences granted by his predecessors. This implies, of course, that indulgences must have been granted shortly after the apparitions of 1531.[17]

In 1754 Pope Benedict XIV decreed that Our Lady of Guadalupe should be the national patroness and made December 12 a Day of Obligation with an octave, and additionally ordered a special Mass and Office. This same pontiff wrote: "In the image everything is miraculous, an image emanating from flowers gathered on completely barren soil on which only prickly shrubs can grow . . . an image in no manner deteriorated, neither in her supreme loveliness nor in its sparkling color . . . God has not done likewise to any other nation."

Pope St. Pius X granted the unusual privilege of permitting Mexican priests to say the special Mass of the Lady of Guadalupe on the 12th day of every month, and Pope Pius VII permanently attached the sanctuary to the Basilica of St. John Lateran. Since St. Peter's is first in rank, St. John Lateran is placed second, making the sanctuary the second ranking church in all Christendom.

[15]Handbook, *Op. cit.*, p. 18.
[16]*Ibid.*, p. 19.
[17]*Ibid.*, p. 122.

Three popes ordered the crowning of the image: Benedict XIV, Leo XIII, and Pius XII. Pope Paul VI reintroduced an ancient custom by sending a golden rose to the shrine and Pope John Paul II, on a visit to Mexico in January 1979, visited the image in its new basilica adjacent to the old church, and paid homage to the 450-year-old relic.

The visionary of Guadalupe, Juan Diego, it should be noted, lived 17 years following the apparition. During this time he was appointed as the official custodian of the tilma and was ever ready to relate the apparitions and to answer all questions concerning the image. He lived in a small room attached to the church and following his death at age 74 in 1548, he was buried in the chapel, as was his uncle Juan Bernardino, who died at age 84 in 1544.

The miraculous image of Mary on the 450-year-old fabric consistently intrigues its viewers, baffles others with its defiance of nature, and above all has inflamed in the hearts of the devout a deeper love for the heavenly Mother and an awareness and appreciation for the supernatural of which this image is a major proponent.

Our Lady of Kazan

A MONG the Russian people the Icon of Our Lady of Kazan is one of the most famous and venerated images of the Blessed Mother.

According to expert opinions the icon dates from the 13th century and was painted on wood in the typical Greek Byzantine style. The image depicts the head and shoulders of the Virgin Mary with the Infant Jesus standing upon her knee. Although the work is almost entirely covered with a rizza of precious gold, the image beneath it is completely painted with pigments that extensive x-ray examinations have indicated are perfectly preserved.[1] Only the faces of Our Lady and the Infant Jesus are visible as is the right hand of the child which is superimposed on the neck of His Mother in a posture of benediction. The golden rizza dates from the 17th century and is encrusted with more than one thousand diamonds, emeralds, oriental rubies, sapphires and pearls.[2]

[1] *The Holy and Miraculous Icon of Our Lady of Kazan.* Archpriest John J. Mowatt, Byzantine Center, Fatima, Portugal, p. 1.
[2] Ibid. p. 2.

While the greater part of the stones have been on the icon for centuries, a few donated stones have been added in recent years.

Thought to have been painted in Constantinople, historians believe it was brought to Russia by way of the Black Sea and the Don River and then to the city of Kazan where it was enshrined in a monastery.

The image was lost in 1209 when the Tartars sacked the city, destroyed the monastery and killed its inhabitants. It was recovered more than 350 years later when the city was being rebuilt following a disastrous fire. The year was 1579.

A child is credited with discovering the image among the rubble of her house that her father was then restoring. Named Matrona, the child of nine told of a heavenly lady who indicated a place where she should dig to recover an icon. Two appearances of the lady were ignored by the parents and neighbors, but when a third vision threatened punishment, they promptly began to sift through the ruins. It was Matrona who unearthed the image, which was wrapped in old rags. Although buried for over three centuries the image was uninjured. News of the miraculous discovery spread throughout the city, bringing thousands to the place of the apparitions. With the archbishop carrying the icon, a solemn procession was formed to escort the image to nearby St. Nicholas Church. Later it was enshrined in the Cathedral of the Annunciation in Kazan. Still later, when a copy of the icon was made and sent to Czar Ivan the Great, he issued orders that the original icon should be enshrined in the convent he wanted built over the place of the discovery. It was in this convent some years later that Matrona and her mother became members and took monastic vows.

When Russia was besieged from within and without by enemies, and several laid claim to the Russian throne, Bishop Germogen called upon the patriotic Russians to fight the impostors and resist the foreign invaders, assuring them that they would be supported and protected by the Mother of God. He was himself imprisoned by Polish troops in 1612 and suffered a martyr's death by starvation. In retaliation, the Russian people organized behind the Greek bishop, Arsenius, who was visiting Russia at the time. In a vision, St. Serge, founder of the Holy Trinity Monastery in Zagorsk, appeared to the bishop and assured him of victory under the protection of Our Lady. Hearing this, the Russians took the holy icon as a victory banner and stormed the walls of the Kremlin, liberating Moscow on November 27, 1612. The Russian troops hailed Our Lady of Kazan as the liberator of Russia while the Church proclaimed October 22 as the feast day to commemorate the victory. The icon was again used as a victory banner by Czar Peter the Great in his battle against the forces of Charles XII of Sweden in 1790. The image experienced a number of transfers to places of honor, each new place seemingly attempting to overwhelm the icon with splendor and expressions of reverence. On the famous Red Square in Moscow, Prince Pozharsky, commander-in-chief of the people's militia, built a basilica dedicated to the Lady of Kazan where the icon was transferred, but when the capital was moved from Moscow to St. Petersburg, Czar Peter built a special shrine for the image and had it removed to this new place of honor.

Following Napoleon's defeat, which was attributed to the intercession of Our Lady, the Kazan Basilica was constructed to house the holy icon. Finally consecrated during the reign of Alexander II, the czar offered all the war trophies and battle flags of the Napoleonic invasion to the shrine as tokens of Our Lady's victory. The icon remained there until the Russian Revolution of 1917. In 1929 the Kazan Cathedral in St. Petersburg (now known as Leningrad) was desecrated and converted into a museum, which it remains to this day.

Although it is uncertain how the image was removed from Russia, it is speculated by some that it was sold after the Revolution, together with other icons, church vessels, religious and national treasures, at a time when the new government was hard-pressed for funds. It eventually appeared in private hands in Poland and then in England in 1935.

In 1960 the icon was loaned to a pious group who brought it in pilgrimage to Russian Orthodox churches throughout the United States in the hope of raising enough funds to redeem it. Solemn celebrations and sacred liturgies were observed during each of its visits. It was also displayed with reverence in the Russian Orthodox Pavilion at the New York World's Fair of 1964-1965. The icon was eventually redeemed by the Apostolate of Our Lady of Fatima and was enshrined on July 26, 1970, in the Byzantine chapel of the Icon of Kazan in Fatima, Portugal.

After more than 50 years of wandering among private owners, the icon is now housed in a holy setting where it is hoped that one day it can be returned to its former sanctuary on Russian soil.

Our Lady of Montserrat

T HERE is historical evidence that a chapel dedicated to the Mother of God was established on Montserrat in the year 888.[1] Two hundred

[1]*Montserrat*, Dom Justino Bruguera, Editorial Planeta, Barcelona, 1964, p. 21.

years later, in 1025, a Benedictine monastery was established there with the Benedictines still maintaining the sanctuary and providing hospitality to the thousands of visitors who journey there each month to honor the ancient statue of Our Lady.

The holy image is a fine example of 13th-century Romanesque art carved in wood. It is in a sitting position and measures 95 centimeters, slightly over three feet in height. In accordance with the Romanseque style, the figure is slender with an elongated face and a delicate expression. A crown rests atop the Virgin's brow and another adorns the head of the Child Jesus who is seated on her lap. A cushion serves as her footstool and she is seated upon a stool that has substantial legs topped by smooth cone-shaped finials. The dress consists of a tunic and cloak, both gilded and plain in design and draped in a stylized manner. A veil covers the Virgin's head under the crown and falls smoothly about the shoulders. This, too, is gilded, but is enhanced with geometric designs of stars, squares and stripes accented in subtle shades. The right hand of the Virgin holds a sphere, while the left reaches forward in a graceful gesture. The Christ Child is similarly dressed except, of course, for a veil. His right hand is raised in blessing while His left holds an object described as a pine cone.

Almost all the statue is gilded except for the face and hands of Mary and the face, hands and feet of the Infant. These parts have a brownish-black color. Unlike many ancient statues that are black, due to the nature of the wood or the effects of the original paint, the dark color of Our Lady of Montserrat is attributed to the innumerable candles and lamps that burned day and night before the image. With the passage of time the smoke seeped into the figure causing it to blacken in a gradual way. Because of this darkness it is affectionately called La Moreneta, The Dark Little One. By virtue of this coloration the Virgin is classified among the Black Madonnas, with the statue being highly esteemed both as a religious treasure and for its artistic value.

Nothing is known of the statue's origin, although legend tells us that shepherds grazing their flocks near Montserrat discovered the wooden statue in a cave amid a mysterious radiance and angelic singing. Ordered by the bishop to carry it to the cathedral, the procession began, but never arrived at its destination, since the statue became increasingly heavy and difficult to manage. With its deposit at a nearby hermitage it remained there until the present abbey was built. While this legend might be questioned, it is believed that the early monks provided themselves with a statue of the Virgin on completion of the original Romanesque church. The statue they secured is thought to be the one now venerated and it is believed that it was placed near an altarpiece or against a wall, since the back of the statue was not carefully completed.

The statue is located in an alcove high in the wall behind the main altar. Directly behind this alcove and the statue is a large room called the Camarin de la Virgen, the Chamber of the Virgin. This chamber can accommodate a large group of people and from here one can pray beside the throne of the Blessed Mother. This room is reached by a monumental marble stairway decorated with carvings and mosaics.

Located about 20 kilometers northwest of Barcelona, in the geographical center of that part of Spain known as Catalonia, the monastery and sanctuary are found against an unusual mountain named Montserrat, a Catalan word for "sawn mountain" since its numerous rock formations appear from a distance like the teeth of a saw. Unlike any other mountains in the world, the formations rise to stupendous heights and are smooth and convoluted as though carved and formed by a prodigious hand. The mountain and those in the area are a perennial attraction to mountain climbers who are challenged by the almost perpendicular rise from the countryside.

Although not located on the peak of the mountain, as are the sanctuaries of Monte Cassino and Le Puy, the monastery is situated high enough from the surrounding area to make one think it safe from attack, yet the monastery suffered almost total destruction during the Napoleonic invasion, a destruction made even more complete by civil wars and revolutionary disturbances. With the desecration of the monastery, the monks deserted to other foundations, but returned with new vitality and completed the reconstruction in a remarkably short time. The buildings that replaced the ancient ones were spared during the Spanish Civil War of 1936-1939 by the Autonomous Government of Catalonia.

The number of historic figures who were connected with the sanctuary or who visited it is considerable. One of its hermits, Bernat Boïl, accompanied Columbus to the New World, thus becoming the first missionary to America. One of its abbots was Giuliano della Rovere, who became Julius II, the Renaissance pope for whom Michelangelo worked. All the kings of Spain prayed at the shrine. Emperor Charles V and Philip II of Spain both died with blessed candles from the sanctuary in their hands. King Louis XIV of France had intercessory prayers said at Montserrat for the queen mother, and Emperor Ferdinand III of Austria made generous endowments to the monastery.

Among saints who visited there can be counted St. Peter Nolasco, St. Raymond of Penafort, St. Vincent Ferrer, St. Francis Borgia,

St. Aloysius Gonzaga, St. Joseph Calasanctius, St. Anthony M. Claret and St. Ignatius, who as a knight was confessed by one of the monks and spent a night praying before the image. A few miles away is Manresa, a pilgrim shrine of the Society of Jesus, the Jesuit order founded by Ignatius which encloses the cave wherein St. Ignatius Loyola retired from the world and wrote his *Spiritual Exercises*. Both Goethe and Schiller wrote about the mountain and Beethoven died in a house in Vienna which was an ancient fief of Montserrat. Additionally, the place was made famous by Richard Wagner, who used the location for two of his operas, Parsifal and Lohengrin. The Virgin of Montserrat was declared the patron saint of the Diocese of Catalonia by Leo XIII and it has always been considered the most celebrated image in Spain.

The sanctuary retains a special power of attraction for many people who consider a yearly visit almost an obligation. Whether individually, in groups or pilgrimages, the sanctuary is always busy with devout souls, some of whom visit the cave where legend tells that the statue was found. Anniversaries, jubilees and family feasts are blessed by a visit to the Madonna and there is a saying that a man is not properly married until he has taken his wife to Montserrat.

Conservative estimates place the number of visitors each year at over a million,[2] a stupendous number considering that the mountain is not situated near well-traveled roads that lead to important cities or villages, but is set apart making a visit almost a deliberate inconvenience.

Our Lady of Pompeii

D ISCOVERED in a junk shop by the Dominican priest Alberto Radente, the painting of Our Lady of Pompeii endured the humiliation of being purchased for the meager sum of eight carlins (the equivalent of one dollar).

Depicting the Blessed Mother and the Child Jesus presenting rosaries to St. Dominic and St. Catherine of Siena, the painting was given by Father Radente to a pious nun, Concetta Delitala of the Monastery of the Rosary at Porta Medina, who in turn presented it to Bartolo Longo on November 13, 1875, for the church he was building in Pompeii.

[2]*What is Montserrat?*, Maur M. Boix, Publicacions De L'Abadia De Montserrat, 1978, p. 32.

At first reluctant to take the portrait because of its historical and artistic flaws, Bartolo Longo finally accepted it, along with the prediction that the Mother of God would perform many miracles by means of it. And so she did from that time to the present.

Some reports have it that a hole marred the painting at the time of its purchase and was the reason for its inexpensive price. Whether the report is true or not, the picture underwent the first of its three restorations a year later. Because the first was hastily and unsatisfactorily accomplished, the second restoration occurred three years later (1879), with a third renovation being completed in the Vatican restoration school almost 90 years later (1965).

Bartolo Longo, an attorney who conceived the plan to erect a church close to the historical ruins that had been resurrected from the volcanic ash of Vesuvius, heard a mysterious voice in October 1872 that encouraged him to a devotion to the rosary. In 1875, the year the portrait was given to him, work was begun on the church which was to be dedicated to the rosary and Our Lady of Pompeii. Eventually Bartolo Longo founded an orphanage for girls and a trade school for orphaned and neglected boys. After his death in 1926 the church was enlarged into a magnificent basilica with the many charities of Mr. Longo being commemorated in brilliant paintings, mosaics, bas reliefs and monuments.

The painting of Our Lady, now beautifully restored, occupies a conspicuous place above the high altar where it captures the attention of tourists who visit there either before or after their tour of the ancient Pompeiian ruins.

The interior of the basilica startles the worshiper with its brilliant paintings of saints, angels, pontiffs, Dominican priests and nuns, and its variously colored marbles. Every inch, it seems, is covered with artistic gildings, intricate carvings, paintings and frescoes that prompt reflective admiration.

Once subjected to neglect, the image of Our Lady of Pompeii now enjoys continual veneration in a setting of magnificence.

Our Lady of Prompt Succor

WHEN the fire of 1812 advanced toward the Ursuline convent in New Orleans, orders were given by city officials for the sisters to evacuate their cloister. Despite strong winds that whipped the flames toward the building and with the danger imminent, a statue of Our Lady of Prompt Succor was placed on a windowsill facing the fire. After the superior, Mother St. Michel, prayed aloud, "Our Lady of Prompt Succor, we are lost unless you hasten to our help," the wind promptly changed, the convent and the properties around it were relieved of danger and the fire died out. Witnesses of this omen attributed the miracle to our Lady and spread the news throughout the city.

The history of the statue now enshrined above the altar of the chapel of the Ursuline convent began in France when the country was just issuing from the great revolution. With few priests and nuns to relieve the young of their religious ignorance, a woman such as Mother St. Michel was a treasure of her country. Described as a woman of rare ability and as a teacher crowned with success, she was asked by the Ursulines in New Orleans to join them in educating Indians and Negroes and to help in administering the boarding school, orphanage and the interests of their order. Despite the circumstances requiring her continued labors in France, she, nevertheless, saw the will of God in the American invitation.

The bishop of France, however, rejected any thought of dispensing with her services and resisted her requests for permission to leave by declaring that such permission could be given only by the pope. This was equivalent to an emphatic refusal since Pope Pius VII was then held a captive of Napoleon and lived under a strict injunction that prevented all communications, even those made by letter. Knowing that a reply from the pontiff was impossible, the bishop felt secure in the condition he expressed. Nevertheless, Mother St. Michel wrote to the pope setting forth her motives for wishing to leave. Before sending the letter she knelt before a statue of Mary and prayed: "O most holy Virgin Mary, if you obtain a *prompt* and *favorable* answer to my letter, I promise to have you honored in New Orleans under the title of Our Lady of Prompt Succor." The letter left Montpellier on March 19, 1809. The favorable reply was received from the pope one month later on April 28, 1809. Although knowing the state of affairs in France and the need for such apostles of the Faith, the pope nonetheless gave his permission and his blessing for the nun to leave France for America with her group of religious aspirants.

Bishop Fournier acknowledged the swift response from the pontiff as miraculous and blessed the statue of Our Lady that Mother St. Michel had ordered to be carved in accordance with her promise to Our Lady. On their arrival in New Orleans December 30, 1810, the statue was solemnly installed in the convent chapel. Homage and veneration to Mary under the title of Our Lady of Prompt Succor has been constant since that time. The chronicles of the Ursuline monastery summarize the graces worked through this devotion with the statement: "Under this title the Most Blessed Virgin has so often manifested her power and goodness that the religious have unbounded confidence in her."

Two years after the installation of the statue in the monastery, the fire that was previously described took place. Shortly thereafter, this devotion was to manifest itself prominently in the history of New Orleans during the war of 1815.

The war began when the British, embolded by their victory over Napoleon's forces, aimed their ambitions at the United States. After raiding Washington and setting fire to the White House, and after attacking Fort McHenry at Baltimore, they planned to conquer the central portion of America by capturing Louisiana. The war was well in progress when the British arrived on the shores of Louisiana. So certain were they of a victory that their ships carried a full staff of civil officials who were ready to administer the province of Louisiana. The expedition was described as being ". . .perfectly appointed in every way, commanded by officers some of whom had grown gray in victory. The elite of England's army and navy were afloat." Transferring to small boats, the troops arrived nine miles below the city of New Orleans on December 9, 1814. During the month, the British attempted several times to attack the city by tangent routes.

The troops that opposed each other consisted of approximately 20,000 well-trained and superbly equipped British militiamen against a scraggly group of about 6,000, among whom were Tennessee frontiersmen, fishermen, farmers, flatboatmen and hurriedly trained city men, all led by General Andrew Jackson (who would later become the seventh President of the United States).

The night before the decisive battle, the wives, mothers and sisters of Jackson's band assembled in the Ursuline chapel before the statue of Our Lady. Thoroughly terrified they prayed to the Blessed Mother throughout the night for the safety of the men and for victory over the British invaders. At dawn, with the sound of cannonfire reaching the city from Chalmette plantation, the women prayed the more fervently. Later, during Mass, a courier rushed into the chapel announcing the defeat of the enemy. A *Te Deum* was immediately entoned amid the most enthusiastic display of gratitude.

The British suffered enormous casualties, with one British writer stating: "They fell like blades of grass beneath the scythe." The American force suffered few casualties. The British withdrew and made no further attempt to capture the city.

General Jackson did not hesitate to admit of a divine intervention on his behalf and went in person, together with his staff, to thank the Ursulines for their prayers and to express his appreciation to Our Lady of Prompt Succor.

During the night of prayer the superior of the Ursulines made a vow to have a Mass of Thanksgiving sung annually should the Americans be victorious. The vow has been honored every year on the anniversary of the battle, January 8, since the year 1815.

Ironically this final battle of the war was fought after a treaty of peace had been signed, a fact unknown by the participants.

In accordance with a decree of Pope Leo XIII issued in November of 1895, the statue of Our Lady of Prompt Succor was solemnly crowned. Another honor was rendered Our Lady when the Sacred Congregation of Rites, acting on the request of the archbishop of New Orleans and two bishops of surrounding regions, approved and confirmed on June 13, 1928, the choice of Our Lady of Prompt Succor as the principal patroness of the city of New Orleans and of the state of Louisiana.

Madonna of Aracoeli

CONSPICUOUS in its position atop the high altar of the Basilica of Santa Maria in Aracoeli is the celebrated portrait that is rivaled by the Madonna's portrait in St. Mary Major Basilica for the title of "Salus Populi Romani" (Salvation of the Roman People).

The image was painted on a block of beech wood and, although it was estimated to have originated in the 11th century, recent discoveries place it as early as the sixth century and connect it with the early Byzantine monks who lived on the hill where the basilica is now located.[1]

In 1348 the image was carried in procession through the streets of Rome on the occasion of a pestilence that visited the city. The short duration of the scourge was credited to the benevolence of the Mother of God.

[1]Santa Maria in Aracoeli Sul Campidoglio, Emanuele Romanelli, Rome, p. 22.

The Vatican Chapter honored the image by crowning it in 1636, but it unfortunately lost this crown to the greed of Napoleon's troops in 1797. With its golden crown restored in 1938, the Roman people were consecrated to the Immaculate Heart of Mary before this ancient image in 1949.

The basilica which honors this picture was built on the site of the ancient Capitoline fortress and symbolizes the triumph of Christianity over the pagan world. In ancient times the church was called St. Mary's on the Capitol, but since the 12th century it has been named Aracoeli (Altar of Heaven), in honor of the altar dedicated by the Emperor Augustus to the Son of God.

It is related that when the people and the Roman Senate were intent on bestowing divine honors on Octavian Augustus (62 B.C.-A.D. 14), the emperor became disturbed and fasted for three days. After this time the sky opened and in a dazzling light the Virgin Mary, standing atop an altar with the Child Jesus in her arms, descended while a mysterious voice entoned the words, "This is the altar of the Son of God." The emperor prostrated on the ground, refused the honor contemplated by the people and built an altar to commemorate this vision. Around the altar was built a church that developed into the present basilica. An "Altar of the Legend of Augustus," embellished with mosaics and carvings in marble, is intact and displayed in the church.

While this legend is regarded by some as ". . . a myth to be regarded as a flower of history, the transformation of fleeting fact into eternal poetry," we find the legend included in the *Universal Chronicles* written in the second half of the sixth century.[2] Without debating the legend's authenticity or the actual occurrence of the vision, it is known that a church dedicated to the Virgin Mary was already in existence on the Capitol at the end of the fifth century. A group of Byzantine monks are known to have lived near the site, and in 883 appeared the first signs of the sons of St. Benedict.

The great basilica in its original form rose during the Benedictine period, to judge from the oldest part of the floor that dates from the ninth and 10th centuries. A papal bull assigning the church and monastery to the Franciscan friars is dated 1249.

The prestige of this basilica is established by its possession of important relics in addition to the ancient portrait. The 15th-century statue of the Child Jesus, arrayed with innumerable golden trinkets, is kept in a chamber near the sanctuary. The history of this statue is treated else-

²*Ibid.*, p. 6

where in this volume. A chapel dedicated to the Empress St. Helena has a grand altar topped by a statue of the saint. Beneath this altar is kept a 12th-century wooden chest, elaborately carved and carefully sealed, that contains some of the relics of the saint.

It cannot be denied that this basilica was built atop a hill since access to its main entrance is gained by climbing a flight of 124 steps, these built by public subscription in 1348.

Our Mother of Perpetual Help

THE Church of St. Alphonsus Liguori in Rome is proud of its possession of the famous portrait of Our Mother of Perpetual Help. Although its origins are unknown it is estimated that it was painted in the 14th or 15th century by a Greek artist.[1] Its documented history begins with the year 1495 when the image, with its history of miracles, was taken from the Isle of Crete to Rome. Four years later it was solemnly enthroned in the Church of St. Matthew on the Esquiline Hill. In the 18th century, when this church was destroyed by fire, the miraculous portrait escaped injury and was secretly taken by the Augustinians to nearby St. Eusebius Church, and later to the Church of St. Mary in Posterula.

When the Church of St. Alphonsus was built in 1855 on land adjacent to the site of the old St. Matthew's, a search was made for the portrait. After its discovery, Father Mauron, superior general of the Redemptorist order, successfully petitioned Pope Pius IX for its return.

The Redemptorists received the picture with great solemnity and joy and permitted an exact reproduction to be made for a church in England in commemoration of a miraculous cure resulting from a novena made in honor of Our Mother of Perpetual Help.

When the Redemptorist Fathers in the United States were asked in 1870 to establish a mission church in Roxbury, not far from Boston, they dedicated their small structure to the Mother of Perpetual Help and received from Rome an exact copy of the portrait that had been touched

---

[1]The assertion that this image was painted by St. Luke is unfounded. Material received from the Church of St. Alphonsus in Rome does not make this claim nor does material published by the Redemptorist order on this subject. See the entry of St. Luke for an elaboration on the subject of St. Luke as artist.

94

to the original. Other copies made at the mother shrine in Rome were touched to the original and sent to other houses of the order.

Papal approbation of the image was acknowledged in 1867 by Pope Pius IX when it was ceremoniously crowned by the Vatican Chapter in recognition of the miraculous nature of the devotion. In 1876 the same pontiff raised the existing confraternity to that of an archconfraternity with the right of affiliating all Perpetual Help confraternities throughout the world.

The Tuesday devotions inaugurated at St. Alphonsus (Rock) Church in St. Louis, Mo., were quickly adopted by churches of the order, and other churches, and took the form of a perpetual novena, a practice that is now observed worldwide.

Countless miracles attributed to the image extend from the time of its documented history in 1495 through the years until the present day. These seem to give ample testimony and proof of the portrait's favor with the Mother of God.

A study of the portrait is necessary to understand its historical and artistic qualities. It is painted in a flat style characteristic of icons and has a primitive quality. All the letters are Greek. The initials beside the Mother's crown identify her as "Mother of God." Those beside the child, "ICXC," are abbreviations meaning "Jesus Christ." The smaller letters identify the angel on the left as "St. Michael the Archangel." He is depicted holding the lance and spear with the vessel of vinegar and gall of Christ's passion. The angel on the right is identified as "St. Gabriel the Archangel." He holds the cross and the nails.

During the time this portrait was painted, halos were not commonly depicted. For this reason the artist rounded the head and veil of the mother to indicate her holiness. The golden halos and crowns were added much later. The Madonna in this portrait seems out of proportion to the size of her Son since it was Mary whom the artist wished to emphasize.

The charms of the portrait are many: from the naïveté of the artist who wished to make certain the identity of each subject was known, to the sandal that dangles from the foot of the Child who grips the hand of His Mother while gazing sideward at the instrument of torture held by the angel. Above all, the expression of the Madonna encourages a sadness on the part of the viewer. With her head gently touching that of her Son, and while surrounded with the instruments of her Son's future sufferings, she seems to gaze plaintively as though seeking compassion from those who look upon her.

Salus Populi Romani
(Salvation of the Roman People)

S INCE A.D. 350, when the Basilica of Santa Maria Maggiore was erected, its greatest treasure has been an image of the Madonna and Child. The portrait has been in the basilica for so long that its origins have been lost although there is no doubt that it was painted in the Greek style. Historians of art have agreed that the portrait is at least 1,500 years old and it is acknowledged as one of the oldest portraits of Our Lady.

The basilica that proudly guards the picture has been known through the years by four names: *St. Mary Major*, since it is the major basilica of Our Lady in Rome and third in importance of all the churches in that city with only St. Peter's and St. John Lateran preempting it; *Basilica Liberiana*, since it was begun during the pontificate of Pope St. Liberius; *Santa Maria ad Praesepe* (St. Mary of the Crib), because it enshrines boards believed to be those of the manger in which Jesus was born; and *Our Lady of the Snows*, because of the legend in which the location for the basilica and the outline of the foundation were indicated by a miraculous snowfall during the month of August.

The name of the portrait is justly deserved. Since the sixth century the Roman population has gathered before the image to pray during times of danger and for the urgent needs of the city. The first of many such gatherings assumed the form of a procession in A.D. 593 when St. Gregory carried the portrait through the streets of Rome when the black plague afflicted thousands. On making their way from St. Mary Major to the Church of St. Peter, the Archangel Michael appeared in a vision above the mausoleum of Hadrian (the present Castel Sant'Angelo), indicating the end of the pestilence. It was to commemorate this vision that a statue of the archangel was erected over the mausoleum.

The portrait was carried in processions innumerable times, the last being in 1837 when Pope Gregory XVI (1834-1846) prayed for the end of the cholera epidemic.

Before this portrait St. Pius V prayed during the battle of Lepanto. The young priest Eugenio Pacelli, the future Pope Pius XII, likewise visited the portrait and celebrated his first Mass in 1899 before the altar Shrine of Mary. In 1939, one of his first acts after his elevation was to pontificate at a Mass of Thanksgiving at the shrine. In 1944, during the second World War, when the city was threatened with bombing, the people of Rome prayed before the image while the battle of Anzio was waged only 20 miles away.

The miraculous snowfall that indicated the location and outline of the basilica in A.D 350 is commemorated in a unique fashion each year on August 5. At a given moment during High Mass a shower of white rose petals flutters down upon the worshipers from the dome of the Borghese chapel.

The original portrait was a full-length depiction of the Virgin sitting on a throne holding the Child Jesus on her lap. Unfortunately fire destroyed the bottom portion and somewhat injured the upper portion, but this was skillfully restored. Many copies of the portrait have been executed and widely distributed, but some are not exactly true to the original although they all have an oriental style. The portraits extend to the hips of the Virgin, the Child Jesus holds a book, and the features have grave expressions. The original portrait in St. Mary Major is jeweled, has Greek letters on either side of the Virgin, and both figures are crowned. The portrait with its Greek letters is reminiscent of the portrait, Our Lady of Perpetual Help.

The Virgin of the Pillar

THE history of the "Virgen del Pilar" (Virgin of the Pillar) of Zaragoza, Spain, and that of St. James the Apostle are inseparable.

Tradition tells us that St. James journeyed to Spain to spread the Gospel and was already there in the year A.D. 40 when he paused to pray beside the River Ebro with seven of his disciples. Our Lady, who was still living in Jerusalem, was at the same time praying for the success of his missionary endeavors when she appeared to St. James. He and the disciples all shared in the vision that was accompanied by celestial music and a radiant light. After words of encouragement and a request for a chapel, the Blessed Mother gave them the small jasper column upon which she stood as evidence of her appearance.

Supported by the vision and the tangible evidence of its authenticity, St. James spread the Faith throughout Spain which is now under his patronage. After dying a martyr's death he was buried at Santiago de

Compostello where his shrine attracted more pilgrimages, by far, than did those of the other apostles.[1]

The chapel that the Virgin requested was soon built over the place of the apparition, but was eventually destroyed as were several succeeding replacements. The pillar survived, as did the ancient statue that had been placed upon it. In fact, the statue survived the invasions of various conquerors: the Romans, Goths, Moors, Muslims and Vandals; and witnessed the invasion of more peaceful throngs: prayerful pilgrims, all the kings of Spain, Queen Blanca de Navarra in 1433, and numerous saints including St. Teresa of Avila, St. John of the Cross and St. Ignatius of Loyola.

The present church dates from the 17th century. In its chapel, amid a splendid setting, stands the statue which seems quite diminutive by contrast. Measuring about 15 inches, it stands upon its jasper pillar that rises about six feet in height. The column is now covered with silver and bronze, but a small portion of the jasper has been left exposed. This section of the pillar is framed by a golden oval and is "worn out due to millions of kisses."[2]

The wall directly behind the statue is of green marble and is studded with 148 stars, 80 of which are jeweled.

The wooden statue is a simple one of the Virgin with a pleasant smile. The Christ Child, who holds a small bird, is supported by the Virgin's left hand while the mantle that drapes all about them is held with her right. On certain days of the month the statue is dressed with a cape heavy with jewels and gold embroidery that partially conceals the pillar. A jeweled crown is placed on both Virgin and Child while a golden burst of an aureole is added to the jeweled halo that is affixed to the marble directly behind the head of the statue.

The Church of the Virgin of the Pillar, built over the place where St. James the Apostle prostrated before the Virgin's miraculous visit, was declared a national museum on May 22, 1904 with an impressive crowning of the Virgin taking place on May 20, 1905.

Persistent reports since ancient times have it that a fragrance of roses constantly surrounds the pillar and is readily perceived by worshipers. A spokesman for the shrine recently attributed the fragrance to the disinfectant that is used daily on the column to discourage the transmittance of disease due to the number of persons who touch and kiss it. Yet, one wonders if the disinfectant used once a day would support a fragrance that would last the whole day and night until the next applica-

[1] See entry of St. James the Apostle elsewhere in this volume.
[2] From papers supplied by the shrine.

tion. One might also consider that the reports of the perfume were made consistently from ancient times when disinfectants were unknown and perfumed samples awaited invention in recent years.

The people of Zaragoza regard the statue as a legacy from their forefathers and demonstrate a tender devotion and a fierce loyalty to it. It is believed that since the Church of the Virgen of the Pillar was the first raised in honor of the Blessed Mother, it will last as long as the Faith. During his historic tour of Spain in November 1982, Pope John Paul II visited this ancient shrine of the Blessed Mother and later the same day recited the Rosary during a worldwide radio broadcast.

Another Virgin of the Pillar, and one that is held in similar esteem, is that which holds sway in France in the great Cathedral of Chartres. Dating from the 16th century, it is a reproduction of a more ancient statue. Having spent several hundred years in various other places in the cathedral, it was placed in its permanent shrine in 1806.

Unlike the pillar in Zaragoza, Spain, this pillar was not miraculously presented, but consists of a column of the old rood loft, its capital being enhanced with touches of gold. The statue itself is made of wood and is quite dark in color. The Christ Child sits upon His Mother's knee and she, in queenly demeanor, holds aloft a jeweled scepter and is crowned as is her royal Son. The visitor usually sees the statue dressed in a magnificent gown of the proper liturgical color.

Like its counterpart in Spain, the column is also worn, but toward the bottom, from the constant displays of affection for the Mother of God. Attached to the walls on either side of the shrine and on the background screen are innumerable silver hearts, each representing the gratitude of a devoted child of Mary. To the side of the shrine is a conflagration of candles burning in petition and thanksgiving.

Before this shrine is situated the glass-sided reliquary containing the pieces of cloth believed to be a veil once belonging to the Virgin Mary.[3]

The Weeping Madonna of Syracuse

THE plaque depicting the Immaculate Heart of Mary was mass-produced in a studio in Tuscany and was shipped along with others of

---

[3] The history of this veil is treated elsewhere in this volume.

its kind to Syracuse, Sicily, where it was purchased as a wedding gift. But after it hung on a wall of the humble home of the Iannuso couple it was singled out for the unexpected and prodigiously shed tears for four days.

The veneration now paid this plaque in a church built especially for its exhibition was approved by three popes but only after an ecclesiastical tribunal scrupulously studied the miracle and had the tears analyzed by scientists, who announced that their composition was exactly like those of human origin. It has been said by authorities that never was a miracle so thoroughly tested or so quickly approved.

The history of the plaque begins with its sculptor Amilcare Santini who modeled it in only three days "under artistic inspiration." It was made of plaster that had been dissolved in water and poured into a mold before it was turned out to dry in the sun. It was sprayed with nitro-cellulose varnish that made it shiny and suitable for painting. After it was colored, varnished and polished, ordinary screws were used to attach it to a panel of black opaline. The panel measured 39 by 33 centimeters, the figure 29 by 22 centimeters.

The plaque was purchased as a wedding gift for Antonina and Angelo Iannuso who were married March 21, 1953. They admitted that they were tepid and neglectful Christians, yet they hung the image with some devotion on the wall behind their bed.

Angelo was a laborer who had taken his bride to live in the home of his brother on Via Degli Orti 11. When his wife discovered her pregnancy it was accompanied by toxemia that expressed itself in convulsions that at times brought on temporary blindness. At three in the morning on Saturday, August 29, 1953, Antonina suffered a seizure that left her blind. At about 8:30 a.m., in Antonina's own words:

"I opened my eyes and stared at the image of the Madonna above the bedhead. To my great amazement I saw that the effigy was weeping. I called my sister-in-law Grazie and my aunt, Antonina Sgarlata who came to my side, showing them the tears. At first they thought it was an hallucination due to my illness, but when I insisted, they went close up to the plaque and could well see that tears were really falling from the eyes of the Madonna, and that some tears ran down her cheeks onto the bedhead. Taken by fright they took it out the front door, calling the neighbors, and they too confirmed the phenomenon. . . ."[1]

Of the many visitors who examined the plaque at close range was Mario Messina, who was highly regarded in the neighborhood. After

[1]The Weeping Madonna, Bulletin of Our Lady of Tears of Syracuse, Twentieth Anniversary Issue, 1973, p. 2.

observing the slow formation of the tears he removed the plaque from the wall, examined it thoroughly and satisfied himself that the tears were not a result of an internal reservoir. After drying the plaque, two tears immediately reappeared.

News of the phenomenon spread quickly throughout the city bringing crowds that forced their way indoors and gathered in the streets around the house. The inspector of security, with the couple's permission, hung the plaque on the outside of the house to satisfy the curiosity of the people, but later, on seeing that the crush showed no sign of diminishing, the picture was taken to the constabulary in an effort to reduce the confusion. The image wept while outside the building and during its transport, but after 40 minutes at the police constabulary, when it did not weep, it was returned to the Iannuso home.

On Sunday, August 30, at 2:00 a.m., the weeping image was placed on a cushion and displayed to satisfy the curious who had remained in the streets throughout the night.

The image was nailed above the main door on Monday where its tears were collected by the people on pieces of cloth and wads of cotton. During this time the curious were satisfied, the skeptics were convinced and many of the sick were healed. Also during this day, to protect the plaque from falling, it was brought to an improvised altar outside the home of the Lucca family who lived directly across the street. Several hours later, after the recitation of the Rosary, it was returned.

Three priests visited the home during this time. One of them notified the Curia, who set about assembling a group of distinguished clergymen, four men of science and three reputable witnesses to comprise an investigative commission.

On the specific instructions of the chancellor of the Curia, the commission gathered at the Iannuso home the morning of Tuesday, September 1, for the purpose of studying the phenomenon and collecting a sample of the tears for chemical analysis. The plaque was examined while it wept and while the liquid collected in the cavity formed by the hand over the heart. The commission examined the smooth finish and found no pores or irregularities on the surface. The backing was removed and the unfinished calcined gypsum was scrutinized and found in a dry condition even though tears collected on the reverse.

Six coats of nitrocellulose colors were counted on the image and these were covered with a coat of nitrocellulose varnish.[2] Using a sterilized pipette, a sample of tears was collected and placed in a sterilized vial that was taken to the provincial laboratory to be examined by doc-

[2] *The Madonna Wept in Syracuse*, Dr. Ottavio Musumeci, Marchese, Syracuse, Sicily, 1963, p. 39.

tors and chemists. One centimeter of liquid was obtained, about 19 to 20 drops.[3]

Following this thorough examination, the image continued weeping for another 15 minutes, but at 11:40 in the morning the tears stopped, never to be repeated.

The sample of tears was compared scientifically with those of an adult and a child. Following a detailed analysis, the conclusion reached by the doctors was that:

"... The liquid examined is shown to be made up of a watery solution of sodium chloride in which traces of protein and nuclei of a silver composition of excretiary substances of the quanternary type, the same as found in the human secretions used as a comparison during the analysis.

The appearance, the alkalinity and the composition induce one to consider the liquid examined analogous to human tears."

The report was dated September 9, 1953 and was signed by Doctors Michele Cassola, Francesco Cotzie, Leopoldo La Rosa and Mario Marietta.[4]

Concerning this commission and the various investigations conducted, we must consider that the Church is never in a hurry to pronounce her judgments on such occurrences and that she acts with maximum caution and prudent reserve and is ready to affirm miracles only after positive and unquestionable proofs have been extended. Nevertheless, sufficient proofs were apparently given since a favorable judgment was rendered in a relatively short time.

The archbishop of Syracuse visited the Iannuso home to examine the plaque and returned another day to recite the Rosary together with the crowd. Various monsignori visited the plaque, some of whom witnessed the weeping. Many cardinals expressed interest, while the archbishop of Palermo, Ernesto Cardinal Ruffini, in a radio broadcast of December 1953 stated, "... after careful sifting of the numerous reports, after having noted the positive results of the diligent chemical analysis under which the tears gathered were examined, we have unanimously announced the judgement that the reality of the facts cannot be put in doubt." Pope Pius XII, in a radio broadcast on October 17, 1954, said, "... we acknowledge the unanimous declaration of the Episcopal Conference held in Sicily on the reality of that event. Will men understand the mysterious language of those tears?"[5]

[3]Ibid., p. 73.
[4]Twentieth Anniversary Issue, Op. cit., p. 10
[5]Ibid., p. 11.

The medical commission that was nominated on October 7, 1953, to examine seriously and scientifically the nature of extraordinary cures worked through the intercession of the Blessed Virgin of the plaque, considered 290 cases of which 105 were of "special interest." These miracles were reported within a few years of the incident.

The first person to experience a miracle of healing was also the first to observe the weeping. From the time Antonina Iannuso first saw the tears she recovered completely from severe toxemia and gave birth to a healthy son on December 25, 1953. Archbishop Baranzini officiated at the infant's baptism.

The same astonishment experienced by the people of Syracuse at the time of the miracle was felt by those around the world who read about the occurrence in local papers, and then heard about it on radio and television. It has been tabulated that reports even reached India, China, Japan and Vietnam. In Italy alone more than 2,000 articles appeared in 225 papers and magazines, while hundreds of articles appeared in 93 foreign newspapers in 21 different nations.[6] Rarely is an event of religious interest given such worldwide attention.

That the events were the result of collective hallucination is rejected by authorities of the shrine since one, then two, then small groups, and finally hundreds of people, including skeptics, viewed the event and the intermittent character of the occurrences. The plaque was seen to weep in several places inside the home and at three places outside; moreover, there was the tangible evidence of saturated cloths and cottons. Hallucinations are to be excluded because of the psychological state of numerous unbelievers who examined the image and even tasted the salty liquid. Moreover, photographs and motion-picture footage of the weeping cannot, of course, be hallucinated.

The question of condensation is likewise rejected since it would have covered the whole statue and would not have originated from the corners of the eyes. Condensation would have collected on nearby objects as well, which did not occur, and if it had been present would certainly not have been salty.

The physicians and scientists who studied the event could offer no natural explanation for the occurrence and deemed it extraordinary in several documents.[7]

The reliquary presented to Msgr. Ettore Baranzini, archbishop of Syracuse, on the occasion of the 50th anniversary of his ordination is of

[6] Musumeci, *op. cit.*, pp. 82-84.
[7] *Ibid.*, pp. 36, 38, 40.

special interest since it contains the tears collected by the medical commission for their chemical analysis. The reliquary is comprised of three layers. The bottom contains, in addition to cloths that had been saturated with tears, one of the vials that contained the tears collected by the commission and cotton wool that absorbed some of the tears on another occasion. The second layer has four panels depicting the events. The third layer has a crystal urn which holds another of the vials used for the collection of the samples. The tears within it are now crystallized. On the 29th of each month, in commemoration of the day the weeping first began, the reliquary is taken in procession during special ceremonies.

The little house on Via Degli Orti 11, where the Madonna first shed her tears, is now an oratory where Mass is often celebrated. The image itself is enshrined above the main altar of the Santuario Madonna Delle Lacrima that was built specifically to accommodate the crowds that continually gather in prayer before the holy image.

Why did the Madonna weep? Many theories have been offered which remind us of the tears Mary shed at the foot of the Cross and of those shed by her during the visions of La Salette. During one of the visions of St. Catherine Labouré, on July 18, 1830, St. Catherine noticed that the Virgin looked sad with tears in her eyes. Perhaps we should pray the words engraved on the base of the reliquary, "Weeping Madonna, take from the hardness of our hearts tears of penitence." And we wonder with Pope Pius XII, "Will men understand the mysterious language of those tears?"

Relics of the Apostles and Evangelists

Bust of St. Thomas

105

St. Andrew

JESUS was walking by the Sea of Galilee one day when ". . . he saw two brothers, Simon, who is called Peter, and his brother Andrew casting a net into the sea for they were fishermen. And he said to them, 'Come, follow me and I will make you fishers of men.' And at once they left the nets and followed him" (Matthew 4:18-21). In this narration from Holy Scripture we are first introduced to Andrew, a follower of John the Baptist and the second apostle called to the ministry.

Although a native of Bethsaida in Galilee, Andrew bore a Greek name that signified "valor" and together with his father, Jonah, and his brother Peter, he lived at Capharnaum and exercised his profession on the Sea of Galilee.

Andrew is mentioned frequently in Scripture, notably on the occasion of the miraculous feeding of four thousand[1] when he told Jesus, "There is a boy here who has five barley loaves and two fish, but what are these among so many?" (John 6:8-9) With the exception of Peter, Andrew presumably exercised the greatest influence among the others as indicated a few days before the Lord's death when certain gentiles asked Philip if they might see Jesus. Philip referred the matter to Andrew as though he were of greater authority (John 12:20-22).

When the apostles set forth to preach the Gospel, it is believed that Andrew labored in Russia, Turkey and Greece where his life ended in the city of Patras in the province of Achaia. It is generally agreed that he was crucified during the reign of Nero by order of the Roman governor Aegeas, by being bound, not nailed, to a cross shaped like an X. His sufferings thus prolonged, he died on November 30 in the year 60. This day of martyrdom is observed around the world as his feast day. Andrew is honored as patron of Russia, Greece and of Scotland, where his feast was regarded as a holy day of obligation until 1918.

In art he is readily identified with his decussate (X-shaped) cross. A monumental statue of the saint with his transverse cross was erected in

---

[1] Four thousand is mentioned in Matthew 15:38 and Mark 8:9, but five thousand is mentioned by John in 6:11 and Luke in 9:14.

106

St. Peter's Basilica in a prominent position against one of the four large supporting walls that face the high altar.

The bones of the saint, now enshrined in Amalfi, Italy, have since ancient times produced a mysterious oil called manna. This phenomenon is explored in the chapter on the manna of the saints which the reader may examine.

Although the feast of St. Andrew is observed on November 30, every January 28, at his shrine in Amalfi, the day is observed in a special manner. On this day in 1846 the relics were rediscovered in a crypt beneath the flooring of the basilica where they had been left undisturbed for over 200 years. As though in gratitude, the manna that appears at intervals never fails to appear on this anniversary date.

When the relics of the saint were removed from Patras to Constantinople in 357, the head was retained by the church in Patras. This relic, in a silver bust reliquary, was brought to St. Peter's for safekeeping in 1464. Exactly 500 years later, in 1964, Pope Paul VI ordered its return to Patras, Greece.

St. Bartholomew (Nathanael)

BARTHOLOMEW'S name is mentioned by Matthew, Mark and Luke in their lists of the apostles. John does not give a specific list, but, in naming the apostles, that of Bartholomew is not mentioned and is replaced with the name of Nathanael.

Scholars consider that Bartholomew and Nathanael are one and the same and regard the name Bartholomew as patronymic, that is, *bar* meaning "son of," and Tolmai or Tholmai being his father's name just as Simon was called Simon bar-Jona, meaning Simon son of Jona. Although not conclusively proved, this theory is, nevertheless, strengthened in that the three evangelists link the name of Philip with that of Bartholomew as though the two were friends, while John links Philip to Nathanael and depicts them as close friends as proved by the incident in which Philip, after his calling to the ministry, immediately sought out Nathanael, who joined him in following the Master (John 1:44-46).

With the exception of the comment made by Jesus concerning St. John the Baptist, ". . . history has not known a man born of woman greater than John the Baptizer" (Matthew 11:11), perhaps none other in

107

Scripture is so honored by a comment of our Lord than Nathanael. The Lord's opinion of Nathanael was made after the previously mentioned incident in which Philip urged Nathanael to see Jesus, whom Philip claimed was the one promised by the prophets. Nathanael complied and on seeing him approach Jesus said, "Behold a true Israelite in whom there is no guile" (John 1:47). A dialogue then followed with Nathanael asking Jesus, "Whence do you know me?" Jesus answered, "Before Philip called you I saw you under the fig tree." Nathanael replied, "Rabbi, you are the Son of God, you are the King of Israel." Jesus then said to him, "Because I said to you that I saw you under the fig tree, you believe. Greater things than these shall you see. . . ." (John 1:47-51)

Compared to the other apostles such as John, Peter and Andrew, the name of Bartholomew or Nathanael is not conspicuous. Apart from being included among the lists of the apostles and the event just listed, Nathanael is named only once more in Scripture and this after the resurrection, when Jesus appeared to him and other apostles on the shore of the Sea of Tiberias and prepared a breakfast of bread and fish for them (John 21:2).

An Eastern legend states that after Pentecost Nathanael met St. Philip at Hierapolis where the latter was preaching. Nathanael then traveled into Lycaonia where St. John Chrysostom claims he spread the faith.[1]

The *Roman Martyrology* states that he also preached the Gospel in India, but the designation of India does not necessarily mean the India of today, since the name was applied indifferently by Greek and Latin writers to mean Arabia, Ethiopia, Libya, Parthia, Persia and the lands of the Medes.[2] From "India" he went into Greater Armenia, a fact confirmed by unanimous tradition and by later historians of Armenia who agreed that the saint both preached and died there. The *Roman Martyrology* agrees that his death occurred in Armenia and adds that he was flayed alive by the barbarians and was finally beheaded.

The relics of the saint were transported to Benevento in the south of Italy near Naples in the year 809, with a portion of them being taken to Rome a century later and placed in the church dedicated to the martyr Adalbert. (The church was later renamed for the apostle.) It was determined in 1740 that both Benevento and the Church of San Bartolomeo, also known as St. Bartholomew on the island, were built by the Roman emperor and German king, Otto III (980-1002). The church is actually located on an island in the Tiber River at Rome. In ancient times the site

[1]*The Lives of the Saints,* compiled by Rev. Alban Butler, revised by Herbert Thurston, S.J., and Donald Attwater, P.J. Kenedy and Sons, New York, 1933, Vol. VIII, p. 290.
[2]*Ibid.,* p. 289.

was occupied by a temple to Aesculapius, the god of medicine. Ruins of this temple can be found in the orchard of the Franciscan monastery that now claims the site.

Once dedicated to the god of medicine, part of the isle is still committed to the sick since a hospital operated by the monks of San Giovanni Calabita is also located there. In recent times part of the Franciscan monastery was seized by civil authorities and divided into homes for elderly Jews although the friars still retain a portion for their use.[3]

The Tiber produced a sudden and disastrous flood in 1557 that damaged the church with its rich mosaics. The relics of the apostle were saved and for safety were placed in St. Peter's while the church was abandoned for several years. The structure was repaired in 1560 and again in 1624. Pope Pius IX financed another restoration in 1882 and donated the present altar under which the relics of the apostle are kept in a large sarcophagus with lamps burning on either side.

St. James the Greater

DURING the Middle Ages the shrine of St. James at Compostela, Spain, was the most popular place of pilgrimage whose importance was preempted only by Jerusalem and Rome. The journey to the shrine was undertaken on sea and land with so many pilgrims trodding toward the north of Spain that churches, hospitals and shrines were established throughout France and Spain on all the main routes leading to Compostela. It is a matter of record that Emperor Charlemagne declared it a legal and moral obligation to give water, shelter and fire to pilgrims on their way to visit the relics of this apostle.

St. James and his brother John were the third and fourth apostles selected by Jesus (Peter and Andrew being the first and second). James was fishing one day with his brother and father, Zebedee, when he received the Lord's invitation. Immediately the brothers followed the Master, leaving their father with the hired hands. St. James apparently occupied a position of some importance among the other apostles, having been allowed to be present at the Transfiguration, at the cure of Peter's

[3]*A Guide to the Churches of Rome,* Mary Sharp, Chilton Books, New York, 1966, p. 53.

mother-in-law and the raising of Jairus' daughter. It was James' mother who asked our Lord for places of honor for her sons, and it was James, together with the others in the Garden of Olives, who gave way to sleep. On the day that he and John asked Jesus to make fire from heaven descend on a village that refused to receive them, Jesus surnamed them Boanerges, "sons of thunder."

Following Pentecost, when the apostles were strengthened in the faith and went forth to spread the gospel, James, it is believed, eventually found his way to Spain. With seven of his disciples he was one day walking along the Ebro River near Saragossa when our Lady, who was still living in Jerusalem, appeared to him and encouraged him in his endeavors. At the place of this apparition a church was built which enshrines, in a special sanctuary, the jasper column that was left by the Virgin as proof of her visit. The story of this vision and the shrine is related elsewhere in this volume.

After laboring for many years in Spain James returned to his homeland and was soon imprisoned by Herod, who had him beheaded sometime between the years 40 and 44. It is believed his remains were returned to Spain after a number of transferences to various sites.

The shrine dedicated to the saint inside the ancient church at Compostela is immediately recognized by the imposing statue of the apostle seated on a throne, a scepter in his hand, a golden halo about his head, and clothed in garments of silver and gold. As though occupying the place of honor requested by his mother, the statue is surrounded by exquisitely sculptured silver.

The visitor is permitted to climb a staircase behind the altar to salute St. James in the century-old manner. Standing behind the throne of the statue, the pilgrim is permitted to kiss the scallop shells embossed on the cape that surrounds the shoulders of the figure.

Scallop shells figure importantly in the story of this saint. No one knows for certain how it began, but pilgrims in days long past were given the shells as proof that they had endured the arduous journey and reached their destination at the altar of the relics. These shells could only be obtained by the genuine pilgrim who wore them on hat or cloak and showed them with pride on his return home. The shells were so highly valued that they were often handed on as legacies in wills.

Below the impressive statue is a crypt reached by a narrow stairway where the bones of the saint are enclosed in a silver reliquary atop a white marble altar. Last examined in 1879, the relics remain on the site where they were originally placed. The veneration of this shrine dates from before the 10th century. It soon reached the height of celebrity and thereafter, throughout the Middle Ages, it was the center of pilgrimage for all of Europe.

Among the countless pilgrims who visited the relics is counted St. Elizabeth of Portugal, the holy queen, who visited Compostela in July, 1324, and of more recent date, the reigning Pope John Paul II, who prayed at the shrine in November of 1982 while on a tour of Spain.

St. James the Less

S T. James is believed to have been the brother of Jude Thaddeus and as such to have been a cousin of our Lord.[1] He is not to be confused with another apostle, James the Greater, who labored to spread the Faith in Spain. To distinguish him from this James, he is called the Less probably because of his age, his stature, or because he was called to the ministry at a later date.

Although no prominence is given to James in the Gospel narrative, he is frequently mentioned in the Acts of the Apostles as the renowned bishop of the church of Jerusalem and is expressly confirmed as such by Clement of Alexandria and the ancient historian Eusebius.

James is the author of the epistle that bears his name in which he stresses the importance of good works. This was highly disputed by Luther, who preached the doctrine of justification by faith alone and who contemptuously discarded James' writings as an "epistle of straw."[2]

We are told in Acts that recognition of James' importance among the apostles was made by St. Peter when he sent a special message to James notifying him of his escape from prison through the intervention of an angel (Acts 12:17). With many of the other apostles, James participated in the Council of Jerusalem about the year 51, and declared that the gentile Christians were not bound to circumcision nor to the observance of the Mosaic Law, though he urged that they conform to certain ceremonies and respect certain scruples of their Jewish fellow-Christians (Acts 15:13-21). After completing his third missionary journey, St. Paul visited James and joined him and the elders in glorifying the Lord (Acts 21:17-20). James enjoyed an unequaled prestige and his contributions to the infant Church were many. St. Paul was careful to remain on good

[1]Butler op. cit., Vol. 5, p. 3, and Matthew 13:55.
[2]Ibid., p. 6

terms with James and he was held in great esteem by the Jewish people.

We learn from Eusebius, bishop of Caesarea (A.D. 260-340), who is known as the "Father of Church History," that James, the Lord's brethren, received the name "the Just" and that:

> ". . . he was holy from his mother's womb, drank no wine nor strong drink nor ate anything in which was life. No razor came upon his head; he anointed himself not with oil and used no bath. To him alone it was permitted to enter the holy place; for he wore nothing woolen, but linen garments. And alone he entered into the sanctuary and was found on his knees asking forgiveness on behalf of the people, so that his knees became hard like a camel's for he was continually bending the knee in worship to God and asking forgiveness for the people. . ."[3]

An account of the saint's martyrdom is related by Hegesippus, a Jewish Christian who lived about the middle of the second century. According to his record, at the time of the Pasch, when all the tribes and the gentiles came together to observe the feast, the Jews, scribes and Pharisees were concerned that the people, thus mingling with the Christians, would provoke disputes. Since James was considered just by all, he was persuaded to climb to the pinnacle of the temple to speak and hopefully to prevent an uprising among the people. While giving testimony to Jesus, the Scribes and Pharisees threw him down and as this did not kill him, they stoned him and completed the martyrdom with a blow to the head.

Josephus, a Jewish historian (A.D. 37-101) mentions nothing about the apostle being thrown down from the pinnacle of the temple, but concurs with Hegesippus that the saint was stoned to death, and assigns the martyrdom to the year 62.[4]

May 3 has been reserved to the saint as his feast day and is jointly celebrated with St. Philip, another apostle. The reason for this association is unknown, although it is speculated that their names were linked when Pope John III dedicated a church to the apostles about the year 565 and transferred the remains of the two apostles to a special altar.

The largest altarpiece in Rome depicts the martyrdom of Philip and James, and is admired in the Basilica of the Holy Apostles, also known as Santi Apostoli. In this same church Michelangelo was temporarily buried and it was in the parish of Santi Apostoli that he lived during his stays in Rome.

When the chapel of the two saints was altered in 1873, the relics of

---

[3]*Ibid.*, p. 4.
[4]*Ibid.*, p. 5.

both apostles were found in a beautiful transparent marble sarcophagus that was placed in the crypt immediately under the high altar.

It is believed the basilica was originally dedicated to Philip and James as evidenced by an inscription long preserved in the church. Later it was regarded as the church of all the apostles as it remains today.

St. John the Evangelist

ST. John was the youngest of the apostles and according to his own account was "the disciple whom Jesus loved." He was fishing with his brother, James the Greater, when both were invited to follow Jesus. He was present at the Transfiguration, at the Agony in the Garden and at the Last Supper when he rested his head upon the bosom of the Lord. During the three hours of our Lord's sufferings he stood beneath the cross with Mary, who was entrusted to his care.

The Acts of the Apostles tells us that he and Peter remained closely united in friendship after Pentecost, going together to the temple to pray. He was present with the others when the apostles held a council at Jerusalem at about the year 51.

Tradition tells us that during the persecution of Domitian, the saint was taken to Rome where an unsuccessful attempt was made on his life by plunging him into boiling oil. The Church of San Giovanni Alla Porta Latina was built in Rome on the spot where this is supposed to have taken place. The first written mention of this church was made toward the end of the eighth century when Adrian I restored it. Almost adjacent to this is the Church of San Giovanni in Oleo that was built to commemorate the event. It was this attempt on the life of the saint that won for the Evangelist the palm of a martyr. According to the *Mirabilia*, the vessel in which the saint was placed was still shown in the 12th century.[1] When this attempt on the life of the saint was miraculously frustrated, he was banished to the island of Patmos where it is thought he received the revelations that were set down in the last book of the Bible called the Book of Revelation, or, sometimes, the Apocalypse.

St. Irenaeus informs us that the Evangelist moved to Asia Minor after the martyrdom of Ss. Peter and Paul. It was there he spent the last decades of his life and it was at Ephesus that he served as bishop.

[1]Sharp, *op. cit.*, p. 98.

A little chapel at Ephesus is pointed out to visitors as the home that John shared with the Blessed Mother. The story of this structure is dealt with elsewhere in this book. It is believed that the Mother of Jesus eventually returned to Jerusalem where she died and was taken bodily into heaven. The place is now occupied by the Church of the Dormition.

St. John's writings are believed to have been set down late in life. His fourth Gospel, three epistles and the Apocalypse were written between the years A.D. 90 and 100.

Although St. John was the youngest of the apostles he was apparently the last to survive and the oldest at the time of death, having died at about the age of 100 years.

St. John's Basilica in Ephesus, Turkey, where the Evangelist was buried, is now in ruins, but the tomb is indicated by a railing of iron and two standing columns. This was apparently situated in a side chapel of the basilica.

It is curious to note that during the apparition of Knock, Ireland, which observed its 100th anniversary in 1979 with ceremonies attended by Pope John Paul II, the Blessed Mother appeared with the two who had protected her during her lifetime on earth, St. Joseph and St. John the Evangelist, who was dressed in Mass vestments and wore atop his head the traditional bishop's miter.[2]

St. Jude Thaddeus

ST. Jude and his brother, St. James the Less, were counted among the Twelve Apostles and are considered to have been blood relatives of Jesus.

The original form of Jude's name was Judas, but this was changed to distinguish him from the betrayer of Jesus although he is sometimes also distinguished in Scripture as Judas Thaddeus, Judas the brother of James, or Judas, son of Alpheus.

Jude is quoted in Scripture only once and this at the Last Supper when he asked the Savior, "Lord, why is it that you will reveal yourself to us and not to the world?" His question prompted a long reply from the Redeemer (John 14:22).

[2]Our Lady of Knock, William D. Coyne, Catholic Book Publishing Co., New York, 1948, p. 28.

114

The saint's name is often linked with another apostle, Simon the Zealous, with whom he labored in spreading the Gospel in Syria, Persia and Mesopotamia. According to the Western tradition that is recognized in the Roman liturgy, both saints suffered martyrdom. Their bodies were temporarily entombed in Mesopotamia and were eventually taken to Rome where they were interred in the old Basilica of St. Peter. When the present basilica was in the process of construction in 1605, Pope Paul V had the relics transferred to a new altar dedicated to the two saints. This is located in an honored position in the left transept.[1]

Small relics of St. Jude have been distributed worldwide, but a major relic, the forearm, is in the possession of the Dominican Fathers at the St. Jude Thaddeus Shrine on South Ashland Avenue in Chicago. Records of this relic trace it originally to the Armenian Dominicans, but when they, together with the Armenian faithful, fled their country in the 18th century because of the Moslem persecution, they settled in Smyrna in Asia Minor and eventually entrusted the relic to the Dominican monastery in that city. Since devotion to St. Jude in Smyrna was then languishing, it was thought best to donate it to a Dominican church where devotion to the apostle was flourishing. Knowing that devotion to St. Jude was greatly exercised in the United States, and knowing that the shrine of St. Jude in Chicago wished to have a larger relic, it was placed in their care with the approval of provincials and major superiors of the order.[2] The selection of this shrine was most appropriate since daily devotions and perpetual novenas have been observed there since 1929.[3]

The relic, now in two pieces, is kept in a silver reliquary in the form of a life-size forearm which is solemnly exposed during public novenas for the edification of the saint's devotees. The hand of the reliquary is partially opened with the forefinger and thumb in an attitude of benediction. The silver is clearly antique, with silversmiths agreeing on its ancient quality and design.[4] A long glass section in the arm portion exposes the relic to view.

St. Jude apparently held a position of minor importance among the apostles since he designated himself as such in his own epistle, and is often referred to in Scripture as the brother of James, giving one the impression his identification depended on James, who was of greater importance (as he must have been, since he was elected bishop of the Church of Jerusalem). While Jude held an inconspicuous position among

[1]*St. Jude Thaddeus*, Rev. Leo C. Gainor, O.P., Catechetical Guild Educational Society, Minnesota, 1956, p. 61.
[2]From information supplied by the shrine in Chicago.
[3]Gainor, *op. cit.*, p. 67.
[4]*Ibid.*, p. 62.

his confreres, it is now evident that he is invoked more than the others, being the special patron and advocate of desperate and seemingly hopeless problems. Additionally he enjoys worldwide popularity with churches, hospitals and numerous shrines dedicated to his honor.

With his partner in missionary endeavors, St. Simon the Zealous, St. Jude's feast day is observed on October 28.

St. Jude is often depicted in art with a likeness of Jesus on a disk being held in one hand, a staff or club in the other, and a flame above his head.

St. Luke

S T. Luke the Evangelist was neither a Jew nor an apostle, but was one of the earliest converts. According to Eusebius, the church historian, Luke was born in Antioch, Syria, although it is mentioned elsewhere that he might have been Greek.

Luke was a physician, St. Paul calling him "the most dear physician" (Colossians 4:14). His medical training is evidenced by his choice of language in his Gospel and in the Acts of the Apostles, which he also composed. It is said that there is nothing more certain in biblical writings than the proposition that Luke was the author of Acts. The historian Plummer claims that the position of St. Luke as the author of Acts, ". . .is so generally admitted by critics of all schools that not much time need be spent in discussing it."

The epistles of St. Paul and the Acts of the Apostles often mentioned that St. Paul and Luke labored together on missionary endeavors and that during Paul's imprisonments, Luke was his faithful friend and frequent visitor.

There is evidence that Luke was not only acquainted with St. Mark, but was also familiar with Mark's Gospel. Of the 20 miracles of Jesus which Luke records, six are not found in the other Gospels, and of the many parables of Jesus recounted in Scripture, 18 are mentioned exclusively by Luke.

As an evangelist Luke must have suffered much for the Faith, but it is unknown if he actually died a martyr's death.

The evangelist is usually depicted in art as a calf or an ox, the sacrificial animal, because his Gospel begins with the account of Zachary, the priest who was the father of St. John the Baptist.

It has been repeatedly suggested since about the sixth century that St. Luke was a painter and sculptor, but there are no works of art supposedly executed by him that sustain historical scrutiny in his favor. It is said, however, that he is considered a *painter in words* because his graphic descriptions of the Annunciation, Visitation, Nativity and other events have become the inspiration and favorite themes of Christian painters.

Little is known about the disposition of his relics until about the year 1463 when Padua and Venice both claimed to have the body of the saint and vied with one another over the authenticity of their relics. The bones in each place were eventually exhumed and carefully examined. Those at Venice were found to be the bones of a young man; those at Padua were of a man who died at a venerable age. Since the skull of the body in Padua was missing, and since the head was then known to be in Rome, the relics in Padua were accepted as being those of St. Luke. The Venetians were so disappointed in having their relics pronounced invalid that they were vehement in their disapproval of the ecclesiastical pronouncement, so much so, that excommunication was threatened on all those who would continue to promote the relics in Venice as being valid.[1] The relics have been enshrined in the Basilica of Santa Giustina above an altar in a side chapel. The tomb is of blue stone decorated with golden panels depicting portraits of angels, the saint and various symbols.

St. Mark

THE ancient historian Papias declared that Mark had not heard the Lord and had not been His disciple. While not counted as one of the Twelve Apostles, St. Mark, nevertheless, was closely associated with them and after learning from them the details of the life of Christ, he set them down in the second Gospel.

It is believed that Mark is identical with "John surnamed Mark" of Acts 13:12-15 and that the Mary whose home was a gathering place in Jerusalem for the early Christians was his mother. We learn that Mark was a cousin of Barnabas with whom he traveled in the interests of the Faith (Colossians 4:10).

[1]*Capo Di S. Luca Evangelista Di Padova E L'Imperatore Carlo IV Re Di Boemia*, G. Prevedello, Abbazia Di S. Giustina, Padova, pp. 3-11.

117

Mark was doubtless a congenial companion, since he also labored and journeyed with both St. Paul and St. Peter. We learn that when Paul was enduring his first captivity in Rome, Mark was a comfort to him (Colossians 4:11). Again, during Paul's second imprisonment prior to his martyrdom, at a time when the evangelist Luke was with him, St. Paul wrote to Timothy pleading with him to ". . . take Mark and bring him with you, for he is profitable to me for the ministry" (2 Timothy 4:11-12).

Papias, as well as the ancient historians Eusebius and Irenaeus, speaks of Mark as the interpreter or spokesman for St. Peter, while tradition tells us the Romans requested that he set down the teachings of St. Peter. This seems to be confirmed by the prominence St. Peter has in his Gospel. It is for this reason that the second Gospel seems to be a record of the life of Jesus as seen through the eyes of Peter.

St. Mark seems intent on proving to the Romans that Jesus is the Savior and that He is divine. For this reason he concentrated more on the miracles of Jesus than on His sermons.

The *Roman Martyrology* tells us that after Mark wrote his Gospel he went on to Alexandria where he became bishop and founded a church. Here he devoted himself to the task of teaching what he had learned from the apostles. Later he was arrested for his faith, was bound with cords and was tortured by being dragged over stones. We are further informed that while in prison he was comforted by an angel and, finally, after an apparition of our Lord himself, he went to his reward.

The relics of the evangelist remained in Alexandria until the year 829 when Venetian merchants purchased them. At Venice the building of the magnificent St. Mark's Basilica was immediately begun as a fitting shrine. A grand mosaic within the basilica depicts this translation of the body of St. Mark.

It is certain that St. Mark has been honored from time immemorial as principal patron of the city, but the legend that St. Mark had once preached in Venice grew up after the removal of his relics and is not regarded as valid.

The relics reclined for many years in the confession of the church, a room that served as a mausoleum located beneath the flooring of the altar. They were removed from there at a later time since in 1808 they were brought to light during enlargements of the choir. The relics are now enshrined under the high altar. A green marble canopy rises above the altar and is supported by Greek columns carved with scenes of the Gospels.

The Basilica of St. Mark, begun in 829 and remodeled and enlarged

118

at later times, was magnificently adorned during the 14th century by seamen and merchants who returned from the Orient and other parts of the world with architectural pieces, valuable stones, bronzes, metalwork and all manner of artful pieces to enhance the prestige of the shrine. Its interior is splendored with mosaics, sculptures and art, and with good reason it is called Chiesa d'Oro, the Golden Church.

Atop a gray column in the Piazzetta di S. Marco in Venice is a sculpture of a winged lion, a symbol reserved to the evangelist since his Gospel begins with a reference to the desert of which the lion is regarded as king.

St. Matthew

MATTHEW is identified as Levi by Mark and Luke and was a Galilean Jew by birth. It is thought that he was called to the ministry during the second year of Christ's public life.[1] His profession was that of publican, that is, a tax collector, and with his office located in Capharnaum, the same city in which Christ preached and wrought miracles, Matthew was no doubt aware of the Savior's activities and doctrines before he was invited to join Him. He apparently knew that his compliance with the Master's invitation would mean the surrendering of a lucrative position for that of poverty.

In his Gospel, Matthew tells of his meeting with the Savior in this manner: "Now as Jesus passed on from there he saw a man named Matthew sitting in the tax collector's place and said to him, 'Follow me.' And he arose and followed him" (Matthew 9:9-10). The Lord's acceptance of Matthew, the tax collector, was a direct challenge to public opinion. As a collector of taxes, Matthew was regarded by both Jew and gentile as an extortionist, a public sinner, traitor and apostate since the collectors gathered the taxes for the Romans and were commissioned by them to raise as much money as possible, thereby acting, in the eyes of the Jews, as subjugators of their own people. The presence of a tax collector in a family prevented a Jew from marrying into it since he was regarded as an outcast. Matthew himself gives proof of the low esteem with which his profession was regarded by quoting the Savior's words, "If you love

[1]Butler, *op. cit.*, Vol. 9, p. 271.

those that love you, what reward shall you have? Do not even the publicans do that?" (Matthew 5:46-47)

Scripture frequently relates the criticisms of those who questioned Christ's association with tax collectors and again Matthew tells us that soon after he began to follow Jesus, Christ went to his home and began eating with Matthew and Matthew's publican friends. "...The Pharisees, seeing it, said to his disciples, 'Why does your master eat with publicans and sinners?' But Jesus heard it and said, 'It is not the healthy who need a physician, but they who are sick. . . . I have come to call sinners, not the just.' " (Matthew 9:11-13)

Perhaps as a gesture of contrition or humility Matthew identifies himself in his list of the apostles as "Matthew, the publican." (Matthew 10:3)

After Pentecost, Matthew, like his colleagues, became a herald of the faith and, after sharing it by word of mouth, finally wrote it down to preserve it for posterity. Concerning this Gospel, the Biblical Commission of June 19, 1911 declared that "... the universal and constant tradition dating from the first centuries and expressed in early writings, ancient codices, versions and catalogues of the Bible, proves beyond doubt that St. Matthew wrote the first gospel as we now have it in our bibles before the year 70."

St. Matthew's Gospel is placed first in the New Testament and was written for Jewish Christians. Because he begins the Gospel with the human genealogy of Christ, Matthew is usually symbolized as a winged man. The characteristic that distinguishes Matthew's Gospel from the others is his frequent allusion to Old Testament prophecies and their fulfillment by Christ, thus showing that Jesus was the Messiah long awaited by the Jews.

The account of Matthew's career subsequent to the Ascension is uncertain as well as the time, place and manner of his death, although it is

Statue of St. Matthew in Rome

120

generally conceded that he was martyred.

The apostle's relics were translated to the West and are thought to have been enshrined in the Cathedral of Salerno, Italy, in A.D. 954. A letter of Pope Gregory VII addressed to the bishop of Salerno, dated A.D. 1080, refers to the relics of the evangelist as being enshrined in the cathedral.

The relics are still venerated in the Cathedral of St. Matthew and can be found under the main altar in the crypt.

St. Matthias

FOLLOWING the Ascension, Peter proposed to the assembled 120 disciples that they choose one from among themselves to fill the place in the apostleship made vacant by the traitor Judas. "Therefore, of these men who have been in our company all the time that the Lord Jesus moved among us, from John's baptism until the day that He was taken up from us, of these one must become a witness with us of His resurrection" (Acts 1:21-22). Two names were put forward: Joseph called Barnabas, and Matthias. After a prayer for God's direction they drew lots, ". . . and the lot fell upon Matthias and he was numbered with the eleven apostles" (Acts 1:26).

Following his selection, no further mention is made of Matthias in the Acts of the Apostles or in the epistles. Clement of Alexandria, however, tells us that the new apostle was remarkable for his insistence upon the necessity of mortifying the flesh to subdue all sensual and irregular appetites, a lesson he had learned from Christ and which he faithfully practiced himself.

All information concerning his life and death is vague and contradictory. One source relates that he preached the Gospel to the barbarians and cannibals in the interior of Ethiopia and won the crown of martyrdom after being mistreated by them. Another tradition maintains that Matthias was stoned at Jerusalem by the Jews and was then beheaded, while the *Greek Menaea* informs us that he was crucified. His body is thought to have been kept in Jerusalem for a time before being transported to Rome, where it is now kept in the Basilica of St. Mary Major. Beneath the high altar is an underground chapel, also called a

121

confession, in which the saint's relics are kept within the smaller altar located there.

The Bollandists cast doubt on the authenticity of these relics and surmise that they might be those of St. Matthias who was bishop of Jerusalem about the year 120, whose history was sometimes confused with that of the apostle.

St. Paul

S AUL was born in Tarsus, a city in Turkey, and belonged to a prominent and devout family of Jews. He claimed Roman citizenship by birth, received a thorough education and, because he considered himself an enlightened Jew, spurned the thought of a Messiah who died ingloriously on a cross. He believed that the religious ideals of Israel were betrayed by those who worshiped such a Redeemer and willfully condoned and participated in the persecution of those who expressed a belief in Jesus of Nazareth. He was present at the death of the Church's first martyr, Stephen, and it was he who held the garments of those who killed Stephen by stoning. "And Saul approved of his death" (Acts 7:60). Saul continued, ". . . harassing the Church; entering house after house, and dragging out men and women, he committed them to prison" (Acts 8:3). On the way to Damascus, ". . . still breathing threats of slaughter against the disciples of the Lord, light flashed about him; he fell to the ground and heard a voice saying, 'Saul, Saul, why dost thou persecute me?' " He was suddenly converted to the Faith and arose an apostle. For three days he remained blind, neither eating nor drinking (Acts 9:1-9). The same voice announced to Ananias on the third day, ". . . this man Saul is a chosen vessel to me to carry my name among nations and kings and the children of Israel. For I will show him how much he must suffer for my name" (Acts 9:15-16).

After Ananias laid hands upon him, Saul (also called Paul) received the gifts of the Holy Spirit, regained his sight, was baptized, and forthwith preached with a restless zeal that Jesus was the Son of God. When he joined the apostles at Jerusalem the fears and suspicions of the apostles regarding the validity of his conversion were allayed by Barnabas who later accompanied him on some of his travels for the Faith.

During extensive missionary journeys Paul suffered shipwreck, repeated imprisonments, a beating with rods and was once stoned and left for dead. After the Apostolic Council of Jerusalem, Paul was accompanied on a journey by St. Luke and according to Paul's epistle to the Romans (Romans 15:24) he set out for Spain where St. James the Greater was laboring for the Faith. He was imprisoned in Caesarea for two years and in Rome he was incarcerated twice, once by Nero who kept him for two years in the Mamertine prison, a place where St. Peter had also been imprisoned.

According to reliable traditions he was beheaded in Rome three years after Peter's death and according to the writings of St. Clement of Rome, it is suggested that Nero was present at Paul's execution.[1] The place of his death is believed to be the site where the Church of San Paolo Alle Tre Fontane is now located. Also called the Church of the Decapitation, it was begun in the fifth century on the spot where St. Paul was beheaded. Situated in the sanctuary are a low marble column to which St. Paul was bound, and a marble slab on which he died. At the back of the church are three small buildings which protect the three miraculous fountains that are said to have bubbled forth when the head of St. Paul made three bounds on the slope. While St. Gregory the Great mentions the beheading of the saint and the place of his martyrdom, he does not mention the bounding of the head; nevertheless, there are three fountains enclosed in monuments of marble, each topped with a head representing that of St. Paul.The actual head of the saint is enshrined together with that of St. Peter in a golden urn that is enclosed in the papal altar of the Lateran.

According to Roman law the bodies of the executed could be given to family or friends for burial. It is believed the body of St. Paul was wrapped in linen and spices and was buried on property belonging to Lucina, a Roman noblewoman. A simple mortuary chapel was constructed over the grave until Constantine replaced it with a basilica that was consecrated by Pope Sylvester I on the same day that St. Peter's was consecrated, November 18, 324.[2] According to the Acts of St. Sylvester, Constantine greatly enriched the basilica while enlargements and endowments were made by many notables, including St. Gregory the Great and Charlemagne.[3] The basilica was repeatedly enlarged and repaired and is known as the Basilica of St. Paul's Outside the Walls (San Paolo Fuori Le Mura). The body is kept beneath a marble slab dating from the

[1]Sharp, *op. cit.*, p. 173.
[2]*St. Paul's Outside the Walls*, Cecilia Pericoli Ridolfini, il Resto del Carlino, Bologna, 1977, p. 3.
[3]*Ibid.*, p. 3.

fourth century which bears the inscription, "Paulo Apostolo Mart." The tomb is located in the center of the apse and has not been disturbed since the third century.

A marble marker inside the Benedictine monastery that is attached to this basilica recalls the consistory in which Pope John XXIII first announced the Second Ecumenical Vatican Council on January 25, 1959.

The 14 epistles left by St. Paul powerfully express the Church's doctrines and have been the consolation and delight of countless saints. St. Jerome remarked that the words of the Apostle Paul seem to him like peals of thunder while St. Chrysostom wondered, "How did this blessed one gain an advantage over the other apostles? How comes it that he lives in all men's mouths throughout the world? Is it not through the virtue of his epistles?"

St. Peter, Prince of the Apostles

WHEN Jesus summoned Simon and his brother Andrew from their boat with the invitation to follow Him, Jesus looked at the older of the two and said, "Thou art Simon, the son of Jonah; thou shalt be called Cephas" (the Aramaic equivalent of the Greek word, Peter, i.e., rock). From that time on Peter, the fisherman from Bethsaida, took his place as the head of the apostolic college and as such appeared in all the Gospel scenes whether witnessing and listening, or provoking the most important statements of the Master.

The Acts of the Apostles (4:13) describes Peter as being "uneducated and ordinary," while historians appraised him as being slow in understanding and hasty in action, unpredictable and weak. To demonstrate these claims there are cited the instances when he sliced off the ear of the high priest's servant at the moment of the Lord's arrest, when he fell asleep instead of keeping watch during Christ's agony in the garden, when he denied Jesus three times after brashly affirming that he would never denounce him, and when he impulsively leapt from the boat on the Sea of Tiberias and started walking toward Jesus only to grow fearful and slip into the waves. The humanity of the saint is likewise portrayed in the Gospels and it is said that we know more about Peter than we do of any of the other apostles. According to one chronicler, Peter's name is mentioned in the Gospels and Acts 195 times, whereas

124

those of the other apostles added together amount to 130 times.[1] He is the only apostle we know for certain had been married.

If the Gospels portray his weaknesses they also report his gift for natural leadership and his love for the Son of God. As the spokesman for the others it was he who made the sublime profession of faith: "Thou art Christ the Son of the living God," to which our Savior replied with the solemn phrase: "Blessed art thou, Simon Bar-Jona, because flesh and blood hath not revealed it to thee, but my Father who is in heaven. And I say to thee, that thou art Peter and upon this rock I will build my church. . . ." (Matthew 16:16-18)

After Pentecost, when he was infused with the gifts of the Holy Spirit and the wisdom required for his future work, Peter once again spoke in the name of the others and converted 3,000 people (Acts 2:41). His authority constantly grew with miracles taking place wherever he went. At times his shadow alone was enough to effect a cure. (Acts 5:15)

Peter's movements after Pentecost are not easily traced. We are told in Galatians (1:18) that three years after Paul's conversion, Paul visited Peter in Jerusalem and stayed with him a fortnight. It is also known that Peter went on missions to Samaria, Joppa, Caesarea, Antioch and Corinth and that he established the Church in Rome where he wrote the two epistles to the Christian communities of Asia Minor.

His sufferings for the Church were great. He endured the hardships of many travels, suffered imprisonment in Jerusalem under the persecution of Herod Agrippa I and again endured imprisonment in Rome under Nero. He was crucified according to tradition, with his head in a downward position, a posture he had requested since he felt unworthy to meet death in the same manner as his Master. This took place on the site of Nero's circus and although the exact year is uncertain, it is believed Peter died between the years A.D. 64 and 69. He was buried on Vatican Hill and it is accepted by many Roman archeologists that the bodies of both St. Peter and St. Paul were conveyed in the year 258 from their respective tombs to the site where the Basilica of St. Sebastian now stands on the Via Appia. Once known as Memoria Apostolorum, the catacombs beneath this basilica testify to their temporary enshrinement since excavations in 1916 revealed graffiti concerning both apostles.

The year that St. Peter's remains were returned to the area of the Vatican is unknown, but Constantine was convinced from strong traditions that the tomb of the first pope was there and proceeded to build a basilica in A.D. 324 directly atop an existing cemetery. The floor of this

[1]*Saint Peter's: The Story of Saint Peter's Basilica in Rome*, James Lees-Milne, Little, Brown and Co., Boston, 1967, p. 23.

ancient basilica has been unearthed several feet below the present flooring of St. Peter's Basilica. (For details of these excavations of the crypt and the details of the Roman cemetery with its shrines, statuary, paintings, mosaics and stucco reliefs, the reader is directed to two excellent books on the subject: *The Shrine of St. Peter and the Vatican Excavations*, by Jocelyn Toynbee and John Ward Perkins, and *Saint Peter's: The Story of Saint Peter's Basilica in Rome*, by James Lees-Milne. Constantine's belief that the apse of his basilica was situated directly above the tomb of the apostle, and the constant tradition that the altar of the present basilica is also directly above the tomb, has been established by the excavations detailed in these two books.)

The tomb of the apostle was located beside a red plaster wall that served as a backdrop and whose construction with pillars and niches indicated a tomb of great importance. Reverently protected by a marble slab, the bones found in the tomb were examined geologically and anatomically and were found to have been the bones of a large man who lived during the first century.

A touching incident regarding this tomb and the saintly Pope Pius XII was revealed by Pope Paul VI on the vigil of the Feast of Ss. Peter and Paul in 1978. Before an audience of 9,000 people, Pope Paul VI related that during the time he served as undersecretary of state at the Vatican he "... had the good fortune to be Pius XII's companion in an archeological exploration. I remember how one evening our venerable predecessor Pius XII said to me, 'Come, let us go to St. Peter.' Then furtively we two passed through corridors, staircases and cubicles to the area of St. Peter's tomb." Pope Paul VI revealed that this secret adventure led Pope Pius XII to begin the extensive excavations previously mentioned that led to the exact location of the apostle's bones.

With the location of the tomb established, Pope Paul VI was able to conclude his narrative by declaring, "Peter is here — here where the documentary, indicative, archeological and logical analyses have indicated."[2]

In addition to the bones of the saint kept in the Vatican, there is also a chair believed to have been used by Peter in the house of Pudens where he lodged on first coming to Rome. Its solid legs of yellow oak have iron rings attached to them through which rods were placed, thus enabling it to function as a portable throne for the early popes. The panels between the legs and the arched back are of acacia wood inlaid with ivory that may have been added in the ninth century. The chair was on exhibit for centuries, but in 1656 it was placed in an inaccessible place where it

[2]*Clarion Herald* (New Orleans archdiocesan newspaper), Vol. 16, No. 21, July 13, 1978.

would be safe yet near those who wished to honor it. At this time Bernini was commissioned to design a monument for it. The decision to safeguard the relic was fortunate since its last examination in 1867 revealed that it had been ruthlessly gouged by relic hunters.[3] Bernini's massive sculpture, found at the westernmost end of the basilica, in the tribune apse, was dedicated on January 16, 1666 amid long and elaborate ceremonies. After being borne on the shoulders of several clerics the chair was placed on the high altar while the papal choir intoned several hymns, including *Tu es Petrus*. After being incensed, the chair was fitted into its place behind Bernini's black, gilt and bronze throne. Until the beginning of the last century it could be seen by visitors who climbed a ladder to the rear.

The Feast of the Chair of St. Peter has been celebrated from the earliest days of the Christian era on February 22. This day is still reserved in the liturgy for its worldwide observance. The feast does not honor the actual chair, which would be ludicrous, but the preeminent position Christ gave to Peter as leader of His Church of which this chair is only a symbol.

The throne of the apostle was not the only piece of furniture taken from the house of Pudens, Peter's former host. During the saint's visit there, a wooden table was used for the celebration of Holy Mass. This was regarded by the gracious host as a treasured relic. It was conveyed to the catacombs and was carefully preserved there through the years of persecution, being used in hiding by the early popes. After a time it was entrusted to the Church of St. Pudentiana, but during the pontificate of St. Sylvester, who reigned from 314 to 335, it was transferred to the Lateran, the Cathedral Church of Rome. A portion, however, was retained at St. Pudentiana's and is kept in a chapel dedicated to the apostle.

For many years Peter's altar was left exposed in the Lateran for the celebration of Mass by the popes. It is now encased in an altar of marble with the original wood still visible. As the principal altar of the Lateran, it is known as the papal altar since the celebration of Mass is reserved there for the pope or his appointed representative.

Atop this altar is a magnificent baldacchino, a Gothic structure resting on four marble columns. In the upper part of this canopy, in a chamber behind a bronze lattice, are preserved the heads of St. Peter and St. Paul which until this shrine was prepared to receive them had been kept in the Sancta Sanctorum, the private chapel of the Lateran palace. They were placed in the Sancta Sanctorum for safety when the Saracens threatened Rome in 846. While they were kept in this private chapel, the

[3]Lees-Milne, *op. cit.*, p. 279.

relics were twice taken in grand processions, first by Honorius III (1216-1227) who carried them to Santa Maria Maggiore to celebrate the arrival of the Crusaders in the Holy Land, and in 1241 by Pope Gregory IX (1227-1241) when it was hoped the relics would inspire the people to resist the troops of Emperor Frederick II who threatened the papal state. The translation of the relics from the Sancta Sanctorum to the basilica took place on Easter Monday, April 13, 1370, under the supervision of Pope Urban V who had erected the Gothic canopy above the altar and the reliquary for the reception of the relics. Almost 500 years later, in 1804, Pope Pius VII (1800-1823) assured himself that the seals placed by Urban V were unbroken. While a more splendid outer covering was being prepared for the reliquary, the cases were opened and the relics examined.

St. Peter's Chair

Also reverently kept in Rome are the chains of St. Peter, which have an unusual story. The pious Eudocia, wife of Emperor Teodosio II, journeyed to Jerusalem and found the chain that had bound Peter during his imprisonment. According to the Acts of the Apostles (12:6), an angel caused the chains to fall from Peter's hands and led him past slumbering guards to freedom. Eudocia sent part of the chain to Constantinople and another part to Rome as a gift to her daughter, Eudossia, who in turn gave it to Pope Leo the Great.[4] In Rome there was already a chain that was greatly prized which had bound the saint during his nine-month imprisonment in the Mamertine Prison near the Forum. When the pope compared the two chains, they miraculously fused together into one unbreakable series of links.[5] Because of this miracle Empress Eudocia built the Basilica of San Pietro in Vincoli (St. Peter in Chains) and dedicated it to the apostle in the year 442. The relic is now kept in a golden urn beneath the high altar, close to the famous statue of Michelangelo's *Moses*.

While the previously mentioned relics are all kept in Rome, a sandal believed to have been worn by the saint on his right foot is preserved in the Holy Chamber of the Cathedral of Oviedo, Spain. Experts describe it as a Roman sandal dating from the first or early second century with the

[4]*San Pietro in Vincoli*, G. Matthiae, Marietti, Rome, p. 5.
[5]*Ibid.*, p. 5.

sole consisting of four layers of leather. This is enclosed in a silver case of the 17th century that has the inscription, "San Pedro Apostol." The historian Rev. P. Carballo, in his work *Asturias Antiquities*, believes that the sandal was a gift from the pope to the king of Spain, a claim that is based on a letter to Alphonsus III of the ninth or 10th centuries.

The Prince of the Apostles has been honored with many churches in Rome, and innumerable churches throughout the world, being named in his honor. It seems quite appropriate that the Basilica of St. Peter, the largest church ever built through the ingenuity of man and so thoroughly touched by artistic genius, should have also been dedicated to him. Because of Peter's simplicity, his sheer humanity, his dedication and his love of the Master, he has endeared himself to all Christians who look toward his Vatican tomb and the basilica above it with a holy reverence.

St. Philip

THREE apostles came from the town of Bethsaida: Peter, his brother Andrew and Philip.

All that is known of St. Philip is revealed in the Gospel of St. John who tells us that before leaving Galilee Jesus found Philip and said to him, "Follow me" (John 1:43). Philip lost no time in finding Nathanael, telling him, "We have found him of whom Moses in the law and prophets wrote, Jesus, the son of Joseph of Nazareth." Nathanael asked him, "Can anything good come out of Nazareth?" To this Philip replied, "Come and see" (John 1:43-46).

Philip is quoted again at the feeding of the five thousand. Seeing the great number of followers Jesus asked Philip, "Whence are we to buy bread for these to eat?" Philip looked about and gave this sensible appraisal, "Two hundred denarii worth of bread is not enough for them, that each one may receive a little." It is Andrew, however, who found the boy with the five barley loaves and two fish (John 6:5-8).

Again Philip is mentioned on the day following the triumphal entry into Jerusalem. When the pagans came to meet Jesus they approached Philip with their request. Philip told Andrew and together they told the Savior (John 12:21-22). Finally at the Last Supper Philip interrupted Jesus during His last discourse with the request, "Lord, show us the Father and it is enough for us." Almost as a rebuke Jesus replied, "Philip, he who sees me sees also the Father." Jesus then continued with a lengthy explanation of this mystery (John 14:6-9).

Apart from the mention of him as being in the Upper Room awaiting the anointing of the Holy Spirit, and what is mentioned above, this is all we know about Philip with any degree of certainty. The church historian Eusebius and other early writers have mentioned a few details which tradition connects with the later life of the apostle. It is believed, therefore, that he preached the Gospel in Phrygia and died at Hierapolis where he was buried.[1] A claim is made that he was crucified.[2]

The relics of the saint were brought to Rome about the year 561 and were entombed with those of St. James the Less within a special chapel in the Basilica of Santi Apostoli where they are still venerated.

An unlikely situation exists in that St. Philip's name was never linked in Scripture with that of James the Less, and it is unlikely they were even remotely related, or together labored in spreading the Faith, yet Philip and James share the same tomb and also the same feast day, May 3.

St. Simon

THE surname "Zelotes" was added to Simon's name because of the zeal he had for the Jewish law and to distinguish him from the other Simon called Peter.

Also identified at times as the Cananean, no mention is made of him in Scripture except that he was adopted by Christ into the group of apostles and that together with the others he received the gifts of the Holy Spirit at Pentecost. His activities after this are unknown although legends abound.

One tradition has it that he labored in the Near East and died by being sawed in two. This is emphasized in art since he is often depicted with the instrument of his death and with a book symbolic of the law that nurtured his zeal. The menology of Basil says that St. Simon died in peace at Edessa, but the Western tradition, recognized by the Roman liturgy, is that he joined St. Jude in Mesopotamia where they labored together for some years in Persia, finally suffering martyrdom at Suanir. This later tradition seems the most probable of all since the relics of both

[1]Butler, *op. cit.*, Vol. 5, p. 2.
[2]*A Catholic Dictionary*, Donald Attwater, The Macmillan Co., New York, 1958, p. 382.

saints were later brought to Rome and entombed in the same altar in St. Peter's. The feast of St. Simon and St. Jude is celebrated on October 28.

St. Thomas

THE former occupation of St. Thomas and the circumstances surrounding his calling are unknown, although it is believed he was a Jew and a Galilean. His name is Syriac for "twin"; Didymus, as he was also called, is the Greek equivalent. Apart from his insertion in the lists of the apostles, the only evangelist who mentions him specifically is John, who quotes his words on three occasions as they were spoken to the Savior or uttered in His hearing.

Thomas is first mentioned at the time of the raising of Lazarus. On learning that Jesus wished to visit the tomb in Judea in the region where Jesus had just escaped His enemies, the disciples warned Jesus that the Jews were still seeking to stone Him, ". . . and dost thou go there again?" When Jesus repeated His intention, Thomas brashly expressed his love for the Master by declaring to the others, "Let us also go that we may die with him" (John 11:8-16).

John mentions Thomas again on the occasion of Jesus' lengthy farewell address at the Last Supper. On telling the apostles that there were many mansions in His Father's kingdom and promising to return one day to take them to His Father's house, He said, "Where I go you know and the way you know." It was Thomas who asked, "Lord, we do not know where thou art going and how can we know the way?" To which the Lord replied, "I am the way, the truth, and the life. No one comes to the Father but through me" (John 14:2-7).

Undoubtedly the best known incident regarding Thomas concerns the apparition of the risen Christ to a gathering of the apostles at a time when Thomas was not with the group. Refusing to believe that Christ was truly risen, Thomas said, "Unless I see in his hands the print of the nails, and put my finger into the place of the nails, and put my hand into His side, I will not believe." Eight days later, during another apparition of the risen Christ, after Thomas was permitted to touch the wounds he exclaimed, "My Lord and My God!" (John 20:24-29)

Following Pentecost the saint is believed to have traveled extensively in spreading the Faith and to have eventually made his way to India. His

131

labors there were later embellished with fanciful traditions that were recorded in *Acta Thomae*, a work subsequently denounced by Pope Innocent I, St. Augustine and St. Turibius of Astorga, and in the decree of Pseudo-Gelasius.[1] A persistent belief known to St. Ephraem, St. Ambrose, St. Paulinus of Nola, St. Jerome and others is that the apostle did, indeed, labor for many years in India. This is regarded by experts in Oriental history to be based on historical fact as is the meeting of the apostle with two kings who reigned there. Additionally this belief seems to be substantiated in our day by the presence in India of natives who call themselves the Christians of St. Thomas, who live along the west coast known as the Malabar coast, and particularly those who live in the state of Travancore. These identify themselves by the distinctive way in which the sari is worn by the women. In India the manner of dress aids in placing people just as an accent betrays the region of a country. The sari worn by the women of India is draped and tucked in ways that are peculiar to the region in which they are native. The descendants of the Christians converted by St. Thomas wear pleats at the back of their sari instead of the front like the others, and are in this way readily identified.[2]

The Christians of St. Thomas maintain to this day that they were evangelized by the apostle himself, and claim an ancient oral tradition that he landed at Cranganore on the west coast and established churches in the Malabar region before passing along the southern tip of India to the eastern coast.

Eight miles outside Madras, near the shore of the Bay of Bengal, is a mount named for the saint where it is believed he suffered martyrdom in the year 72[3] by being pierced by the sword of a pagan. Located on the spot is a stone engraved with a cross which was seen to ooze blood on December 18, 1558, and to continue on that day each year with various interruptions until the year 1704. The phenomenon first occurred during the celebration of Mass and lasted four hours. Diocesan authorities certified that at the end of this bleeding the stone turned a glistening white before returning to its original black.[4]

The apostle was buried at Mylapore, now a suburb of Madras, where the Cathedral of St. Thomas of Mylapore was erected over his grave.

From earliest times the Christians of St. Thomas aspired to make at

[1]Butler, *op. cit.*, Vol. 12, p. 217.
[2]*India*, Taya Zinkin, Walker & Co., New York, 1965, p. 8.
[3]Butler, *op. cit.*, p. 216.
[4]*Soul Magazine*, John M. Haffert, ed., Ave Maria Institute, Washington, N.J., 1978, Vol. 29, No. 4, p. 17.

least one visit to the tomb during their lifetime, and to aid the poor financially in this endeavor was regarded as a sign of special piety. The custom was later relaxed after the schism of 1653 when some of the Christians, were divided into different rites and later into reforms and Protestant sects.

The mount on which the saint was martyred remains a place of pilgrimage as is the tomb which contains certain relics of the saint. During the fourth century the bulk of the relics was taken overland from India through Persia and Mesopotamia to Edessa where they arrived on a July 3 according to the *Martyrology*. After a time the relics were taken by sea around Greece to Ortona on the eastern shore of Italy where they arrived in 1258.

The relics of St. Thomas are kept in the crypt of the Basilica of Ortona; the head is kept apart in a silver bust reliquary. The bones have been examined on several occasions throughout the years and numerous indulgences have been awarded by various popes to those who visit the saint's remains.

Relics of Bible Figures

Statue of St. Anne at her shrine in Canada

St. Anne

JUDGING by the dispersion of St. Anne's relics, the mother of the Blessed Virgin was revered from the earliest days of Christianity.

When the Christians ventured forth to spread the Gospel to foreign lands, a considerable portion of the relics of St. Anne was given to a group which included St. Anne's two cousins, both named Mary, and a relative named Maximin. In leaving their native land they evidently felt they could not bear to be eternally separated from all contact with their blood relatives, especially since this contact was also their closest link with their Savior. For this reason they were given a considerable portion of the relics and these they placed in a coffer made of cedarwood.

Together with their precious cargo the group crossed the Mediterranean and landed at Marseilles, France. The two Marys settled at Marseilles among humble fisherfolk, but Maximin pushed further inland to the little city of Apt. In time the region around Marseilles was subjected to repeated invasion and siege, and fearing for the safety of the relics they were entrusted to Maximin in the bishopric of Apt where they could be more properly enshrined. Here in the eighth century the relics were visited by Charlemagne who saw for himself the words inscribed on the ancient winding sheet that embraced the relics, "Here lies the remains of St. Anne, Mother of the Glorious Virgin Mary."[1] During this visit Charlemagne distributed portions of the relics to friends, reserving for himself a portion that was destined for Aix-la-Chapelle. He prepared an inventory of the relics, sent a copy to the pope and entrusted the greater portion to the bishop of Apt and his successors. Since this visit by the great Charlemagne, the sanctuary of Apt has been regarded as the principal resting place of St. Anne. It has been noted that if Charlemagne had doubted the validity of the relics at Apt, he would have instigated a search for them in the Holy Land as he had already done for those with lesser contact and relationship to the Savior. It has been claimed that Charlemagne held the grandmother of Jesus in high esteem, his devotion being exhibited by the embroidered figure of St. Anne on his coronation robes.[2] His contemporary biographer, Kleinclausz, recorded that Charlemagne again visited the shrine in the year 801.

[1]*St. Anne, Grandmother of Our Savior*, Francis Parkinson Keyes, Julian Messner, Inc., New York, 1955, p. 109.
[2]*Ibid.*, p. 181.

A portion of the post at which Christ was scourged is said to have been taken to Rome in 1223 by John Cardinal Colonna. It is now kept in a small chapel in the Church of St. Praxedes.

137

The Last Supper chalice, known as the Holy Grail, is the subject of numerous legends. The cup is displayed in a chapel of the Cathedral of Valencia, Spain.

A piece of the true cross is contained in the crucifix at right displayed at the Cathedral of Oviedo. Other relics of the cross of a notable size are found in the Cathedral of Trier, Notre Dame in Paris, the Cathedral of Ghent in Brussels and at the Vatican.

Pictured below is the tomb of St. John the Apostle (square, fenced-in area) at Ephesus.

The unusual statue of the Child Jesus is called the Holy Infant of Aracoeli, and dates back to the 15th century.

A reliquary containing bones of St. James the Greater may be viewed in a shrine in the ancient church of Compostela, Spain.

This statue of Our Lady of Montserrat is found in a chapel dedicated to the Mother of God in the year 888 on Montserrat. Legend says the wooden statue, gilded except for the faces and hands, was found by shepherds in a cave amid a mysterious radiance and angelic singing.

The house below was built on the site and foundation where it is believed the Blessed Virgin Mary spent her final days on earth in Ephesus, Turkey.

This statue of Our Lady of Guadalupe in Zaragoya, Spain
(one of two Our Lady of Guadalupes), was discovered at the
entrance of an underground cave after "a radiant lady"
appeared to a cowherd in 1326 and indicated where he
should dig to unearth a treasure.

The body of St Bernadette, now covered with wax, was found to be incorrupt 30 years after her death. A museum containing the body and many relics and artifacts is housed at St. Gildard Convent in Nevers, France.

A habit and veil worn by St. Thérèse of Lisieux.

A cascade of hair shorn from St. Thérèse when she entered the convent was saved by her father. It is now on display at the Carmel in Lisieux.

Our Lady of Perpetual
Help is the title of the
Italian icon at left.

Displays and reliquaries containing relics and artifacts of St. Teresa
of Avila are maintained at three locations in Avila.

One of the dearest relics in Assisi is this 1224 blessing to Brother Leo in the handwriting of St. Francis of Assisi. The black writing is that of St. Francis; the red letters are by Brother Leo attesting to the authenticity of the blessing.

The gray habit worn by St. Francis is displayed in the Basilica of St. Francis in Assisi.

St. Stephen of Hungary's crown, scepter and globe.

The Shrine of the Three Kings is located in Cologne, Germany.

St. John Neumann rests below the alter in a crystal-clear
casket at the shrine of the Church of St. Peter the Apostle in
Philadelphia.

This miraculous crucifix was given to St. Collete by St. Vincent Ferrier, a Spanish Dominican. It is still used on the altar of the Monastery of St. Claire in Besançon, France.

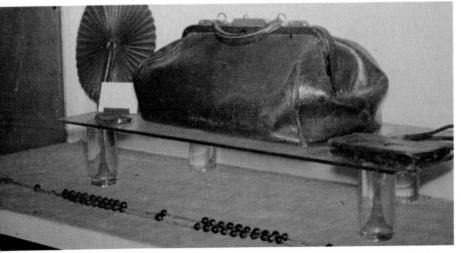

Some of Mother Cabrini's personal effects, including a valise, her rosary and a fan, are preserved and displayed in her hometown of Lodi, Italy.

An ostensorium in Lanciano, Italy, contains a Host turned to flesh and five pellets of blood. The history of the host turned to flesh and the wine turned to blood is detailed in Eucharistic Miracles, page 11.

An urn containing St. Peter's chains is on display in the Basilica of St. Peter in Chains in Rome.

One of the oldest churches in Jerusalem is that which bears the name of the Savior's grandmother. Dating from the time of the Crusades, tradition dictates that it was built on the site of the home of Joachim and Anne, parents of the Virgin Mary.

While it has been accepted on good authority that not all the remains of the saint were removed by those who journeyed to Marseilles, it seems that another collection of St. Anne's relics were taken from her sepulcher in Nazareth and brought to Constantinople in 710. In time the relics were shared with others until many churches in just a few centuries boasted of possessing particles. One of these is St. Anne at Auray. As the principal saint of Brittany, this shrine of St. Anne is located at Auray on the southern coast of the peninsula. In July there is an impressive procession of those who have received answers to their prayers. This festival is unique in that the participants carry emblems of the favors granted.

Of all the churches dedicated to the saint, and of those that safeguard her relics, none can claim as many miracles as can that of the Basilica of St. Anne de Beaupre in Canada. Beaupre (which means "lovely meadow") owes its foundation to a vow made by a group of Breton sailors who landed there in 1658 after being saved from shipwreck through the intervention of St. Anne, to whom they pledged a votive offering. Begun as a small chapel, the first miracle was reported even as the building materials were being assembled. Louis Guimont, a poor cripple who despite his affliction insisted on carrying stones to the site, was suddenly and miraculously cured before the eyes of his fellow workers, thus beginning the stream of miracles that continues to the present day.[3]

Today's grand basilica contains ten chapels, one of which honors the mother of the Virgin Mary. A major relic consisting of a fragment of the wristbone is exposed on the altar of the saint. In front of this altar stands a column of yellow onyx which supports the miraculous statue of St. Anne holding in one arm the child Mary, the hand of the other arm pointing heavenward to the source of all blessings. Golden crowns adorn their heads while rays of gold burst from behind to proclaim the glory enjoyed by both. At the base of the column is a railing where crutches and braces have been placed by those who have been awarded tangible evidence of St. Anne's power. Here the good saint's devotees continually gather.

In all, there are seven main relics of St. Anne at Beaupre, but the relic of the wristbone is the one honored the most. Presented to the basilica

[3]St. Anne de Beaupre in Canada, Catholic Digest, Inc., St. Paul, Minn., 1957, pp. 51-52.

by Pope Leo XIII it was removed in 1892 from the Basilica of St. Paul Outside the Wall in Rome.[4]

It has been estimated that more than 30 million people have visited the shrine in the 300 years of its existence.[5]

St. Anne was named patroness of Canada, an honor she shares with St. Joseph.

The Shrine of the Three Kings

IN Cologne Cathedral, behind one of the largest high altars in Christendom, stands the golden shrine of the Three Magi. Resembling a miniature church, the reliquary consists of three separate shrines, two at the bottom level and a third above them. Inside, in addition to the relics of the three kings, are the relics of St. Nabor, St. Felix and St. Gregory of Spoleto. Three large jewels on the front end of the shrine signify the location of the crowned heads of the three holy kings.

The medieval legend of the relics relates their finding by Empress Helena at the beginning of the fourth century and their transport from Constantinople to Milan and thence to Cologne in 1164.

Measuring 210 centimeters long, 110 centimeters broad and 153 centimeters high, the reliquary originated between 1181 and 1230 with some of the gems and cameos being donated by King Otto IV. The shrine was renewed between 1961 and 1973.

Decorated with intricately enameled pillars, brilliant stones, enamels, filigree plates and embossed metal strips, the golden scenes that surround the reliquary depict the Creation, the life of Christ, the salvation of the world and the last judgment. Individual figures represent the prophets, priests and kings of the Old Testament as well as the apostles, angels, the Virgin Mary with Child and, of course, the three kings presenting their gifts. In all, a veritable history of the world and its redemption.

The German kings after their coronation in Aachen came to Cologne in order to pay tribute to Christ with their gifts, and to receive His confirmation as Otto IV did for the first time when he donated the gold and jewels for the front end of the reliquary. Since the three kings were the

[4]Keyes, op. cit., p. 23.
[5]Ibid., p. 123.

first monarchs to be recognized by Christ, so, too, the Christian kings of Germany wished a similar recognition.

Lazarus

THE traditions regarding the relocations of the relics of St. Lazarus are varied, but most concur that the relics of the man who was once raised from the dead by Jesus Christ, eventually found their way to Autun, France. The account favored by the cathedral in which the alleged relics were enshrined is the following:

The Greek Church believed that sometime after the dispersion of the apostles on their missionary endeavors, and during the early days of the Christian suppression, Lazarus, together with other Christians, was cast adrift by hostile Jews in the hope that they would perish at sea. For this reason the boat was described as being flimsy and leaky. The boat sailed from Jaffa to Larnaca on the island of Cyprus where Lazarus disembarked and lived for more than thirty years. He was eventually buried there after suffering for the Faith. His tomb was miraculously discovered in 899 and his relics brought to Constantinople by order of Emperor Leo VI. The journey of these relics is complicated; however, it has been proved that the cult of Lazarus was in full progress in Autun, France, as early as the 10th century. The relics were first venerated in the Church of St. Nazaire where they rested in a sarcophagus to the right of the high altar. A short distance from this church another church was built and dedicated to St. Lazarus. Consecrated by Pope Innocent II on December 28, 1130, it was later designated a cathedral in 1195.

When the church of St. Nazaire fell into disrepair, the relics of Lazarus were solemnly transferred to this cathedral bearing his name, and were placed in a tomb situated in front of the central apse. In the 18th century the tomb was dismantled and the pieces sold for reasons not specified. Whether or not the relics are retained by the cathedral is unclear.[1]

---

[1]This account of St. Lazarus is summarized from papers supplied by the Cathedral of St. Lazarus at Autun, France.

Mary Magdalene

M ARY Magdalene, the public sinner who was converted by Our Lord and thereafter demonstrated her love for Him in dramatic scenes as recorded in Scripture, evidently wished to travel for the Faith. Like the apostles and disciples who dispersed following Pentecost, she, together with several companions, crossed over to France, then known as Gaul. She traveled some 40 miles inland and spent the next 30 years in a grotto of the mountain chain now known as La Sainte Baume (or "holy balm"). The mountains were named, of course, to commemorate the spikenard, a fragrant ointment, or balm, which she once poured over the head of Jesus (Mark 14:3-9). She died on her way to a nearby village of Villalata where she was buried by Maximin,[1] one of the disciples.

In A.D. 415 the Cassian monks built a monastery in Villalata and named it "St. Maximin." They became the guardians of four marble sarcophagi — one of which held the body of St. Mary Magdalene.

When the Saracens invaded that part of France in 710 and destroyed all Christian symbols, the monks, on December 6 of that year, removed the remains of St. Mary Magdalene to another tomb to conceal her identity. Before fleeing, they buried the four tombs under mounds of earth where they remained hidden for five centuries.

A nephew of King Louis of France, together with a crew of workmen, searched for the tombs and found them on December 9, 1279. Under the watchful gaze of Church dignitaries and royal emissaries the tomb of Mary Magdalene was opened. Inside were found a piece of bark dated December 6, 710, and a small parchment hidden in a ball of wax that identified the relics as those of Mary Magdalene. A great odor of perfume emanated from the tomb even before it was opened and this lasted for many days. It was found that part of the lower jaw was missing. This bone was later discovered in the basilica of St. John Lateran in Rome where it was venerated as a relic of the saint. It was thought that the Cassian monks removed this bone and sent it to Rome in 710 as a relic in the event the body was destroyed by the Saracens. Pope Boniface VIII (1294-1303) requested that the bone be matched against the jaw of the relic in St. Maxim. Since it fitted perfectly, the pontiff issued a papal bull in 1295 confirming the authenticity of the relics.

[1]It is not known if this is the same Maximin mentioned in the history of St. Anne's relics.

The rediscovery of the remains attracted thousands of pilgrims throughout the years, including popes, kings and crusaders as well as many persons later canonized by the Church.

The remains of the saint were placed in a tomb above an altar in the crypt in May of 1280 where they are still kept. The Dominican Fathers, who were made custodians of the Basilica of St. Maximin and the guardians of the relics in 1295, retain the privilege to this day.

The repercussions of the French Revolution spread to the shrine in 1789. Everything in the grotto and basilica was either destroyed or plundered, but the relics of St. Mary Magdalene remained secure.

In addition to the relics of the saint in the Basilica of St. Maximin, other relics of the saint have been honored at Vezelay, France, where they were reported to be in the Cluniac Abbey as early as the year 1050. The history of these relics is lost, but it might be speculated that the Cassian monks, during the Saracen threat, sent not only a relic to St. John Lateran, but other relics further inland for safety.

At Vezelay a political dispute between the Duke of Nevers and the Order of Cluny over the administration of the abbey resulted in disaster for the relics when the duke, enraged because the pope sided with the order, took his revenge by breaking into the sanctuary in 1116 and damaging the relics. Whether some were retained for the veneration of the pilgrims is unclear; however, a disastrous fire that engulfed the monastery four years later on July 27, 1120, killed a thousand people who were praying there, and might well have destroyed what little remained of the relics.[2]

As though to compensate for its ill fortune, the abbey was later visited by several notables. In the presence of King Louis VII and Queen Eleanor of Aquitaine, St. Bernard in 1142 read the papal bull that launched the Second Crusade. Before starting the Third Crusade Philip Augustus, King of France, and Richard the Lion-Hearted met at Vezelay, made peace with one another and together took up the sword in defense of the Holy Land.[3] St. Thomas à Becket was likewise a visitor. On Pentecost in the year 1166 he pronounced excommunication against the clerics who, to gratify King Henry II of England, had violated the rights of the Church.

In 1876 the future Cardinal Bernadou, archbishop of Sens, determined to restore the shrine of St. Mary Magdalene at Vezelay and brought there a relic donated by Martin IV.

[2]*Monastery and Cathedral in France*, Whitney S. Stoddard, Wesleyan University Press, Middletown, Conn., 1966, p. 18.
[3]*Ibid.*, p. 18.

Devotion to St. Mary Magdalene at Vezelay has steadily declined through the years, but the homage paid the saint at Villalata is still vigorous.

In the grotto where the saint lived for 30 years a Mass is offered daily in her honor, and, in addition, all the Dominican priests of the French province of Toulouse offer Masses to the patroness of the province, St. Mary Magdalene. The saint is likewise remembered by the Dominican contemplative sisters in their Convent at St. Maximin.

Miraculous Statues of the Infant Jesus

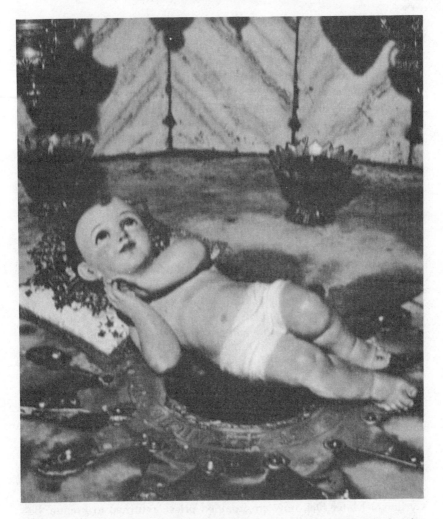

A statue of the Child Jesus is situated on a star which marks the place where Jesus was born. On the star it is written in Latin: *Hic de Maria Virgine Jesus Christus Natus Est*

Statues of the Infant Jesus

WHILE countless statues of the Christ Child are venerated during the Christmas season, two statues in particular enjoy recognition throughout the year and experience a worldwide reputation. The better known is the statue of the Infant Jesus of Prague. Although kept in Czechoslovakia the statue is of Spanish origin and was given to a Spanish princess by her mother as a wedding gift. It was brought to Prague by the bride, Maria Manriques, after her marriage in 1556 to Vratislav of Pernstejn, a Czech nobleman. The statue once again served as a wedding gift when it was given to Maria's daughter, Polyzena, upon her marriage to Zdenek of Lobkovice. On being widowed in 1628 she resolved to make the statue available to all believers by donating it to the Carmelites of Prague and the Church of Our Lady of Victory. Her words at the time proved prophetic: "I hereby give you what I prize most highly in this world. As long as you venerate this image you will not be in want." When special devotions were instituted in honor of the Child Jesus, the community that had been enduring hardships soon prospered.

The Child Jesus was particularly dear to one of the novices, Cyrillus à Mater Dei, who was delivered of interior trials by means of this devotion. The future history of the statue would in all probability have suffered if it had not been for this holy Carmelite.

At the beginning of the disturbances attending the Thirty Years War the novitiate was removed to Germany in 1630. With the absence of the novices and Brother Cyrillus, the devotions before the statue were gradually neglected until the prayers were abandoned altogether. Need and distress once more returned. Eventually the invading army of King Gustavus Adolphus of Sweden took possession of the churches in the city, plundered the Carmelite monastery and threw the image of the Infant Jesus on a heap of rubble behind the high altar. For the next seven years the statue lay forgotten by all. On the feast of Pentecost in 1637, Cyrillus à Mater Dei, now an ordained priest, returned to Prague. Because hostile armies still overran the city, the community was in distress until Father Cyrillus remembered the prosperity and peace they enjoyed while devotions were observed to the Infant Jesus. He searched for the

160

lost statue and eventually found it almost buried in dust and debris. Made of wood and coated with wax, the image had miraculously suffered little from its neglect except for its two hands, which were missing. Cyrillus placed the statue atop an altar in the oratory and reorganized devotions to it. One day, while praying before the statue, he distinctly heard these words: "Have pity on Me, and I will have pity on you. Give Me My hands, and I will give you peace. The more you honor Me, the more I will bless you."

When the money intended for the repair of the statue was spent on a replacement, the Infant manifested His displeasure by causing the new statue to be shattered by a falling candlestick. Once again the original statue was the object of their veneration, but when additional funds for the necessary repairs were slow in coming, Father Cyrillus again heard the voice: "Place Me near the entrance of the sacristy and you will receive aid." When this was accomplished the full cost of the repairs was promptly donated.

The needs of the community were always met through the continued devotion to the Child Jesus, and such were the favors granted that replicas of the statue were made for those who wished likewise to benefit in diverse areas of need.

The Holy Infant owes part of its fame to the practice of the Sisters of the Congregation of Angelical Maids who adopted the practice of clothing the statue several times each year in the proper liturgical color. The most beautiful garment is an ermine cloak placed on the statue the first Sunday after Easter, which is the anniversary day of the coronation of the statue by the bishop of Prague in 1655. During the Christmas season the statue is clothed in a dark green robe made of velvet and richly decorated with golden embroidery, a gift of the Empress Maria Theresa on the occasion of her coronation as queen of Bohemia in 1743. The Infant's wardrobe contains more than 50 dresses, the oldest being a dark red brocade dating from about the year 1700.

Since the time of its ecclesiastical approbation in 1655, replicas of the statue always represent the royal status of the Child. Crowned and clothed in a mantle of fine fabrics, the statues hold a sphere representing the world in the left hand while the right hand is raised in blessing.

Standing a mere 19 inches high, the statue is known throughout the world, with the word "miraculous" generally added to its title.

The original statue of the Infant Jesus is enshrined in a side chapel in the Kostel Prazskeho Jezulatka, the Church of the Infant of Prague.

Another statue that has earned considerable recognition is that of the Christ Child of Aracoeli. This crowned, bejeweled life-size figure of the Child Jesus is venerated in a special chapel of the Basilica of Santa Maria in Aracoeli, Rome. It was carved in Jerusalem at the end of the year 1400 from the wood of an olive tree grown at Gethsemane. According to tradition it was carved by a Franciscan friar, but its coloring was completed by the hands of an angel. The jewels that adorn it were donated by people from around the world in gratitude for favors received and in testimony of their affection.

Following an ancient custom, the statue is often relieved of its golden weight and is carried on request to the bedside of the sick.

While the churches in Rome vie with one another in assembling the most beautiful Christmas crib, the most famous is unquestionably the one in which this image is located. The statue is placed in its historic crib scene on Christmas eve by members of the Presidential Guard during impressive ceremonies. Some years the statue is placed on the lap of a statue of the Blessed Mother, at other times it reposes in a manger.

From Christmas until the Epiphany the church resounds with the voices of the children of Rome who visit the crib to recite poems, sing hymns and play music in honor of the Christ Child's birth.

The statue is apparently revered throughout the world as evidenced by the many letters requesting graces and relief of temporal cares. These letters are kept at the side of the glass case in which the statue is protected.

Crosses and Crucifixes
as Relics

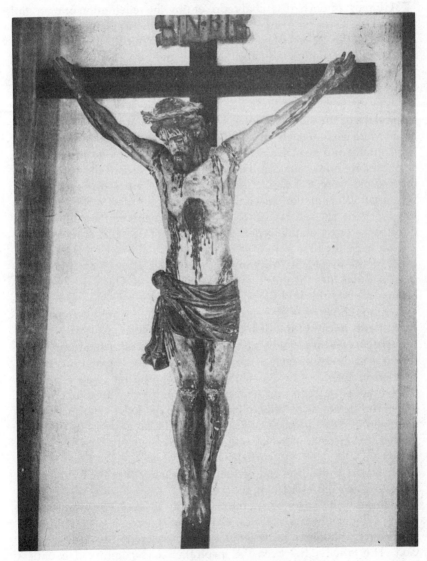

Crucifix used by St. John of the Cross

The Cross and the Crucifix

T HE most important symbol representing the redemption of mankind was used since the early days of the Church, but then only in secret, because of the threats of violence that existed during the days of persecution. Even though used clandestinely, and principally on sepulchral monuments, the Christian felt obliged to disguise the signs in artistic and symbolic ways.

One of the oldest of these was the anchor that is found carved on the stone slabs of the oldest sections of the Roman catacombs. Various other forms were used, namely the addition of bars of different lengths placed horizontally or diagonally at random heights along the vertical bar. Such examples are numerous and their renderings are artistically varied. Four other types were: (1) the "chi-rho," a P superimposed over an X that was used often in the catacombs; (2) the X, or decussate cross, also known as the St. Andrew's Cross because it is believed the saint suffered death on a cross of this type; (3) the Greek T (or tau) cross which is known to be the first cross used on a religious habit when it adorned the cloak of the hermit St. Anthony of Egypt (A.D. 251-356); and (4) the most popular form of the cross, the Latin cross, in which the transverse beam is set two-thirds of the way up the vertical.

Although we have many carved crosses dating from the fourth century, it was not until the fifth century that Christian art broke from its former fears and was boldly presented to the world atop monuments and this, it is said, was a result of two historical events. The first was the apparition of the cross to Constantine the Great during a battle in which the symbol appeared in the heavens with the words, "In this conquer." When the cross was placed on his banner, he did indeed conquer the enemy who greatly outnumbered his forces. The other event involved his mother, St. Helena, in which she discovered the Holy Cross in Jerusalem.

It was not until the end of the sixth century that the figure of the Redeemer was represented on the cross.

Through the years both crucifixes and crosses have adorned vestments, religious habits, rosaries, altars, tombs, and have stood proudly atop church buildings to designate their consecration to the service of God. The crucifix has been the inspiration and comfort of countless saints and the subject of innumerable works of art. It was the crucifix that often prompted the saints to works of virtue and it has been by means of the crucifix that the Savior at times communicated with his saints.

Of these incidents perhaps the most famous occurred when St. Francis of Assisi, at the beginning of his conversion to holiness, wandered into St. Damian's church which was then in a sorry state of disrepair. Kneeling before the Byzantine cross with its painted image of the crucifix the saint prayed, "Great God, and You, my Savior, Jesus Christ, dispel the darkness of my soul, give me pure faith, lasting hope and perfect charity. Let Thy Will, O God, be my will; make me and keep me Thine, now and forever."

In response, a voice proceeded from the crucifix and repeated three times, "Francis, go and repair my house which you see is falling down." Understanding the words to mean the church building in which he was praying, and not the Church in general which some believed was intended, Francis secured funds for the necessary building materials by selling bolts of fabrics from his father's store, thereby placing himself on the shadowed side of his father's disposition which instigated his disinheritance.

Another incident is recorded in the life of St. Thomas Aquinas (d. 1274) who was a philosopher, theologian and is now regarded as a doctor of the Church. At the age of five, according to the custom of the time among the sons of nobility, he was sent to receive his training from the Benedictine monks at Monte Cassino, but later, being attracted to the Order of Preachers he received the habit of the Dominican order. He was once the student of St. Albert the Great and received his degree on the same day as did another saintly friend, St. Bonaventure. Engaged in preaching, teaching and writing, his counsels were sought by both the faithful and the scholar while his company was often requested by the pope.

Although the saint lived less than 50 years, he composed more than 60 works, some of great length. Of these the most famous are the *Summa Contra Gentiles* and the *Summa Theologica*. Historians tell us that the saint had the ability to dictate to several scribes at the same time.

His biographers relate that he was often found in ecstasies. On one occasion at Naples in 1273, after completing his treatise on the Holy Eucharist, his brethren found him in ecstasy before a crucifix and heard a voice coming from the image of the crucifix saying: "Thou hast written well of me, Thomas; what reward wilt thou have?" To which Thomas replied, "None other than Thyself, Lord."

While St. Thomas is considered the luminary of dogmatic theology, his counterpart in the field of mystical theology, St. John of the Cross, likewise was favored with a similar experience and this, too, as a result of his writings.

The saint's brother, Francisco, tells us that during his last visit with the saint, John took him by the hand and led him into the garden. When they were alone the saint related the following, as recorded by Francisco:

"I wish to tell you something that happened to me with Our Lord. We had a crucifix in the monastery and one day, when I was standing in front of it, it occurred to me that it would be more suitable to have it in the church. I was anxious to have this crucifix honored, not only by the religious, but also by the people. I carried out my idea. After I had placed it in the church as fittingly as I could, and whilst in prayer before it one day, Christ said to me, 'Brother John, ask me for what you wish and I will give it to you for the service you have done me.' And I said to Him, 'Lord, what I wish you to give me are sufferings to be borne for your sake and that I may be despised and regarded as worthless.''[1]

On yet another occasion a crucifix figured prominently in the life of the saint. Once when St. John was engaged in contemplative prayer the crucified Jesus appeared to him in a corporeal vision, covered with wounds and blood. Following the ecstasy John sketched the Redeemer in pen and ink on a piece of paper only five inches long, and presented the drawing to his spiritual daughter, the nun Ana Maria of Jesus, to whom he confided the vision. Because the head of the crucified in the drawing is inclined, the face is not visible, but the shoulders that bore the scourging are prominently exposed. When held sideward the full impact of the drawing is strengthened since the body drags away from its support with the arms stretched to the extreme. Although its anatomy is "occasionally at fault," it was always highly respected by artists who have studied it throughout its existence. The piece of paper upon which the image is impressed is now quite yellow and is reverently guarded in a golden reliquary at the Convent of the Incarnation in Avila.

When St. John of the Cross was canonized in 1726 the ceremony was shared with St. Peregrine Laziosi who, coincidentally, was also favored with a vision of Christ on the Cross.

Born in Forli, Italy, in 1265, Peregrine was taught the ways of prayer by his devout mother, but instead of being influenced by her, he preferred to devote his time to athletic endeavors and won the acceptance of his peers by indulging his impestuous nature. His talent for leadership

[1] *St. John of the Cross*, Father Bruno, O.C.D., edited by Father Benedict Zimmerman, O.C.D., Sheed & Ward, 1936, p. 319.

was spent in heading a faction fostering civil discord and opposition to the pope. When the pope sent St. Philip Benizi to Forli as an apostle of peace, Philip, in the presence of his followers, listened to the holy man as he preached to a gathering in the public square, then displayed his contempt by striking the saint soundly in the face. With shouts of approval the crowd set upon the saint with other abuses, forcing him from the city. As can be expected of a saint, Philip Benizi prayed for Peregrine's return to virtue. Some years later, through the workings of grace, he welcomed Peregrine into the Servite order at Siena. After serving the congregation as a lay brother for 12 years, Peregrine prepared for ordination and was eventually sent back to Forli to found a house of the order. Once again Peregrine became a leader in his hometown, but this time as an influence for good. Eighteen years after Peregrine rebuffed a papal representative in the person of St. Philip Benizi, Peregrine was himself delegated a papal representative by Pope Boniface VIII to proclaim the pardon of Forli.

The number of those he converted to the Faith was outstanding, his work among penitents and sinners was extensive, his travels on errands of mercy were numerous and his miracles were countless.

When Peregrine was about 60 years of age he was stricken with a cancer of the right leg which pained him, but did not interrupt his works of mercy nor his customary exercises of virtue. Not content with the penances he had already imposed upon himself, he continued his labors until gangrene consumed the flesh of his leg to the bone. So heroically did he bear this trial that his confreres compared his patience to that of Job. The amputation of the leg was eventually recommended as the only means of preserving his life.

On the eve of the operation St. Peregrine visited the chapter room of the monastery to pray before a painting that depicted the Crucifixion. We are told that he remained praying there throughout most of the night. Whether in a dream or in a vision, Christ appeared to stretch His hand from this painting and touch the saint's diseased leg which was afterward discovered to be completely healed with not the least trace of the former ailment. The renowned surgeon, who was scheduled to perform the amputation, arrived the next morning for the operation and promptly acknowledged the miraculous nature of the cure. Because of this miracle, countless victims of cancer devoutly pray to St. Peregrine for similarly successful cures.

The lives of the saints are resplendent with incidents in which the cross or the crucifix figured prominently, but one of the most interesting involved St. Camillus de Lellis (1550-1614) whose love and devotion to

167

the crucifix was emblazoned in red on the front of the robes worn by the members of the order he founded, the Servants of the Sick. The cross of red cloth was meant to inspire the sick and dying to sentiments of confidence and contrition. This was the first time the symbol of the red cross was used as a sign of organized charity, almost 300 years before the establishment of the International Red Cross Organization.

As a child Camillus was vivacious and troublesome and by the time of his adolescence he was already a compulsive gambler. As a young man of 19 he joined his father in the military service and fought in two battles. One, occurring in 1571, was that at Lepanto in which the fervent recitation of the Rosary by the townspeople is credited with the miracle that enabled the Christians to defeat the Turks, who threatened an invasion of eastern Europe. Thousands of Christian slaves on Turkish galleys were liberated, with the infidels suffering their first great defeat at sea.

At the time of his discharge from the military, Camillus had gambled away his inheritance and his equipment and took to begging on the steps of the Cathedral of Mafredonia. It was here that a parishioner offered him a position as a mason's helper and in this capacity he came into contact with a Capuchin priest through whose counseling he experienced a complete reform and a rekindling of faith. His entrance into religious life was abbreviated by a recurring ulceration of his leg which had at one time interrupted his military career. He applied for treatment at a hospital in Rome, but was so dissatisfied with the servants' lack of cooperation and constant unfaithfulness to duty that he began the establishment of an order whose members were to bind themselves by a fourth vow — to the charitable care of the sick and dying, a vow still made by members of the order, in addition to those of poverty, chastity and obedience.

With the encouragement of his confessor, St. Philip Neri, he commenced studying for the priesthood and was ordained in 1584.

During the early days of his nursing order, when he diligently worked to improve the condition of the hospital which he served as director, many opposed his efforts. Whether they were the employees who resented the correction of their slovenly execution of duty or whether it was others, it is known that enemies one day entered the oratory of the congregation, removed the crucifix from the wall, cast it aside and disturbed the contents of the room. The discovery of the vandalism greatly troubled the saint who reverently removed the crucifix from this room to another. During the night, while complaining and praying before this crucifix, he saw the body of Christ move, detach one arm from the affix-

168

ing nail and reach toward him. At the same time a voice came from the crucifix with great clarity and spoke words both consoling and reassuring, "Do not be afraid. Persevere. This is My work, not yours."

The crucifix is now enshrined in the principal church of the order, the Church of St. Mary Magdalene in Rome. Unquestionably one of the most beautiful in that city, it also contains the enshrined relics of the saint.

Needless to report, the order flourished following the vision of the crucifix. At the time of the saint's death there were 330 professed members who labored in 15 cities in Italy.

The red cross still decorates the front of the habits worn by members of the order, with smaller versions being distributed to those who request them. Made of felt they measure an inch and a half in length and are blessed with special prayers that were inserted in the Roman Ritual. Their popularity dates from 1601 and is due to a miracle in which God seemed to give His approval. While the Camillians were busy with the sick during the battle of Canizza, a tent in which the brothers stored their equipment burned. Everything was destroyed except a red cross that had been attached to a habit. One of the officers asked for the cross and wore it as a breastplate, remaining unharmed for the remainder of the foray. Replicas have been propagated by the millions throughout the world procuring benefits of resignation, conversion and recovery for the sick.

Perhaps the most unusual incident involving a cross is the one mentioned in the history of St. Colette (1381-1447), who was devout from early childhood. When her parents died during her adolescence, she distributed her belongings to the poor, entered the Third Order of St. Francis and retired to a hermitage on the advice of her guardian, the abbot of Corbie. Here she led a most austere and sacrificial life that proved a preparation for the trials that awaited her.

It is recorded that Colette had a vision of the Seraphic Father, St. Francis of Assisi, who charged her to restore the rule of St. Clare to its original severity. Many of the great religious orders, it would seem, experienced periods of great activity following their original founding, but at one time or another a degeneration of their original fervor was noted following the death of the founders or their immediate successors. Those who restored the orders to their original ideals must necessarily have been persons of great courage and advanced spirituality. Such was St. Colette, who has been known since the mid-15th century as the reformer of the Poor Clares.

Encouraged by her spiritual director, she ventured forth following

169

the vision to receive the necessary authority from Peter de Luna, an anti-pope residing at Avignon, who was acknowledged by the French as pope under the name of Benedict XIII. Impressed by her mission, her humility and sanctity, she was made superior general of the whole Order of St. Clare with plenary powers to enforce whatever regulations she deemed necessary for the glory of God and the good of the order. Thus endowed, she restored many convents and even houses of the Friars Minor, although suffering ill-will, violent opposition and rebuffs.

Besides restoring those convents already in existence, St. Colette founded 20 new houses, with some selecting the name of Colettine.

In conjunction with St. Vincent Ferrer she helped heal the great schism, in which three laid claim to the papacy, by diplomatically arranging a new election in which Pope Martin V was selected.

The saint was frequently discovered in rapture following Holy Communion. Her sanctity was confirmed during a vision when she received from heaven a gold crucifix which contained, in a locket, a fragment of the true Cross. Called the Cross from Heaven, its upright measures 0.035 millimeters and the crossbar 0.008 millimeters. On one side are five precious stones: a blue stone on each extension, and a red stone in the middle. This relic is conserved at the Monastère de Ste. Claire in Besançon which also has a crucifix presented to St. Colette by St. Vincent Ferrer. Considered to have been his mission cross, it now serves as the altar cross in the sisters' chapel. Relics of St. Colette are kept with great care in a golden reliquary at the Monastère de Ste. Claire in Poligny, France.

The good Lord also communicated through the crucifix to St. John Gualbert, St. Thomas of Villeneuve and St. Vincent Ferrer among others. Likewise, numerous are the incidents in the lives of the saints in which the crucifix was the instrument through which devotion was increased, miracles were effected and graces flowed.

Buildings as Relics

The Portiuncula

Holy House of Loreto

S INCE the 15th century, and possibly earlier, the Holy House of Loreto has been numbered among the most important shrines of Italy. Believed to have been the house of the Blessed Mother in Nazareth, the little structure is now encased in richly sculptured marble and stands within a splendid basilica that has attracted many saints and popes throughout the centuries, as well as pilgrims from around the world.

The story of the Holy House begins at the time of St. Helena, about the year 330, when the saint was industrious in her efforts to preserve the places made sacred by the presence of Jesus and His Mother. To safeguard the house of the Blessed Mother in Nazareth St. Helena built a church around it, with the Holy House and adjacent grotto situated in its crypt.

The Holy House was first mentioned by St. Epifanio (315-403) while Arculfo in 670 also testified to the existence of the house as it was enclosed within a church situated near the center of Nazareth, a fact agreed to by Bede the Venerable in 720, and St. Willibaldo (700-781).[1]

We are told by Godfrey of Beaulieu, the biographer of St. Louis, king of France, that he witnessed the visit of St. Louis to the Holy House in 1251 as it was enshrined in the crypt of this church in Nazareth. For this reason the likeness of St. Louis was painted on one of the walls.

When the Moslems menaced the Holy Land in 1291, the Holy House suddenly disappeared from Nazareth on the night of May 10 and was found at Tersatto, Italy, some 60 miles south of the Yugoslavian border. To the surprise of the townspeople a small church with a campanile was seen on land that had been barren the day before. An examination revealed that the walls measured 16 inches in thickness and were constructed of a reddish-colored stone. The wooden roof had been painted blue and was decorated with golden stars. The building measured 31-1/4 feet in length by 13-1/3 feet in breadth with a height of 28 feet.[2] There was only one door. This was located on the northern side while the western side contained the only window. The door was just over seven feet in height and had a width of four and a half feet.[3] In the

---

[1] *La Tradizione Lauretana*, Congregazione Universale Della Santa Casa, Loreto, Italy, 1977, p. 27.
[2] *The House of Loreto*, Kenneth MacGowan, Congregazione Universale Della Santa Casa, Loreto, Italy, 1976, p. 4.
[3] *Ibid.*, p. 4.

interior were found earthenware vessels, a stone altar, a wooden cross bearing the inscription "Jesus Nazarenus Rex Judaeorum" and a cedar statue representing the Virgin Mary with her Divine Child in her arms, clothed in robes and adorned with golden crowns.

The pastor of the nearby Church of St. George, Alexander Georgevich, was as perplexed as the people and feared a deception of the devil. It is reported that while he prayed for enlightenment, the Blessed Mother appeared to him and cured him spontaneously of an illness that had afflicted him for many years.

The house remained at Tersatto for three years before it disappeared as suddenly as it had come. To compensate for the loss, Nicholas Fragipani built a small church modeled on the Holy House and erected a stone bearing the inscription:

> The House of the Blessed Virgin came from Nazareth to Tersatto on the 10th, May in the year 1291 and left on the 10th, December 1294.

During the night of December 10, 1294, shepherds keeping a night watch over their flocks near Recanati, Italy, saw a house as it was being borne across the sea, and watched as it settled to earth four miles away. Villagers soon determined from the interior that the structure had been used as a church. Thousands flocked to satisfy their curiosity, but when bandits became a hindrance the house was miraculously transported to a nearby hill. Here it remained only a brief time before moving during the same year to its last and present location in Loreto where it positioned itself partly on a road and partly on a field. A hermit who lived on the slopes of Mount Urso, Paul of the Woods, was favored with a vision of the Blessed Virgin who identified the house and its origin.

The route traditionally accepted as that taken by the Holy House along the eastern seacoast gave rise to the centuries-old custom, still observed, of the devout ringing bells and lighting bonfires on the night of December 10 to commemorate the journey and to light the way taken by the angels.

A mere 16 years after the translocation, the first papal recognition of the Holy House was made by Clement V in 1310 who issued a papal bull in which he granted concessions to the German pilgrims who had made vows at the shrine.[4]

According to documents in the archives of Recanati, the interior of the house was described in 1315 in a legal procedure against members of the Ghibelline party who had entered the Holy House for the purpose of

[4]*The Authenticity of the Holy House*, Father Angelo Maria D'Anghiari, O.F.M. Cap., Congregazione Universale Della Santa Casa, Loreto, Italy, 1967, p. 22.

stealing the ornaments and the gifts of the faithful. In this public record the stone altar was mentioned and a description was given of the statue of the Virgin and Child, thus proving that the sanctuary was flourishing 20 years after its translation to Loreto.

As described in these legal papers, the statue was made of wood, was brown in appearance, and was part of the Holy House during its mysterious travels. In height it measured two feet eight inches and depicted the Divine Child in the Mother's arms with one hand raised in blessing. The other hand held the globe of the world. In 1797, when the area was invaded by Napoleon's troops, the French army sacked the Holy House taking its treasures and removing the statue which eventually found its way to the Louvre. Through the influence of the pope it was returned to the sanctuary in 1801. This original statue was unfortunately destroyed by fire during the night of February 23, 1921. The new statue of Lebanese cedar is identical to the one destroyed having been modeled after engravings. It was crowned in the Sistine Chapel by Pius XI.

Fearing that the little church standing without a foundation might collapse or be affected by the hazards of nature, and owing to the respect paid it by the people, a protective wall was constructed about it in 1295 by the people of nearby Recanati. When the work was completed it was found that the newly constructed brick walls had mysteriously separated from the original walls.

The little house stood within this brick enclosure and comprised the sanctuary sought by pilgrims until construction of the great basilica was begun in 1468. When the sanctuary was protected by this basilica the little house was enclosed within a casement of white marble in 1525 on the authority of Pope Clement VII. Sculptured by some 30 artists, this casement is composed of reliefs that represent various scenes from the life of the Blessed Mother and the translation of the house, while figures of ancient prophets are displayed at intervals between the panels. Clement VII provided for the convenience of pilgrims by closing the only doorway and constructing three others. The displaced materials were

Due to the great number of miracles worked in the Holy House, the records that were first kept eventually proved laborious and time-consuming, and were discontinued. Likewise the many pilgrims who visited the shrine cannot be numbered. It has been tabulated, however, that more than 200 persons who have been canonized, beatified or declared venerable have been to the Holy House, including St. Francis Cabrini, St. Alphonsus Liguori, St. Charles Borromeo, St. Francis de Sales, St. Ignatius Loyola and St. Thérèse of Lisieux who described her visit in her autobiography. Thérèse wrote, "How deep was my emotion when I found myself under the same roof as the Holy Family, contemplating the walls upon which Jesus cast His sacred glance." The saint seems to have given us the reason for the miraculous preservation of the little home when she added, "Jesus is content to show us His home so as to make us love poverty and the hidden life."[5]

Since the first papal recognition of the sanctuary by Clement V in 1310, some 47 popes have confirmed the Holy House by either the presenting of gifts, the granting of privileges, exemptions and indulgences or by papal bulls and documents both in solemn or simple form.[6] Papal visitors to the sanctuary number 13, including Pope John XXIII who journeyed there on October 4, 1962, one week before the opening of the ecumenical council (Vatican II) so that he might pray for the success of this endeavor. Another papal visitor was Pope John Paul II who prayed in the sanctuary on the feast of the Nativity of the Blessed Mother, September 8, 1979, before his historic trip to Ireland and America. Declaring that "every home is above all the sanctuary of the mother," he added that the shrine is ". . . the house of all and the house of each one." In his address the pope also remarked that the Holy House was ". . . the first temple, the first church on which shone the light of the maternity of the Mother of God."

A number of official investigations concerning the authenticity of the Holy House have been initiated beginning in 1296 when a deputation of 16 competent and respected men were assigned the task by the authorities. After journeying to the Holy Land to examine the place where the Holy House had originally stood, they concluded that the Holy House was modeled after the one-room dwellings common during the time of Christ and that based on identical measurements and other features the dwelling had indeed come from Nazareth, ". . . an assertion that found confirmation in miracles without number."

Another investigation was authorized in 1524-1534. Pope Clement VII dispatched three chamberlains to Tersatto to examine the structure built over the place where the Holy House had temporarily rested. These measurements coincided with those of the House of Loreto. At Nazareth the foundation where the Holy House had originally stood was examined and this was again found to tally exactly with the measurements of the house. An examination at a much later date proved that the stones and mortar of the Holy House were not known locally in Loreto, but were common to and chemically identical with those of Nazareth.

[5]*Story of a Soul: The Autobiography of St. Thérèse of Lisieux*, John Clarke, O.C.D., ICS Publications, Washington, D.C., 1975, p. 129.
[6]*The Catholic Encyclopedia*, The Encyclopedia Press, Inc., New York, 1911, Vol. 3, pp. 455-456.

Still another investigation was made after the fire of 1921 that destroyed the original statue. The technical findings made during the archeological examination of April 1921 and July 1922 were summarized in a letter to the bishop of Recanati by Architect F. Mannucci. In this document he stated:

> The making of the walls necessarily required a foundation that assures a solid support, or at least a ground preparation capable of making possible the horizontal strata. On the contrary, the walls of the Holy House have no foundation at all nor any preparation of the soil beneath, which is loose and powdery. In some points the walls were found to be completely isolated from the soil underneath. One can therefore certainly conclude that the Holy House could not have been constructed on the site where it is now located. . . . The quality of the construction of the walls made in horizontal rows and joined with an excellent quality mortar, indicates that they were certainly made by able hands and it would be unrealistic to believe that, if they were built on the site, the person who designed or supervised the work would have ignored the nature of the soil to the point of neglecting the most elementary rule in planting the building on dusty ground. . . . It therefore must have been transported.
>
> It is surprising and extraordinary that the Holy House, though it has no foundation and stands on loose unfirm soil and is partially overburdened by the weight of the vault constructed in place of the roof, has been preserved unaltered without the slightest indication of yielding nor even the smallest sign of damage to the walls.[7]

A more recent archeological study commenced on the evening of May 7, 1962, after several years of preparation and study. Undertaken with pontifical approval, the work continued for three years until June 29, 1965. Performed in secrecy by a restricted circle of archeologists, engineers and ecclesiastics, the excavation and exploration of the subsoil was made during the evening hours from eight until midnight during the hours the basilica was closed to visitors. As a result of this endeavor there remains beneath the Holy House an "archeological zone," a system of tunnels which the scholar of today can visit in absolute safety.[8]

The results of this study were published in several journals and the book, *Contributi Archeologici Per La Storia Della Santa Casa Di Loreto*, which is detailed with diagrams, sketches, maps and photographs and with information regarding the primitive aspects of the monuments, the

[7] *Loreto: The Shrine of the Holy House*, Father Fabian Urbani, O.F.M. Cap., Ed., Loreto, Italy, 1973, Vol. 6, No. 4, pp. 70-71.
[8] MacGowan, *op. cit.*, p. 27.

structure's transformations and restorations. This detailed study, wholly favorable to the traditions of Loreto, established the fact that the Holy House stands without foundation and that the structure is actually four walls thick, that is, the first being the walls of the Holy House, the second, although not touching it, consisting of the brick wall constructed by the people of Recanati, a wall that serves as a support for the marble screen and the marble covering itself. The floors have been reworked several times. The present flooring was installed in 1939.

Among other interesting findings, the archeologists discovered coins of the Republic of Ancona of the 14th century in a cavity of the Recanati wall while several similar coins were found under the stone altar. Also found, and this at about 2.20 meters below the flooring, were graves dating to the time of Imperial Rome.[9]

The Holy House standing beneath the dome of the basilica has prompted Pope Pius IX to exclaim, "Of all the shrines consecrated to the Mother of God, the foremost one that shines in incomparable splendor is the Holy House of Loreto."[10] Pope Pius XI commented, "As far as the authenticity of the Holy House is concerned, there are many good reasons for acknowledging it, but no valid reasons for denying it."[11]

While other popes have similarly exclaimed their devotion to the Lady of Loreto and defended the authenticity of her little home, the pilgrim is alerted to the sacredness of the place he is to visit by a notice above the door, "Tremble all you who enter here, because this is the holiest place on earth."

Our Lady's House at Ephesus

IN recent years a little building in Ephesus, Turkey, has received considerable recognition since it is believed to have been the home Mary shared with the Apostle John toward the end of her life on earth. Unlike the sanctuary of Loreto, however, no claim is made that the walls of the sanctuary are the original ones. The details of its history are sketchy, but it is known that after the Crucifixion, in accordance with the direction of

[9] *Contributi Archeologici Per La Storia Della Santa Casa Di Loreto*, Nereo Alfieri, Edmondo Forlani, Floriano Grimaldi, The Shrine of Loreto, Loreto, Italy, 1977, pp. 32-3.
[10] D'Anghiari, *op. cit.*, p. 30.
[11] *Ibid.*, p. 32.

the dying Savior, the Apostle John took Mary into his care and later brought her to Ephesus to avoid an intense persecution. After the deaths of both Mary and John the house they occupied apparently fell into ruin, but the foundation remained. Since time immemorial this foundation had been a place of pilgrimage for Christians as well as Moslems who recognize Mary as the mother of the prophet Jesus. Here, in accordance with a diagram made by Anne Catherine Emmerich (1774-1824), a German Augustinian nun who was favored with numerous visions of the life of Our Lady, the house was reconstructed on the original foundation.

The little house is called Panaya Kapulu, the house of the Holy Virgin. It has become the object of so many pilgrimages that the Turkish authorities have built an excellent road to its entrance. It is estimated by one authority that 10,000 people of all faiths visit the shrine each week.

Also at Ephesus is the first church believed dedicated to Our Lady where 160 bishops assembled in A.D. 491 under the direction of Cyril, patriarch of Alexandria, for the third ecumenical council. During this council the divine maternity of the Blessed Mother was proclaimed. Pope Paul VI celebrated Mass in this church on July 26, 1967 after he visited the Holy House where he prayed before the image of the Virgin.

Another notable visitor was Pope John Paul II who visited the house of Ephesus in November 1979.

St. Paul lived at Ephesus for three years and later, after moving away, addressed one of his epistles to the Ephesian church. Two other epistles were addressed to Timothy, a native of Ephesus to whom St. Paul entrusted the Church of that region. The amphitheater where St. Paul preached in the city is an attraction to pilgrims.

The Portiuncula

WHEN St. Francis came upon the little church called the Portiuncula, it belonged to the abbey of Benedictine monks of Monte Subasio. The little structure, whose name means "little piece," stood forsaken and in ruinous condition on a plain two miles from Assisi. Because of its condition and remoteness it appealed to the saint, who was pleased that it had been dedicated in honor of Our Lady of the Angels, believed to have been so named for the angels who bore Our Lady aloft at the time of the Assumption.

The saint repaired the church as he had previously reconditioned two others and fixed his abode beside it. Here, on the feast of St. Matthias, in the year 1209, his way of life was revealed to him. During Mass that day, the Gospel of St. Matthew was read, ". . . As you go, preach the message, 'The kingdom of heaven is at hand.' . . . Do not keep gold, or silver, or money, nor two tunics, nor sandals, nor staff. . . . Behold, I am sending you forth like sheep in the midst of wolves" (Matthew 10:7-17). Thereafter, he adopted the undyed woolen dress of the shepherds and fastened it about his waist with a cord.

Francis eventually visited the Benedictine monks on Monte Subasio, who offered him the Portiuncula upon the condition that it remain the principal church of his order. The saint refused to accept ownership, and each year sent a basket of fish to the monks in payment of the rental fee. In return, the monks replied with a barrel of oil. This custom of exchange was later revived between the friars of Santa Maria degli Angeli and the Benedictines of San Pietro of Assisi.[1]

During a summer night in the year 1216 Francis was praying in the Portiuncula when he received a vision of Our Lord, who requested that he ask the pope for an indulgence that whosoever should visit the chapel, having confessed his sins for which he had expressed sincere sorrow, should receive complete remission of the punishment due them. Although such a request was unknown at the time, Pope Honorius III, nevertheless, granted this concession on Francis' personal request, but limited its exercise to one day in the year, namely the anniversary of the date on which the Portiuncula chapel would be consecrated. Since the chapel was consecrated on August 2, the indulgence, called the Portiuncula indulgence, or the pardon of St. Francis, was gained for centuries from Vespers of August 1 until sunset of August 2.

At first only those visiting the Portiuncula could gain the indulgence, but later the privilege was granted to any church associated with the Franciscan order. In regions where Franciscan churches, convents or friaries have not been established, bishops now have the authority given by a papal decree of 1911 to designate a church of their choosing.

According to legislation now in force, the Portiuncula indulgence can be gained only once each year on August 2 or the following Sunday, with the permission of the bishop. The conditions are, in addition to

---

[1] *Butler, op. cit.*, Vol. 10, p. 43.

freedom from attachment to sin: (1) reception of the sacrament of penance and the Eucharist on or near the day; and (2) a visit to the church on the day, during which an Our Father and the Creed are offered for the intention of the pope.[2]

The saint's affection for the Portiuncula was evidenced during his final illness when he asked to be carried there so that he might die in his humble cell. After his death on Saturday, October 3, 1226, the little chapel, measuring about 22 feet by 13-1/2 feet, became entirely inadequate to accommodate the throngs of pilgrims. An edifice was built over the Portiuncula and the adjoining cell in which the saint died. This gradually developed into the basilica that is visited by countless pilgrims each year.

The Portiuncula stands beneath the cupola of the Basilica of Santa Maria degli Angeli. The interior of the little building is dominated by an altarpiece of the Annunciation painted in 1393 by Hilarius, a priest of Viterbo.

Under the bay of the basilica's choir, resting against the columns of the cupola, is preserved the cell in which St. Francis died.

A new altar was consecrated and a papal throne added to the basilica when St. Pius X, by means of a brief dated April 11, 1909, raised the sanctuary to a "patriarchal basilica and papal chapel."

[2]*Catholic Almanac,* Felician A. Foy, O.F.M., Ed., Our Sunday Visitor, Inc., Huntington, Ind., 1973, pp. 373-374.

Relics of Blood
The Phenomenon
of Liquefaction

The coagulated blood of St. Januarius is shown as it liquefied during a ceremony in Naples

The Blood Miracles of Naples

THE phenomenon involving the liquefaction of blood, while perhaps not exclusively confined to the kingdom of Naples, seems to have occurred there more frequently and to have been more regarded there than in other Italian cities or other lands. Why this city should claim this distinction is unknown, but it is a matter of well-documented history that the blood of several saints and holy persons has liquefied at various intervals, under diverse situations, at different seasons of the year and in varied ways.

The practice of gathering blood for relics, admittedly a most repulsive action, nevertheless was a common practice beginning in the days of persecution when the early Christians soaked cloths in the blood shed by martyrs or, if possible, actually collected the liquid in flasks to keep as devotional items. Through the years, especially around Naples it would seem, blood was collected from holy persons recently deceased with the specimens being carefully kept.

While it is known that blood once removed from the body soon coagulates and eventually spoils, and since this natural reaction was common knowledge among the medical faculty of the Middle Ages, a claim made by them of prodigious liquefactions can hardly be ignored and would seem to indicate a transcendence of their experience. In our own day, those specimens that are still active are deserving of careful scientific investigation.

In the three articles written on this subject in 1927 for *The Month*, an English magazine, Rev. Herbert Thurston, S.J., mentions a number of holy persons whose samples of blood liquefied in the past. Some of these were lost, others have failed in recent years to liquefy, and because the author could not locate those which would seem to be still kept, we will focus our attention on the facts of the three most important cases in which the liquefaction of blood continues to our day, to be witnessed and studied by interested parties.

Of these three examples the best known is undoubtedly that which concerns St. Januarius (St. Gennaro). The recurring miracle of the liquefaction of his blood 18 times a year is often reported in the secular as well as the religious press, and is the occasion of great gatherings in the Cathedral of Naples. Here the people pray fervently while the resident cardinal, who usually presides over the ceremony, holds the vials of

182

blood. The miracle occurs when the bust reliquary containing the head of the saint is brought near. When the liquefaction is accomplished in full view of the spectators, the cardinal announces, "The miracle has happened," words that cause great rejoicing and the chanting of the *Te Deum.*

The saint's history begins with the Roman Emperor Diocletian, whose persecution during the dawning years of the fourth century made martyrs of innumerable Christians. Among his victims was counted St. Januarius, who was serving as bishop of Benevento. The imprisonment of the bishop occurred in A.D. 305 when he journeyed to Pozzuoli to offer encouragement to Sossius, a deacon who had been imprisoned. The bishop was soon arrested together with several ministers who had labored beside the saint in the service of the Church. After their decapitation the bodies were removed to various cities. St. Januarius' body was taken to Benevento, then to Monte Vergine and lastly to Naples where it was entombed in the main church of the city, with two vials of his blood that had been collected by devout followers. Around this tomb the great cathedral was constructed. Here Januarius was honorably remembered by the faithful of the city.

In the 14th century there occurred a phenomenon that was to attract curiosity throughout the centuries until even today the happenings provoke worldwide interest.

The year was 1389. A procession was making its way about the cathedral when the priest holding the flasks containing the saint's coagulated blood noticed that the contents began to liquefy and bubble. Since then the blood has repeated this phenomenon 18 times each year: on the Saturday before the first Sunday in May and the eight days following; on the feast of the saint, September 19, and during the octave, and on December 16.

The blood has failed to liquefy several times, each time coinciding with the outbreak of disease, famine, war or political suppression. It is for this reason that Neapolitans rejoice at each liquefaction.

There are actually four divisions of the saint's relics. The bones are kept separately while the head is enclosed in a magnificent silver bust that is enshrined a distance from the relics of blood. The liquefaction takes place when the vials are brought in close proximity to the silver bust containing the head. The blood is kept in two vials. The smaller contains only a trace of blood, but the larger measures four inches in height and about two and a quarter inches in diameter and is usually a little more than half filled with coagulated blood that appears as a hard dark mass. The flasks are hermetically sealed and are solidly fixed side

183

by side within a ring of silver and crystal sides that has a sticklike handle at the bottom. The crystals on either side of the ring protect the vials and permit their viewing. This is kept in the main altar of the Chapel of the Treasury in the Cathedral of Naples.

On the feast days of the saint the silver bust that contains the head is exposed upon the altar or taken in procession. Prayers are recited while the priest or cardinal holds the reliquary of blood by its handle in full view of the assembly while making certain that the glass is not touched. After an interval of a few minutes or perhaps even an hour, the mass is seen to gradually detach itself from the walls of the flasks and to liquefy, frequently bubbling and frothing. The vials are then brought to the faithful for their veneration. In the evening the reliquary is put into a silver case and placed inside the altar where the next day the blood might be found coagulated or it may be found in a liquid state and might remain so for days or months.

Every possible argument has been presented by skeptics, but all have been dismissed in view of the contrary reactions of the blood whose liquefaction occurs under the most diverse circumstances and physical conditions. The phenomenon has no need of special conditions to verify itself. For example, the liquefactions occur at different temperatures as indicated by the records kept for more than a century, and by the studies of Professors Pergola, Punzo and Sperindeo who concluded that there is no direct relation between the temperature and the time and manner of liquefaction. The blood may liquefy at temperatures of 77 degrees or higher with the phenomenon taking as much as 20 to 40 minutes, while a smaller amount of time may be required when the temperature is 15 or 20 degrees or less.

Those reluctant to admit the supernatural quality of the happening have argued that the press of the spectators, the lights and candles on the altar or the warmth of the priest's hands have helped in producing the heat that encourages liquefaction. Since the miracle occurs several times each year in various seasons, and since the blood is protected by two layers of glass and since there is no constant point at which the liquefaction takes place, the miracle is contrary to every physical law that exists regarding the temperature needed to liquefy a substance. Likewise there have been occasions when the blood has failed to liquefy under apparently ideal circumstances. The theory of heat or the lack of it affords no adequate explanation of the phenomenon observed.

After the liquefaction the blood frequently presents a variation in volume since at times it decreased while at other times it almost doubles its size, nor does it necessarily return to its original volume. Sometimes the coagulated blood occupies half the vial while at other times it occupies almost the entire space.

A truly mystifying condition exists with regard to its weight. In experiments conducted in 1902 and 1904 the reliquary was weighed in a delicate balance. It was discovered that its weight was no more constant than its bulk, that is, its weight might increase as much as 25 grams, thereby defying physical laws. The strangest element is that there is often an increase in weight when the mass actually decreases, and a decrease in weight when the volume increases — this in direct opposition to the laws that dictate an increase in weight with a corresponding increase in mass.

The color of the coagulated blood changes from dark rouge, almost black, to a bright vermillion that appears opaque when held to a light. Its viscosity changes as well. Sometimes the mass is almost gummy, at other times fluid, and it is independent of any movement that occurs to the reliquary.

Sometimes the blood does not entirely liquefy and maintains a hard globule in the middle of the liquefied part, this condition lasting a day, weeks or sometimes months with no explanation being formulated by scientists for this behavior.

The impossibility of a natural explanation increases by the fact that the substance contained in the vials is true blood. This has been confirmed by the constant tradition and by the documents that are impossible to refute. It is likewise confirmed by scientific research, especially that of 1902 when Professor Sperindeo was permitted to pass spectroscopic beams of light through the liquefied material. This test yielded the distinctive lines of the spectrum of blood with definite characteristics of hemoglobin.

The truly prodigious conditions that scientists could not explain was why the blood sometimes forms tiny bubblets that rise to the surface and collect into a foam, nor why, when it bubbles, it becomes a crimson color while at other times the color of the liquefied material is dull and its movements sluggish.

Skeptical scientists from time to time have attempted to reproduce a liquid with similar characteristics by the mixture of various chemicals, but they have consistently failed to produce something that not only changes from a solid to a liquid form, but also changes its weight, volume and color.

Unable to disqualify the miracle with arguments of a scientific nature, some have grasped elsewhere, even offering the improbable explanation that the blood is affected by some form of psychic force, that the concentration and will of the expectant crowd are held responsible for producing the physical action that their minds and wills demand. This is dismissed since the liquefaction has often happened unexpectedly and in the presence of only a few spectators.

While scientists have been unable to explain how the phenomenon can be accounted for, the mysterious liquefaction of the blood of St. Januarius that has occurred for almost 600 years remains a challenge to the skeptic and a true phenomenon to the believer.[1]

The second blood miracle under consideration involves St. Pantaleon who was born in Nicomedia, Turkey, of a pagan senator and a Christian mother. When he began studying medicine he proved so intelligent and competent that he was permitted to practice his trade before the completion of his formal studies. His reputation was such that he eventually became the physician to Emperor Galerius Maximian. Although raised as a Christian he soon became influenced by the activities and "false wisdom" of the court and unhappily fell into apostasy. A zealous Christian named Hermolaos awakened Pantaleon's conscience by prudent admonitions, and brought him again to the practice of virtue.

When Diocletian's persecution began in Nicomedia, Pantaleon distributed his wealth and possessions to poor Christians and was soon betrayed by envious fellow physicians. The emperor, whom he had medically treated, urged him to apostatize to escape certain martyrdom, but Pantaleon refused and was arrested together with Hermolaos and two others. After bitter sufferings his companions were beheaded, but Pantaleon's ordeal lasted one day longer. He was reportedly subjected to six different attempts on his life, by burning, molten lead, drowning, wild beasts, the wheel and the sword. He was finally beheaded. St. Pantaleon is one of the Fourteen Holy Helpers since he regularly treated the poor without payment.

Having died in the year 305, his cultus was firmly established 300 years later when his relics were diffused to many parts of Italy and France. The greater portion of his relics are in the church of Lucca where in 1715 they were scientifically recognized. Doctors found that the bones belonged to a male of young age and that the burns found thereon confirmed the report of the partial cremation of the martyr's body.

According to the practice during the times of persecution, the blood was collected by those who held the heroes of faith in high esteem. So it was that a pious lady of Nicomedia gathered the blood of Pantaleon and

[1]This information is derived from papers provided by the Cathedral of Naples.

186

kept it in her home. Apparently the blood displayed some unusual activity since merchants of Amalfi, Italy, heard of it and journeyed to Nicomedia to obtain it. The blood relic was brought to Ravella, 22 miles from Naples, where records of 1112 reveal that the blood was there in the cathedral consecrated to St. Pantaleon.

The flask that contains the blood is artistic, flat on top with a narrow neck, and is quite old as can be seen by its primitive composition. The crack in the glass on the left side of the flask was caused in 1759 by a priest who held a candle too close while he was examining the condition of the contents. Fearing that the blood would seep through, the priest made a hasty vow that if no blood escaped he would have a statue made of the saint. This he did as documented by the inscription on the plaque attached to it. In 1781 the ecclesiastical authorities decided to purchase a new crystal, but circumstances never permitted it. It was assumed, therefore, that the will of God, as well as that of the saint, meant for the blood relic to remain in the plain cracked flask that is the original container.

In this ampule the blood is clearly divided into four strata. The lowest level seems to be of sand or dirt mixed with blood since it is dense and dark. The second strata which is as deep as the width of a finger appears to be composed of dirt, but with a greater amount of blood. The third strata is pure blood of a ruby color when melted and this strata is below the highest level which consists of a whitish foam.[2]

The blood occupies only half the container when the blood is inactive. In the empty portion traces of fat and blood can be seen adhering to the glass. When the liquefaction takes place, the strata of pure blood turns transparent and ruby colored like fresh blood while the little bubbles reach almost to the top of the ampule. On the upper part of the glass flask there is a large spot of dark blood that turns wet and reddish at the time of the miraculous liquefaction.

It is important to note that the flask cannot in any way be touched or turned or shaken. It is absolutely untouchable since it is held firmly between the two iron clasps of its reliquary and is secure in its position.[3]

The feast day of the saint is July 27. The blood may liquefy on that day, but sometimes does not. It may gradually begin to liquefy at the beginning or middle of July, and may continue for a month or longer, sometimes for only a week or a few days. This unusual aspect of the

---

[2] *Un Testimone S. Pantaleone, Profilo Agiografico e Analisi Del Miracolo del Suo Sangue*, D. Giuseppe Imperato, Cattedrale di Ravello, Italy, 1970, p. 70.
[3] *Ibid.*, p. 90.

miracle has been documented since 1577.⁴ The blood is not coagulated or hard as would be normal. It is not dried or corrupted, but has been kept in a perfect state of viscousness, in an almost fluid state. It is indeed extraordinary that this sample of the martyr's blood has remained in this condition for over 18 centuries.

The third example of a blood relic that liquefies is that of St. Patricia who was born in Constantinople and was a niece of the Emperor Constantine.

Educated in the imperial court and trained in the Christian religion by a pious woman named Aglaia, she took a vow of virginity at an early age and was obliged to flee her home to avoid marriage to a suitor who had been selected for her. After the death of her father she returned to Constantinople where she renounced all her worldly possessions and distributed her wealth to the poor. Patricia then embarked with Aglaia on a ship bound for Rome, but a violent storm forced them to land at Naples. The rock upon which they landed was afterward called *Castel dell'Ovo*.

After a few months of penitential life she fell ill and died a saintly death at the age of 21. Her body was placed on a cart drawn by oxen for transport to the cemetery, but the animals wandered through the streets of Naples finally stopping at the church dedicated to the martyr-saints Nicandro and Marciano. Some time before her death, Patricia had visited that shrine, signing a cross on the doorstep and saying, "Here my body will rest." With her burial in this church her prophecy was fulfilled. The religious who cared for the shrine soon adopted the name *Patrician Sisters*.

A translation of her relics is reported to have occurred in 1549. Since 1625 she has been honored as one of the patrons of the city of Naples. In 1864 the convent was suppressed forcing the sisters to transfer to the Monastery of St. Gregorio Armeno where they are still located, together with the relics of the saint.

St. Patricia's relics are enclosed in a glass case decorated with gold, silver and precious gems, which the devout visit with great reverence. Frequently they witness the liquefaction of the saint's blood that was first activated a hundred years after her death.

A Roman knight suffering from long and unbearable pains was cured before the reliquary after fervent prayers. Wishing to secure a relic, he obtained permission to spend the night in prayer before the shrine. When all alone, and out of an excess of devotion, he opened the glass

⁴*Ibid.*, p. 74.

case and drew a tooth from its socket. At once he saw red blood flowing as from a living body. The next morning he was found in a faint on the floor.

The bishop and the clergy hastened to the church and with the sisters they discovered that warm blood continued to issue. It was at once collected and placed in two ampules.

The miracle has been renewed for 12 centuries. Not only every year on the feast of St. Patricia, August 25, but frequently in the presence of pious pilgrims who come to pray. The dry mass of dark blood in the ampules is seen to liquefy slowly, increase in volume and fade to a ruby red. It then reacts in all aspects as fresh, living blood.

The authorities, both ecclesiastical and civil, have investigated the phenomenon more than once and have concluded that the liquefaction cannot be explained by science and is, therefore, a genuine miracle.

In the city of Naples, every Tuesday is dedicated to St. Patricia. On that day large crowds venerate the saint while a priest blesses them with the ampules containing the miraculous blood.

The miracle occurs so frequently that tourists are almost constantly streaming to view the liquefaction, since the occurrence is often mentioned on travel itineraries.

The cloistered Sisters Adorers of the Blessed Sacrament have been the custodians of the relics for many years.[5]

[5]The information about the miracle of St. Patricia was obtained from papers supplied by the Monastero S. Gregorio Armeno.

The Manna
of the Saints

Part of a collection of ampules containing oil from St. Walburga

The Manna of the Saints

I N the Old Testament, manna is described as "like coriander seed with the appearance of bdellium" (Numbers 11:7). It might be said that manna took the form of small clumps, tiny and granular, that appeared like white seeds somewhat resembling hoarfrost.[1] Although a substance almost similar to this was found in a few rare cases, and only for a short period of time on the relics of certain saints, the use of the word *manna* has been adopted to describe an oil which appeared on, and often flowed from, the relics of many saints. The word *manna* has been borrowed, since the formation of this oil is as mysterious and miraculous as was the creation of the Old Testament food that was supplied for the Israelites during their wanderings in the wilderness.

The oil that has been observed originating from the relics of saints generally takes the form of a colorless, odorless, tasteless fluid that has occurred in different countries with various atmospheric conditions and under circumstances that are considered unfavorable and unusual, as we will soon learn.

The first reported case of this mysterious fluid seems to have involved the relics of St. Andrew the Apostle. When the apostles set forth to preach the Gospel, it is believed Andrew labored in Turkey and Greece where his life ended in the city of Patras on November 30 in the year 60. It is generally agreed that he was crucified by being bound, not nailed, to a cross.

Sometime later, the anniversary of his death was marked in a special way in the church where his remains were entombed in Patras, Greece. A Greek text regarding this event was obtained and translated by St. Gregory, bishop of Tours, before he died in 594. The document related that a miracle was accomplished by the apostle in the form of manna that presented itself either in the form of a powder or a perfumed oil that flowed from the sepulcher. It was related further that for years the oil was so abundant that at times it dripped from the tomb and flowed halfway down the aisle of the church.

The relics were first moved from the city of his martyrdom in the year 357 when they were deposited in the Basilica of the Apostles in Constantinople. The phenomenon continued, prompting Cardinal Baronio to comment at the time that the entire Christian world knew about the substances that collected on the apostle's tomb. The manna was gathered as a relic and as such was distributed.

Before Constantinople was completely occupied on the occasion of the fourth Crusade in 1204, Cardinal Peter of Capua collected the bones of the apostle in a silver urn and brought them to safety in Italy where he placed them in the Cathedral of Amalfi.

A century after their transportation from Constantinople to Amalfi, the phenomonon was again noticed. An elderly gentleman worshiping in the church was somehow alerted to the miracle and notified the priest, who looked inside the tomb to discover the presence of a white granular substance. The townspeople were informed of the miracle and converged on the site. The substance was applied to areas of pain with one man's sight being restored after several years of blindness.

Even though the phenomenon continued, it seems from records kept by the basilica that the tomb eventually was "lost to oblivion" until the second day of January 1603 when a stonemason by the name of M. Scipione Cretella, while working in the church, discovered a slab of marble with the inscription *Corpus S. And. ap.* Beneath the slab was an urn. He duly notified the priests who in turn notified the bishop. A document was drawn before a notary and was signed by the bishop, mayor and many witnesses. This document was placed within the urn which was once again buried and apparently forgotten.

The relics were again delivered from obscurity on January 28, 1846 when restorations were being conducted in the church. Work on the flooring was progressing very slowly since the masons had heard that a treasure had been buried centuries before. While excavating they found a dry wall from which one of the masons removed some stones. This revealed the marble slab and the urn of the apostle. News of the finding brought priests and villagers who escorted the urn in solemn procession to the sacristy. Since this was conducted late at night the bishop was not informed until dawn. On this day, January 29, in the presence of the archbishop, the document of 1603 was found in the urn and read, followed by an official recognition of the relics. Another document was drawn and signed by those present except three workers and the sacristan who were unable to write. After the two documents were placed in the urn, the relics were removed to the main altar where they are still situated. From that time on, the manna has been collected punctually on the 28th of January when the substance never fails to appear. Some years there is a great quantity; other years, less.

The urn containing the relics of the apostle is located within the hollow of the altar. A silver basin is kept beneath this to collect the manna. The urn with the relics and the basin that collects the fluid is reached by way of a circular hole at the back of the altar.

In addition to January 28, the anniversary when the relics were found in the Basilica of Amalfi, the manna is also collected during the main holidays of the basilica: the 26th of June and during the month of November, which is dedicated to the apostle, and especially November 30, the anniversary of his martyrdom.

A chronicle started by Bishop Bonito in 1908 kept a record of the phenomenon and is maintained to the present time. In this diary under the 29th of November, 1909, it was recorded that the miracle of the manna was of such an amount that two silver bowls and a glass vial were covered with droplets. The entry for January 28, 1910, tells us that one of the basins was covered with a dew while the crystal vial was almost dry. On the 28th of January, 1912, the drops were spilling from the vial.

What occurred on November 20, 1915 is of great interest since the canonical secretary, Antonelli, tried to collect the manna, but was disappointed. Acting on an inspiration he and those with him began to recite the *Miserere*. After the third recitation of this prayer the manna began to collect. During later times it was found that the recitation of the Creed also brought about a collection of the dew. Even today, if the manna fails to appear (with the exception of January 28 when it always appears), the Creed is recited with miraculous results.

During the jubilee year of the episcopate of Archbishop Marini, on June 26, 1929, Cardinal Ascalesi, archbishop of Naples who was in attendance, endeavored to collect manna but found none. During the services the next day the crystal vial had dew both inside and out.

An exceptional amount was found on January 28, 1933, so much so that 15 vials were filled with it.

While some may argue that the manifestation is a natural phenomenon, it should be considered that the chronicle, which is still kept, presents a phenomenon that has been constant, not related to season, not fixed to a liturgical rite, and is collected at all times of the year. Moreover, it has occurred in three countries: Greece, Turkey and Italy, all of which differ environmentally and climatically.

Just as Jesus multiplied in Andrew's presence the five barley loaves and two fish, so it seems that the Lord has multiplied in a wondrous way the phenomenon of the manna of St. Andrew — a manifestation that has spanned more than 14 centuries.[1]

[1]The information concerning the manna of St. Andrew has been taken from papers supplied by the Basilica of Amalfi entitled, *Voce Del Pastore Amalfi*, dated October 1973, February 1979 and March 1979.

Unlike the manna of St. Andrew the Apostle that appeared both in liquid and powdery form, the secretions exuding from the bones of St. Nicholas are presented only as a liquid and have been a curiosity for more than 1,600 years.

The names of two cities have been appended to that of the saint's, Myra, where he served as archbishop, and that of Bari, where his remains are enshrined, the saint being known both as St. Nicholas of Myra and St. Nicholas of Bari.

Few saints have enjoyed as great a popularity as Nicholas, who has been known for centuries as the progenitor of Santa Claus. His reputation for gift-giving originated from the dowries he secretly provided for three girls whose impoverished father was despairing of providing dowries large enough to satisfy suitors, and was plotting to confine them to a house of evil reputation. The first two dowries, consisting of bags of coins, were thrown anonymously through the open window of the father's room and resulted in the eventual marriage of the two oldest girls. When the third bag was thrown, the father discovered the identity of the benefactor and fell at the archbishop's feet in profound gratitude for having saved his daughters from sin.

The saint's attraction to young children seems to derive from the incident in which he reputedly restored three murdered children to life.

The saint's reputation for sanctity does not rely solely on these incidents of charity. The saint was born at Patara in Lycia, a province of Asia Minor (Turkey) where St. Paul planted the seeds of the Faith. When the episcopal See became vacant in Myra, which was the capital of the district, Nicholas was elected to the office and soon became renowned for his deeds of charity and extraordinary piety. The Greek *synaxaries* tell us that St. Nicholas suffered imprisonment and tortures for the Faith during the persecution of Diocletian and was finally released when Constantine assumed the imperial throne.

Traditions are unanimous in telling us that St. Nicholas died in the year 342 and was buried in Myra where a basilica was later built over his tomb. His memory was so nourished in the hearts of the people that by the 10th century an anonymous Greek wrote of him: "The west as well as the east acclaims and glorifies him . . . in the farthest parts of the earth his name is revered and churches are built in his honor . . . the Scythians know him as do the Indians and the barbarians, the Africans as well as the Italians." This was recorded in the 10th century before the removal of his relics to Italy. It seems he was similarly well known in England during the Middle Ages since the estimates given us indicated that 400 churches were dedicated to his honor in that country alone. The popularity of the saint was enjoyed even in Russia where curiously enough he is the patron saint, an honor he shares with St. Andrew the Apostle whose relics, as mentioned previously, display a similar phenomenon.

His patronage of sailors is probably due to a legend that concerns seamen, troubled by a fierce storm, who prayed to the saint for deliverance and were not only favored with a vision, but were also brought safely to shore. In addition to being the patron saint of seagoers, he is also the patron of numerous other professions, as well as countless countries, dioceses and churches.

When the shrine at Myra fell into the hands of the Saracens in 1034, several Italian cities vied for possession of the relics because of the saint's popularity and the phenomenon that attended his remains. Bari won the treasure and arranged to have the relics removed in secret. On May 9, 1087, the remains arrived at Bari where a great devotion had been fostered for the saint. A new basilica was built to enshrine the relics with Pope Urban II presiding over its consecration. Veneration among the people was greatly increased as were the number of miracles attributed to the saint.

The oil that exuded from the saint's bones was first observed in Myra. From that time to this it has been called unction, myrrh, medicinal liquor, balm, manna or oil. Yet another name was given it in 1304 when Carlo II d'Angio presented the church with a sizable donation. He is recorded as having said, "I wish to endow the church of Bari which has the bones of St. Nicholas that exude distilled bone oil." Scientists of recent date, including Professor Filippo Neri, director of the Institute of Hygiene of the University of Bari, examined the manna and came to the conclusion that it is a combination of hydrogen and oxygen, and because of its extremely low content of bacteria the product was declared biologically pure.[2]

According to the observations of a priest by the name of Lequile, the manna can be seen to distill from the pores of the bones separately, little by little until each increases to such a size that it touches another, collects and then drops.[3]

What causes the liquid to appear? Humidity, saturation and condensation have been suggested, but all have been discredited by the custodians of the relics and respected scientists who have studied the matter.

[2]*La Manna di S. Nicola Nella Storia Nell'Arte Nella Scienza*, P. Pio Scognamiglio, O.P., Societa Tipografica Editrice Barese, Bari, Italy, 1925, p 68.
[3]*Ibid.*, p. 67.

We should first consider that the tomb of the saint is about 90 centimeters deep with the walls of marble measuring 15 centimeters thick. The interior is little influenced by outside temperatures nor can it be penetrated by humidity.

The manna has always been observed to collect among the bones and never on the walls of the tomb nor around the small hole through which the interior of the tomb can be viewed. This small hole, cut into the altar table is securely closed when not in use. If humidity, saturation or condensation were being considered, it would seem probable that these conditions would make themselves known around the hole and along the inside walls.[4]

The geographical location does not figure in this since the same phenomenon should also occur in other tombs or caverns around Bari which does not happen. Before the remains were even placed in the marble tomb, history tells us that rivulets were observed coming from the bones — the one from the head, looking like oil, and that from the feet, having the appearance of water. The suggestion that location is responsible is improbable since the event was observed in Myra, Turkey, before the translation, and is probably the reason the fame of the saint had extended so far from his place of labor. While the relics were in Myra a knight is reported to have taken a tooth from the saint's skull which he placed in a small golden case. From this tooth a clear liquid was seen to form.[5] Additionally, a group of people actually stole some fragments of bone and placed them in a bag with the intention of taking them away. The bag at one point was found saturated with liquid.[6] We have here instances where the manna was collected in two different empires, and both inside and outside places of enshrinement.

While excavation work was undertaken with the intention of strengthening the foundation of the basilica, water was seen coming from the ground a considerable distance from the tomb. A test was immediately conducted to learn if the manna had originated from a spring. Results were found to be negative because the marble resisted such a leakage and because the water from the ground was salty while the manna was tasteless. For an entire month this spring was made available to all who wished to repeat this experiment.

From various other studies it was determined that the manna was not sea water, water from rain, water from infiltration or water from a

[4]*Ibid.*, pp. 70-71.
[5]*Ibid.*, p. 71.
[6]*Ibid.*, p. 71.

spring.[7] Moreover, wherever it is kept, in containers well closed or not, small containers or large ones, whether exposed to light or dark, for a short or long period of time, even for a century, the taste or smell of the manna is not altered.[8]

When the Dominicans were installed as custodians of the basilica in 1951, the presence of manna was observed, as it was again in 1953 when the tomb was opened in preparation for the restoration of the entire basilica. Between the fifth and sixth of May of that year, in the presence of a pontifical commission, the archbishop of Bari and distinguished members of the Dominican order, a scientific examination was conducted. The bones were found immersed in a clear liquid measuring two centimeters in depth.[9] After being examined, the bones were placed in a metal case made of zinc, and were covered with linen cloths. This was removed for safekeeping from the crypt beneath the basilica to the treasure room on the superior floor where they were placed for veneration atop the altar. Shortly thereafter they were placed within the altar where they stayed until the work was completed in 1957.

The removal of the bones from the tomb in the crypt marked the first time they were transferred since their placement there in 1087. After the removal of the relics, the place was examined with strong lights. No breach was found in the thick walls through which outside waters could penetrate and it was established that the liquid must have derived from the bones alone.

With the placement of the relics in the altar on the main floor of the basilica, the bones did not secrete oil for a period of four years. This was the fourth time mentioned in their history when the liquid was not formed. The first interruption occurred in Myra in the year 887 when a legitimate successor of the saint was expelled from office. The cessation of manna was taken as a protest and appeared again when the bishop was reinstated.

The second instance occurred in the year 1086, the year before their transference to Italy when the translation of the relics was contemplated. The third interruption occurred in 1916-1917 which was taken as another protest against the blood that was being needlessly wasted in the First World War. The fourth cessation occurred during this restoration of the basilica that lasted from 1953 to 1957.

[7]*Ibid.*, p. 72.
[8]*Ibid.*, pp. 70-73.
[9]*Solemni Celebrazioni Per La Reposizione Delle Sacre Ossa di S. Nicola*, A Cura dei Padri Domenicani Della Basilica di S. Nicola di Bari, Italy, 1957, p. 101.

With the completion of the work, the zinc urn that contained the bones was removed from the chapel of the treasury and was brought back to the crypt where it was again examined in the presence of church officials. The cloths that had been wrapped around the bones were dry and manna was not found at this time.

Anticipating the criticisms of disbelievers who credited the phenomenon to the penetration of outside waters, the bones were placed in the original tomb of the main altar of the crypt which had been rendered immune to water infiltration by procedures that further guaranteed its security.

A grand celebration lasting from April 29 until May 9, 1957 was observed for the recognition of the fine improvements made to the ancient basilica. Solemn pilgrimages were held and sacred liturgies were celebrated in both the oriental and Roman rites. After these solemn functions the bones exuded manna for a few months and then ceased. Concerned by this fifth interruption, two Dominican priests, Armando Bezzeccheri and Battista Mezzanotte continually checked for the return of the manna through the small round hole in the altar.

This they continued to do until April 10, 1961. On the 28th day of the same month when the Dominican Father Ahlheid came to Bari to conduct a novena to the saint, he wanted to see for himself if the manna had returned and actually discovered it. Cotton balls that were lowered through the opening and then drawn upward were found completely saturated, thus signaling the absolute return of the miraculous event. Exactly six months later, on October 28, 1961, so much of the fluid had collected that 15 cubic centimeters were gathered into bottles.

It should be considered by those who believe the manna to be the result of humidity, saturation or condensation, that at the time the manna ceased to collect between the years previously mentioned, but especially the latter period which lasted a full four years, such conditions as humidity, saturation or condensation had every opportunity to exert their influence, but did not. It seems entirely unexplainable why the bones, while being retained in the same crypt, should again resume production of manna from 1961 until the present day.

In this consideration of manna three geographic locations are represented: Myra in Turkey, Bari in southern Italy on the shores of Adriatic Sea and St. Andrew in Amalfi, Italy, near the Gulf of Naples. Yet a fourth location should be included, Eichstatt in southern Germany where a similar event occurs involving the remains of St. Walburga.

This saint was an Englishwoman who belonged to a family of saints. Her father, St. Richard, was the West Saxon king and St. Boniface was a kinsman who is credited with persuading her two brothers, St. Willibald and St. Wunibald, to join him in evangelizing Germany.

St. Willibald became the first bishop of the diocese of Eichstatt, which he founded in 741. Walburga's other brother, St. Wunibald, after his ordination, founded in Heidenheim, in the diocese of Eichstatt, a Benedictine double monastery, for men and women, a separate arrangement in one foundation that was customary at the time, particularly in England. Wunibald governed the monks while his sister, Walburga, who had taken the veil in England, journeyed to Heidenheim to rule as abbess of the nuns. On the death of Wunibald, St. Walburga governed both groups for almost 25 years until her death on February 25, 779.

Even before her burial various religious and lay people were favored with visions of the saint surrounded by a wonderful light and crowned with a halo. First buried at a monastery in Heidenheim, her remains were transferred to Eichstatt between 870 and 879 where they were placed beside those of her brother in the Holy Cross Church where the Church of St. Walburga stands today.

When a portion of the relics was transferred to the newly established convent at Monheim, the relics of St. Walburga were already secreting "pearls" according to the record kept by Wolfhard of Herrieden in the year 983. Two years later this same historian described in four volumes all the saint's miracles that occurred at this location.

When Holy Cross Church fell into decay and a new structure was built around 1035, the remains were again exhumed and placed in a shrine especially built to house the relics. This shrine is situated in a chapel directly behind the main altar. The remains were not placed beneath the altar, but above it in a recess like a tabernacle.

Before this exhumation the public was not aware of the strange occurrence, but in 1075 another historian from Herrieden wrote that "a clear liquid like fresh water flows today from the tomb containing her revered remains, much in the same manner as the flow of oil from St. Nicholas' tomb in Bari. It is a continuous flow wonderfully effective and a cure for many ills."[10]

The recess where the relics are kept and the oil collected consists of a tabernacle with two sections, one above the other. The bones are kept in a bowl made of precious metal that is on the higher level. Silver pipes are connected to holes in the bottom of the bowl and these pass to the lower level where a silver shell is located for the collection of the oil. Thus the oil that collects on the bones drips through the pipes into the

[10]*St. Walburg Eichstatt Kloster- und Pfarrkirche*, Abtei St. Walburg, Eichstatt/Bayern, Germany, 1967, p. 24.

dish below, where the Benedictine nuns collect it and distribute it in tiny ampules to the faithful who believe in its effectiveness, as so many have believed since the last quarter of the 11th century.

The oil is crystal clear with no color, taste or odor. Since its first discovery the liquid has been identified as an oil because of its slow development and because of its use as a medicinal ointment, but the liquid more accurately resembles water.[11]

The prodigious flow of oil from the bones of the saint who died 1,200 years ago is rendered still more phenomenal in that the oil flows each year from October 12, the day her remains were transferred to the present location, until February 25, the anniversary of the saint's death, when it abruptly stops. This four-month activity has been carefully observed for several centuries.

"Strange is it that in joyful times the oil flows freely and in sad times the oil flow stops." The oil failed to flow, for example, when the nuns had been falsely accused by Bishop Antony Knebel von Katzenellenhogen in 1713 and started flowing again when the nuns' good name was restored. The collection of the liquid at other times of the year has marked extraordinary occurrences. Closer to our own time, on the 7th of June, 1835, the oil started flowing at its proper time as a sign of approval when King Louis of Bavaria reopened the monastery for new members after the monastery had been condemned to extinction.[12]

The monastery of Heidenheim, founded by St. Walburga's saintly brother, and governed by her for so many years, was seized by the Lutherans in 1626. The great church formerly connected to the monastery is now the parish church of the Protestants. The Catholic population of the city now numbers barely 200 souls. The shrine of the saint, nonetheless, is under the watchful eye of the Benedictine nuns.

Medical science is unable to explain why the bones of St. Andrew, St. Nicholas and St. Walburga should secrete a liquid, especially since the saints all died so long ago — St. Andrew dying in the first century, St. Nicholas in the fourth and St. Walburga in the eighth century; nor could they explain why the fluid collects at certain times that would seem unfavorable for its formation.

Another example of the formation of manna, but one which has not continued as does the preceding cases, concerns St. Gerard Majella, a humble lay brother who is invoked by mothers around the world for protection against all dangers that attend maternity — this because of a

---

[11]*St. Walburg V. et Abb. O.S.B.*, Eichstatt, Germany, 1935, p. 16.
[12]*Ibid.*, p. 17.

miracle he performed in favor of a woman in the agony of a difficult delivery.

Born in Muro, a small town to the south of Naples, Gerard was the son of a tailor and upon the father's death was apprenticed to another. After becoming proficient at the trade he offered himself to the Capuchins, but was refused as being too young and delicate. After serving the local bishop as a servant, he labored as a tailor in his own business freely distributing his earnings among three interests: his mother and three sisters, Masses for the souls in purgatory and alms to the poor. During a mission given by the priests of the newly founded Congregaton of the Most Holy Redeemer he pleaded with the priests to accept him despite his delicate appearance and was sent to a house of the order with the written message: "I send you a useless brother." Engaged first as a gardener and sacristan, his submissive, humble and obedient manner led some to wonder whether he was "a fool or a great saint." St. Alphonsus, the founder of the order, immediately recognized his saintliness and shortened his novitiate. During his three years as a professed brother he served the community as tailor, infirmarian, companion to the priests during their journeys, and during the needful times that afflicted the new community he also begged for the needs of his brethren.

The saint possessed a number of supernatural favors: ecstatic flight, bilocation, the gifts of prophecy and healing, multiplication of food and infused knowledge. So many miracles were performed through his intercession that one biographer wrote that several large volumes would be needed to tell them.

Suffering from consumption he died in a house of the order in the small village of Caposele at the exact time and date he predicted, midnight of October 15-16, 1755. The "squallida celletta," the squalid cell, wherein he died, was transformed into a chapel in 1796 with marble walls of pink, white and gray. Beneath the altar is a statue of the saint reclining in an attitude of blissful repose. The expenses of decorating this chapel were assumed by a grateful client who had been cured through the saint's intercession from a grave form of meningitis.

Atop the hill against which Caposele is nestled stands the Basilica of Materdomini which contains the sanctuary of the saint. Beneath the altar of this sanctuary is the urn which guards his remains.

Because the saint died from consumption, his personal effects were burned to prevent the infection of the congregation. The only relics existing are a colored handkerchief, two white collars, two instruments of penance, a piece of wood from his first casket and two autographed letters.

One hundred years following his death the ecclesiastical authorities ordered the recognition and examination of the relics as required for the process preceding beatification. After the bones were placed in a vessel a perfumed oil was seen to proceed from them and collect in such abundance that a basin was filled to overflowing. The excess was gathered with great care on handkerchiefs and linens of which the sick "soon proved the virtue." On October 11, 1892 the remains were again examined by ecclesiastical authorities and two physicians. Since the bones were found more or less humid, they were dried and placed in a casket ornamented with white silk. Four hours later the casket was again opened. Once more, to the amazement of all, a white oil possessing a sweet scent was seen to ooze from the relics and cling like droplets of dew upon the silk lining. After a rigorous examination the physicians drafted an official report stating that the formation of the liquid was beyond the natural order.[13]

The first miracle submitted for the approval of the Congregation of Rites was effected by the application of this mysterious oil on a dying man who was instantaneously restored to health.

Persistent reports have it that the oil still exudes from the relics, a claim that is negated by the priests of the shrine. In the souvenir shop attached to the basilica are sold small bottles marked "Oil of St. Gerardo." This is not oil that proceeded from the bones, but simply blessed oil that the faithful use as a devotion to the saints.[14]

Canonized in 1904 by Pope St. Pius X, St. Gerard was acclaimed toward the end of his 29 years of life the most famous wonder-worker of the 18th century and prompted Pope Leo XIII to exclaim that he was "one of those angelic youths whom God has given to the world as models to men."

While the four preceding examples represent oil that originated from the bones of saints, and in three cases those that have continued to collect to modern times, other liquids regarding other saints have been incorrectly likened to a similar miracle. This error, wholly unintentional, began as far back as the days of St. Paulinus of Nola who died in A.D. 431. The custom that prevailed at the time was to pour oil or water over the relics of martyrs and to collect the liquid in vases, sponges or cloths. These relics, called *oleum martyris*, were distributed as a remedy against sickness. This custom was extended to the relics of saints, especially to

[13]*Life, Virtues and Miracles of St. Gerard Majella*, A Lay Brother of the Congregation of the Most Holy Redeemer, Mission Church, Boston, Mass., 1907, pp. 227-228.
[14]From a statement of a represenative of the shrine.

relics of St. Martin of Tours as recorded by Paulinus of Périgueux who wrote about the practice in A.D. 470.

Another example still incorrectly identified as oil from the bones involved the oil of St. Menas, a Libyan martyr whose tomb was a popular place of pilgrimage in the fifth and sixth centuries. Flasks of oil that had been given to pilgrims were found in Africa, Spain, Dalmatia, France, Italy and Russia. This oil was taken from lamps that burned before the sepulchre — a practice that is still popular at the shrines of some saints. According to the inscriptions on some of the flasks, the contents might have contained water from a holy well near the shrine of St. Menas. These flasks were given as souvenirs much as shells were given to pilgrims at the tomb of St. James the Apostle in Spain, which was also a popular place of pilgrimage. It is understandable that these flasks of lamp oil, in time, were mistaken for oil that issued from the bones of the saints, especially after such genuine miracles became popular knowledge.

The list of those early saints whose histories include the mention of oil is lengthy, but because of the practice of using oil from lamps, water from wells or oil that was poured over relics, it is unknown if the bones of any of these saints actually produced oil as do the relics of Ss. Andrew, Nicholas and Walburga whose histories have been well documented and the miracles repeatedly witnessed.

The mysterious formation of a similar oil, frequently perfumed, is known to have proceeded from some of the incorrupt bodies of saints. In only a few cases, however, did the liquid continue to exude to modern times.

Blessed Raymond Capua, who was the confessor of St. Catherine of Siena as well as the confessor at the convent where the incorrupt body of St. Agnes of Montepulciano was kept, himself saw and recorded that the body of St. Agnes produced a liquid substance that issued from her feet and hands in slow but steady droplets that were collected in crystal vases by the sisters. [15]

During the exhumation of the body of St. Camillus de Lellis 11 years after his death, a pure, fragrant oil was seen to issue from his body, an occurrence that continued for nine days. A similar manifestation occurred to the body of St. Paschal Baylon. Although the body of this saint had been covered with lime during its exhumation eight months after burial, a crystalline liquid was seen to distill from the face and hands of

---

[15]*The Incorruptibles*, Joan Carroll Cruz, Tan Books and Publishers, Inc., Rockford, Ill., 1977, pp. 106-108.

the perfectly preserved body. Likewise a clear oil was seen to proceed from the bodies of St. Julia Billiart and St. Mary Magdalen de'Pazzi.[16]

The incidents of such an oil exuding from the bodies of saints are numerous and have been carefully observed and documented, but we will now consider three examples in which the oil has continued to collect to the present.

In Toledo, Spain, a clear oil accompanied by the fragrance of roses and jasmines still proceeds from the incorrupt body of Venerable Mother Maria of Jesus, a companion of the great St. Teresa of Avila. The oil that issued from the body of Blessed Matthia Nazzarei of Matelica, Italy, who died in 1320, flowed intermittently from her hands and feet for centuries, but had flowed continuously since the year 1920 until the relic was enclosed in plastic a few years ago. The oily substance was accompanied with traces of blood which the sisters described as "blood-fluid." Its formation was witnessed and affirmed by numerous doctors and ecclesiastical authorities. It had been noticed especially at times prior to deaths of members of the community or before the outbreak of wars, plagues or events of epic proportions.[17]

The oily substance that has aroused considerable interest in recent years is that which exuded from the perfectly preserved body of St. Sharbel Makhlouf who died in 1898. First noticed during the examination of the body four months after death, it was seen to originate from the pores of the body as perspiration mixed with blood. The liquid was so plentiful that the garments of the body were changed twice a week and these were eventually cut into pieces and distributed to the sick. The saint's body was placed in a special chapel in 1927, and 23 years later, in 1950, a liquid was found dripping from the bottom of the casket, an observance that prompted another exhumation of the body.

The fluid that dripped from the tomb was so plentiful that it actually ran in a thin stream through the chapel where the body was kept and into the oratory. The body at this time was again found in perfect preservation with the garments soaked with the sweat of liquid and blood. During its yearly examination the fluid was found to collect in the bottom of the casket to a depth, at times, of about three inches.[18] The blood fluid continued to exude from the body for 67 years, but at the time of the beatification in 1965 the body was found to have completely decayed. The fluid had, of course, ceased by that time.

[16]*Ibid.*, pp. 36-37.
[17]*Ibid.*, pp. 37 and 110.
[18]*Ibid.*, pp. 295-296.

These appearances of oil from sanctified bones and bodies, while wholly unexplainable by physicians and scientists, is likewise mystifying to the Church, but it would seem that the Lord wishes to draw attention to these, His faithful sons and daughters, and to anoint their remains with an oil of special origin.

As early as the eighth century, St. John Damascene recognized this phenomenon. His observation would seem as appropriate today as it was then: "Christ gives us the relics of saints as health-giving springs through which flow blessings and healing. This should not be doubted. For if at God's word water gushed from hard rock in the wilderness ... yes, and from the ass' jawbone when Samson was thirsty, why should it seem incredible that healing medicine should distill from the relics of the saints?"

Relics of the Saints

St. Agatha

THE waist-length statue of St. Agatha of Catania is adorned with countless jewels presented to her by devotees who have received favors, and by those who were grateful for her intercession in sparing them from the violence threatened by Mount Etna.

Agatha's beauty and family position proved to be the detriment that led to her martyrdom. Having heard reports of her virginal purity and physical charm. She was brought before Quinctianus, a magistrate during the persecution of Decius. His advances were refused, as were the attempts to have her engage in the activities of an immoral house. After being confined for a month in this evil place her virginity was maintained. She prayed all the more for endurance to undergo all her trials for the love of God, much to the chagrin of Quinctianus, who turned from passion to cruelty.

Her tortures were severe. It is recorded that she was scourged, her sides were torn with iron hooks, she was burned with blazing torches and as a final indignity, her breasts were cut from her body. Quinctianus, still bent on satisfying his revenge had her rolled on burning coals, to which were added broken potsherds. She expired after affirming her love and trust in God. The year was A.D. 251.

First-class relics of the saint are kept in various reliquaries, but the skull and principal relics, said to be incorrupt, are kept in the gem-encrusted reliquary that is exposed on various occasions at Catania, Sicily.

Agatha's name was inserted in the Canon of the Mass, and it occurred in the calendar of Carthage about the year 530. It is also included in all the Latin and Greek martyrologies. Because Agatha has been credited with arresting the eruptions of Mount Etna, she is invoked against the outbreak of fire. She has been designated one of the patronesses of nurses and is invoked against breast diseases.

207

St. Agnes

THE name of Agnes, meaning "pure" in Greek, seems appropriate for one who has been regarded among the foremost of the virgin martyrs of the primitive Church.

Both St. Ambrose (d. 397) and St. Augustine (354-430) agree that Agnes was 13 at the time of her death. Pope Damasus tells us that immediately after the promulgation of the imperial edict against the Christians, Agnes voluntarily declared herself a follower of Christ. She was subsequently threatened with fire and then confinement in a house of immorality. She proclaimed her confidence that God would protect her body from defilement and refused the suitors who offered her proposals of marriage. Her only concern was the defense of her modesty, since she was disrobed before the gaze of a heathen audience. Her flowing hair is said to have sufficiently concealed her nakedness.

St. Ambrose tells us in his sermon, *De Virginibus* of 377 that, "This child was holy beyond her years and courageous beyond human nature. . . . She stood, prayed, and then bent her neck for the stroke. . . ."

The saint died in Rome about A.D. 305. Burial was in the cemetery (afterwards called by her name) beside the Via Nomentana.

A basilica, *Sant' Agnes Fuori Le Mura*, was erected over her tomb before 354 by Constantia, the daughter of Emperor Constantine. The saint is entombed within a silver shrine given by Pope Paul V (1605-1621) that is located in the center of the crypt immediately below the main altar of the basilica.

The Sancta Sanctorum at the Lateran is in possession of the head of the saint, discovered in 1901 when Pope Leo XIII gave permission for the examination of the treasury after it had been closed for a number of years. According to archeologists, the dentition (teeth) of the skull showed conclusively that it belonged to a child of about 13 years and was declared from other studies to be authentic. It was further observed that the body was found without a head when the relics of the saint were examined in her church in 1605.

Since the fourth century, the saint's feast day has been observed on January 21. On this day each year two white lambs are offered in her basilica during High Mass and are cared for until the time for shearing. Their wool is woven into the pallia given to archbishops throughout the Church as symbols of the jurisdiction that ultimately derives from the

Holy See. A pallium, a band measuring three inches wide and decorated with six purple crosses, is placed over the head and worn about the shoulders atop the chasuble. Today an archbishop cannot exercise his function until he receives the pallium and may wear it only on special occasions. It is always buried with him. The investiture of the pope with the pallium at his coronation is the most solemn part of the ceremony and is a symbol older than the wearing of the papal tiara.

St. Aloysius Gonzaga

ST. Aloysius has been presented by the Church as the patron of youths, a designation rightly deserved since from his earliest years he practiced virtue and an orderly prayer life that was unusual for a child of his years. He experienced a spiritual quickening and a sudden development of religious faculties when only seven years of age. According to his confessor, St. Robert Bellarmine, the saint never committed a mortal sin, and one wonders if he even committed a deliberate fault, so conscientious was he of the condition of his soul.

As the son of the marquis of Castiglione, he was often obliged to appear in court, but he despised such activities and resolved to enter the Society of Jesus. His mother rejoiced in his vocation, but his father and members of his family strenuously objected. After repeated delays he was permitted to resign the marquisate of Castiglione, relinquishing the right of succession to his brother, and entered the Jesuit novitiate during his 18th year. Two years later he pronounced his first vows and in a few months received minor orders. The saint served in Naples, Milan and Rome, performing menial tasks and observing austere penances.

During an epidemic of the plague in 1591 he begged permission to serve the stricken, and being of a delicate constitution fell victim to the disease and died at Rome, being at the time but 23 years of age.

The relics of the saint are now kept in an artistic urn beneath the altar of his monumental shrine in the Church of St. Ignatius in Rome. Here also are kept, in their respective shrines, the relics of St. John Berchmans and St. Robert Bellarmine. The room used by the saint during his stay in Rome has been converted into a chapel which tourists may visit.

The Basilica del Gesu Vecchio in Naples has two interesting relics of the saint: a small sample of his blood and a book, both of which are kept in appropriate reliquaries.

The saint was canonized in 1726.

Bl. Anna Maria Taigi

A NNA Maria merited recognition by the Church by being an exemplary wife and mother amid poor and trying circumstances. The daughter of an unsuccessful apothecary, she was taken from her native Siena to Rome where her father sought new employment. She worked at various occupations to assist her family financially, and was married in 1790, at the age of 21, to a butler, Domenico Taigi, who caused her considerable anguish because of his exacting and temperamental attitudes. Three of her seven children died in infancy. Those she raised to maturity were provided with the most complete religious and secular education.

In addition to many voluntary penances, Anna Maria patiently endured aridity of spirit, nursed her mother through a lengthy and repulsive illness, performed her duties as housewife and mother, saw to the needs of her quarrelsome husband, and struggled to maintain peace among members of the family in their overcrowded home. In spite of this seemingly uncongenial atmosphere, she was frequently in ecstasy, worked miracles of healing, foretold deaths, read hearts, and as a tertiary of the Third Order of the Most Holy Trinity, she perfectly fulfilled the obligations of the rule.

Shortly after her marriage she was favored with a constant vision of a luminous disc, somewhat like a miniature sun, that maintained a position before her. Above the upper rays was a large crown of interwoven thorns with two lengthy thorns on either side curving downward so that they crossed each other under the solar disc, their points emerging on either side of the rays. In the center sat a beautiful woman with her face raised toward heaven. In this vision Anna Maria saw things of the natural, moral and divine order and could see present or future events anywhere in the world, as well as the state of grace of living individuals and the fate of those departed. Anna Maria saw this vision for 47 years, a period spanning the length of her marriage.[1] Because of her infused knowledge she was frequently consulted by distinguished persons, including Pope Leo XII, Pope Gregory XVI, Napoleon's mother and Cardinal Fesh. Among her friends can be counted St. Vincent Pallotti, St. Gaspar del Bufalo and St. Mary Euphrasia Pelletier.

Anna Maria died on June 9, 1837, and was buried in a cemetery on the outskirts of Rome. When her popularity became widespread and miracles were occurring through her intercession, her body was removed to the city in 1855, 18 years after burial. Discovered incorrupt at this time, it remained so when it was placed in the Basilica of San Chrysogono three years later. The body of Anna Maria is no longer incorrupt, but her bones are well arranged and enclosed in a figure representing her. This is seen in a glass-sided reliquary beneath an altar of the basilica.

Among those who testified during the Process of Beatification was her husband, Domenico, then 92 years of age, who gave his wife a glowing tribute, as did two daughters who gave evidence of their mother's heroic virtues.

Anna Maria was beatified on May 30, 1920, by Pope Benedict XV, who later designated her a special protectress of mothers.

St. Anthony of Padua

A LTHOUGH born in Lisbon, in 1195, to parents of Portuguese nobility, Anthony, nevertheless, derives his surname from the Italian city of Padua where he spent the last years of his life. Anthony joined the Canons of St. Augustine and was ordained at Coimbra at the age of 25. At Coimbra he witnessed the transfer of relics of five Franciscans who had suffered martyrdom in Morocco. Hoping to offer the sacrifice of his life to Our Lord in a similar manner, he confided his desires to mendicant Franciscans who came to his monastery to beg alms. He was encouraged to join their order, and after overcoming some opposition he received the Franciscan habit. Having been given the name

[1]*La Beata Anna Maria Taigi, Madre di Famiglia,* Msgr. Carlo Salotti, Libreria Editrice Religiosa, Francesco Ferrari, Rome, 1922, pp. 273-278.

Ferdinand at his baptism, he adopted the name of Anthony in honor of St. Anthony of Egypt, the patriarch of monks.

Within a short time he was permitted to embark for Morocco where he intended to preach the Gospel to the Moors, but a severe illness totally incapacitated him for months and necessitated his return to Europe. He was brought to Messina in Sicily when contrary winds drove his vessel off course. From there he made his way to Assisi, where a general chapter was held in 1221 presided over by St. Francis and Brother Elias.

He was thereafter appointed to the lonely hermitage of San Paolo near Forli. What is certain is that no one suspected the intellectual and spiritual gifts of the young priest, who was content to wash the pots and dishes after the community meals. His theological knowledge and rhetorical talents were realized at the time of an ordination. Through a misunderstanding, none of the priests were prepared to deliver the customary address, and excused themselves on that account. Anthony was finally chosen to speak according to the inspirations of the Holy Spirit. His address was so eloquent and fervent, and displayed such an understanding of spiritual doctrines that he amazed and impressed all his listeners.

Commissioned as a preacher, he was sent to northern Italy and France. He founded the theological studies of the order and taught theology at Bologna, Montpellier, Toulouse and Padua. He is said to have radiated holiness that attracted crowds who braved all inconveniences to hear him speak. When the churches could not hold the vast numbers, he preached in the marketplaces, and it is related that when heretics at Rimini refused to hear him, the fish rose from the Marecchia River at the sound of his voice and remained in orderly ranks until the saint finished his discourse.

Anthony's last assignment was at Padua, but he died in 1231 next to the Poor Clare convent at Arcella outside the city. He was then only 36 years of age. At Arcella, the room in which the saint died was made into a simple oratory, with the altar marking the place of his death.

So much grief was displayed at his death, and so many miracles were performed, that an ecclesiastical examination of his holiness was initiated almost immediately and culminated with his canonization within a year of his death.

Early pictures of the saint depict him with a lily or a book emblematic of his knowledge of Holy Scripture, and he is also represented with the Infant Savior because of a report by a Count Tiso, who had donated a hermitage to the Franciscan order on property that he owned.

212

On visiting the hermitage the count saw a brilliant light at the door and fearing a fire he opened it, thus revealing the saint in a rapture with the Holy Child on his arm.

The saint is regarded as the patron of social outcasts, the poor and imprisoned, all of whom he showed devotion during his life. Alms especially given to obtain his intercession are called "St. Anthony's Bread." It is uncertain how the saint came to be connected with the recovery of lost items, but an aged story relates that a novice once ran away carrying off a valuable psalter used by the saint. It was promptly returned after Anthony recited prayers for that intention. Another tradition that extends to the 17th century relates that the celebrated Franciscan of that period, Elbart of Temeswar, in praising Anthony declared that, "Just as during life the Lord glorified St. Anthony by giving him the grace of bringing back straying souls, so now, after his death, He gives him the power of restoring lost items."

Pope Gregory IX, who knew the saint well, called him the Ark of the Testament because of his singular knowledge of Holy Scripture. He was likewise recognized by Pope Pius XII, who numbered him among the doctors of the Church in 1946.

Confreres of the saint, aided by the people of Padua, began building a basilica the year after the saint's death. In 1263 his body was transferred there in the presence of St. Bonaventure, who was then the master general of the order, and was later a bishop and cardinal. When the sarcophagus was opened the tongue that had so eloquently proclaimed the Word of God was found perfectly incorrupt. This was removed by Bonaventure and is now kept in a golden reliquary in the treasury chapel of the basilica in Padua where it is on constant display. A second recognition of the remains occurred in 1350 when the jaw and forearm were removed for placement in reliquaries.

The tomb of the saint, called the Ark of St. Anthony, is made of green-veined marble and is positioned so that pilgrims may walk around it. The rear of the tomb has been worn smooth by the contact of faithful hands. On some days visitors pass the tomb at 2,000 or more an hour, while the saint averages approximately 370 letters received daily from all parts of the world.[1]

In Lisbon a splendid church was built to enclose the site of the saint's birthplace.

St. Anthony's popularity has been described as "The Anthony Phe-

[1]*Columbia Magazine*, New Haven, Connecticut, Vol. LIX. No. 6., June 1979, pp. 8 and 11.

nomenon" and it is a rare church that does not have an altar, statue or picture of the saint.

The 750th anniversary of St. Anthony's death was observed in 1981 with grand celebrations, the most important of which was the opening of the sarcophagus for the first time since 1350. Having obtained the permission of Pope John Paul II, the tomb was opened on January 6 under the watchful gaze of a pontifical delegation and distinguished Church officials. Present also were almost 200 others, including professors of anthropology and anatomy and doctors of medicine from the University of Padua.

Inside the double wooden caskets were found three bundles wrapped in red damask with gold trimmings. One contained the habit in which the saint had been buried, the other two contained bones and the skull.

After the lapse of 750 years the pathologists and anatomists readily identified the saint's vocal cords that were perfectly preserved. These are now kept in a unique container in the reliquary chapel beside the incorrupt tongue of the saint. The reliquary consists of an open book of silver with golden letters on each page. Golden flames rise from the center of the book and encircle a crystal glove under which the relics may be seen. It comprises a fitting memorial for the saint who was an outstanding preacher of Holy Scripture.

St. Benedict and St. Scholastica

THE oldest account of the life of St. Benedict is that written by St. Gregory the Great in his second book of *Dialogues*. It is rather a character sketch of the saint illustrating primarily the miracles, rather than a chronological account of Benedict's career. From the *Dialogues* we learn that Benedict was the son of a Roman noble of Norcia, a small town near Spoleto, and was born about the year 480. He was educated in Rome, but at the age of about 20 he feared contamination from the godlessness of his schoolmates who imitated the vices of their elders, and abandoned everything, even the prospect of a career as a Roman noble, and fled to the mountains some 30 miles from Rome. The saint first settled in a village named Enfide with his elderly servant. Here he worked his first miracle by restoring to perfect condition an earthenware wheat sifter that the servant had accidentally broken. The attention this miracle prompted drove Benedict still farther and higher into the mountains to a remote area known as Subiaco. On his way to this place he met the holy monk, Romanus, whose monastery was on a mountain overlooking a cave. Romanus gave Benedict a religious habit and indicated the cave where Benedict would find the isolation he desired. Romanus assisted Benedict in every way and even provided him with food by letting a basket down from the cliff above.

The saint lived in the cave for three years, until his virtues became known to a group of monks whose abbot had just died. Despite his objections they insisted that he rule over them, and he did so for a time until it soon became evident that Benedict's strict notions of monastic discipline did not suit their laxity. They conspired against him and at last put poison in his wine. When the saint made the sign of the cross over the cup according to his custom, it broke into pieces. Reminding them of his warning that his ways and theirs would not be compatible, he left for Subiaco, not to seclusion, but to begin the work for which God had prepared him during his hermitage.

In an effort at ending the capricious rule of superiors in different families of monks who were dispersed in the monasteries of the region, and to control the license of their subjects, he envisioned a unification of the monastic system, united together by fraternal bonds in the exercise of regular observances. To this end he gathered all who would obey him and built 12 monasteries for them and his disciples. In each he placed a superior with 12 monks who followed the example of St. Benedict's virtues and deeds.

It is cited as a miracle that the saint eliminated the deeply rooted prejudice against manual work that was considered degrading, servile and a condition peculiar to slaves. The saint believed that labor was not only dignified, but a great disciplinary force for human nature, idleness being its ruin. He, therefore, made work compulsory for all who joined his community. The motto of the order has always been *Ora et Labora.*

St. Gregory, in his *Dialogues*, relates that a wayward priest in a neighboring village became envious of the increasing number of Benedict's disciples and his growing influence, and made vile attempts at scandalizing Benedict and the monks. To prevent further persecution Benedict left Subiaco about the year 529 and turned toward Monte Cassino, whose lands had been given him by the father of a disciple. Here the inhabitants of the region were accustomed to offering sacrifices in a temple dedicated to Jupiter and Apollo. The saint overturned the altar, broke the idols and in their place erected two oratories that he dedicated to St. John the Baptist and St. Martin of Tours. As a result of generous donations, there gradually arose about these structures the great building of Monte Cassino, the most famous abbey the world has known.

Unlike the small monasteries Benedict had built at Subiaco, the saint now assembled his monks in one great establishment. It is almost certain that the saint at this time composed his famous Rule that prescribes a life of liturgical prayer, study and work, lived socially in a community under a common father.

Not merely content with overlooking the welfare of his brethren in the abbey, he likewise was solicitous for the population of the surrounding country. He cured their sick, relieved the distressed, distributed alms and food to the poor, and is said to have raised the dead on more than one occasion. He likewise read hearts, prophesied, bested the devil in several trials and once, through his prayers, was miraculously supplied with 200 sacks of flour during a time of need.

The year of the saint's death is placed about the year 543. Just before he died we hear for the first time of his sister, Scholastica. St. Bede, among others, accepts the tradition that she was Benedict's twin. It is also felt that she belonged to a community of nuns who were influenced by St. Benedict and his Rule.

According to St. Gregory, Scholastica was visited by her brother once a year and met with him for the last time a few days before her death on a day "when the sky was so clear that no cloud was to be seen." The sister begged her brother to stay longer,

> ". . . but no persuasion would he agree unto saying that he might not by any means tarry all night out of his abbey. The nun, receiving this denial of her brother, joining her hands together, laid them upon the table, and so, bowing down her head upon them, she made her prayers to Almighty God, and lifting her head from the table there fell suddenly such a tempest of lightning and thundering and such abundance of rain that neither Venerable Benedict nor his monks that were with him could put their heads out the door."[1]

Three days later, Benedict beheld the soul of his sister in the form of a dove ascending to the heavens. The saint had the body of his sister brought to the abbey for burial in the grave he had provided for himself.

---

[1]*The Catholic Encyclopedia*, Op. cit., Vol. II, p. 471.

Six days before he died, he gave orders to have the sepulchre opened so that he might be buried with his sister,

> ". . . and forthwith falling into an ague, he began with burning heat to wax faint, and when the sickness daily increased, upon the sixth day he commanded his monks to carry him into the oratory where he did arm himself by receiving the Body and Blood of Our Saviour Christ; and having his weak body holden up betwixt the hands of his disciples, he stood with his own hands lifted up to heaven; and as he was in that manner praying he gave up the ghost."[2]

The saint's prophecy that Monte Cassino would be destroyed and then restored was realized four times, the first destruction taking place about the year 581 at the hands of the Lombards. Saracen hordes overtook and damaged it in 883, and in 1349 a violent earthquake razed it to the ground. Its most complete destruction occurred on February 15, 1944, when it was bombarded during the Second World War. German forces and the Allies each blamed the other for the damage. The Germans, it seems, had occupied caves along the mountain and commanded a view of the countryside that enabled them to monitor the progress of the Allied forces, who were intent on reaching Rome. Repeated attacks against the Allies resulted in many deaths until it was thought best to destroy the abbey, where it was believed the German forces had established a headquarters. Much to the outrage of those who learned about it, the abbey was thoroughly damaged.

Faithfully and magnificently rebuilt with the financial aid of the Italian government, it is reminiscent of a motto on one of its coats of arms *Succisa Virescit* (Struck down it comes to new life).

During the aerial and land bombardments, the tomb of St. Benedict and St. Scholastica beneath the high altar of the church remained almost untouched. In 1950 they were submitted to canonical inspection and in 1955 were replaced in a richly decorated urn in the same niche under the main altar. To this tomb came Pope Paul VI on October 24, 1964, to preside over the consecration of the altar and the rebuilt church. Pope Paul again honored St. Benedict by visiting the Sacro Speco, the Sacred Cave at Subiaco, on September 8, 1971. The two churches that were built here above the cave of the saint are one atop the other and were likened to a swallow's nest by Pope Pius II in 1461. The two churches and several chapels seem precariously assembled against the face of the mountain. In the lower church is the entrance to the Sacred Cave where Benedict lived for three years.

[2] *Ibid.*, Vo. II, p. 472.

Monte Cassino is not the only abbey to claim possession of the saint's relics. Saint-Benoît-sur-Loire in Fleury, France, maintains that it had possession of the relics since the end of the sixth century when Monte Cassino was ravaged by the Lombards. Mommolus, the second abbot at Fleury, is said to have effected the transfer of the relics which brought great prestige to the abbey. French piety has always surrounded the relics at Fleury and even attracted St. Joan of Arc after the Battle of Orléans in 1429. A plaque in the church commemorates her visit.

Since claims are firm at both Monte Cassino and St. Benoit that they possess the relics of the saint, and since the remains at Monte Cassino are incomplete, we can only assume that a portion was retained at St. Benoit at the time of the return of the relics to Monte Cassino. Each abbey, however disputes the other's claim.

At Benoît-sur-Loire the relics are kept in a reliquary that was designed and assembled in 1964 and are kept in the crypt within a cluster of pillars that support the central portion of the church.

The reigning pontiff on March 23, 1980, visited "the cradle of the Benedictine Order," Benedict's hometown of Norcia, to participate in the 1,500th anniversary celebration of the saint's birth.

St. Bernadette Soubirous

THE celebrated visionary of Lourdes was born on January 7, 1844, the first child of François and Louise Castérot. Although registered under the name of Bernarde-Marie, she was known by the name of Bernadette. She was afflicted with asthma from childhood and was such a poor student she was delayed from making her First Holy Communion until the year 1858 when she was 14 years old. On February 11 of that year, while on an errand to gather firewood, the first of her visions of the Mother of God took place. In all, the Virgin Mary appeared to Bernadette a total of 18 times.

By identifying herself as the Immaculate Conception, the Mother of God confirmed the pious belief that Pope Pius IX four years earlier had elevated to a dogma of the Catholic Church — a truth that all Catholics are obliged to believe.

From the time of the first apparition curious visitors to the Castérot home grew in numbers until July of 1860 when the situation became intolerable. Curé Peyramale solved the problem by placing the visionary as a boarder in the boarding school of the Sisters of Nevers located in Lourdes.

On January 18, 1862, Monsignor Laurence, who was entrusted with the task of studying the validity of the visions, concluded in his official document,

> "We judge that Mary Immaculate, Mother of God, really appeared to Bernadette on the 11th February, 1858, and on following days to the number of 18 days in all, in the Grotto of Massabielle, near the town of Lourdes, that this apparition is endowed with all the characters of truth and that the faithful are justified in believing in it with certainty."

Although the Blessed Mother never suggested that Bernadette should become a nun, Bernadette felt this to be her vocation and applied for admission to the novitiate of the order of the sisters who were caring for her. The day before leaving Lourdes for the motherhouse at Nevers, some 300 miles away, Bernadette visited the grotto for the last time. She always claimed that "The grotto was my heaven."

During the 13 years of her religious life, Bernadette served the order as assistant sacristan and an assistant nurse in the infirmary. She was a conscientious Religious, as recorded by the mother general in a letter to Curé Peyramale dated November 13, 1868: "This dear child remains what you desire her to be. She is pious, a good nun, always simple and modest."

To the accusation by a Doctor Voisin, who declared publicly that "The miracle of Lourdes was vouched for on the word of a child suffering from delusions," Doctor Saint-Cyr, the convent doctor at St. Gildard, countered on September 3, 1872,

> "Sister Marie Bernard is twenty-seven years of age, and is small and weak in appearance. She is endowed with a calm and gentle nature, she looks after her patients with great intelligence without omitting an iota of the prescriptions I give her; for that reason she has acquired great authority. I have absolute confidence in her. You can see that this Sister is far from being erratic. I would add to this: that her calm, simple and gentle nature does not dispose her in any way to be led in this direction."

The saint's life as an invalid began in November 1875, with crises alternating with rare alleviations. "My hand trembles like that of an old woman," she confessed to a correspondent in 1876 while she, as the oldest child in the family, was occupied by family cares and grieved by numerous deaths in her family.

Having suffered torments from tuberculosis of the lung and a tubercular tumor of the right knee, the saint received Extreme Unction for the fourth time in her life on March 28. On the 16th of April, after kissing the crucifix sent by Pope Pius IX, she died after twice praying, "Holy Mary, Mother of God, pray for me, a poor sinner." Bernadette was 35 years of age.

Unlike the popular movie version of the saint's life in which she died reclining in bed while being assisted by her parish priest of Lourdes, Curé Peyramale, the saint actually died while sitting in an armchair, her feet on a footstool, in order to relieve her attacks of near suffocation. The curé was not at her side, having died on September 8, 1877, two years earlier.

Thirty years after her death the body of the saint was discovered incorrupt, although slightly emaciated, during an official recognition of the relic as required for the Cause of Beatification. During the year of her beatification, 1925, the body, with the face and hands now covered with wax, was ceremoniously transferred to the chapel of the Convent of St. Gildard where it has been exposed in a glass-sided reliquary.

The relics of Bernadette are numerous. At Lourdes one may see the rosary held by Bernadette during the visions, as well as her white cape and black shoes. Visitors are permitted to enter the prison-home where Bernadette and her family lived. One may also pray before the grotto with the niche where the Virgin stood.

A museum with many artifacts and relics is maintained at St. Gildard in Nevers. Here is kept a large glass-covered case containing the armchair on which the saint sat at the time of her death, and the stool upon which her feet rested. The traveling bag, purse and umbrella Bernadette used during her trip from Lourdes to Nevers are displayed with a letter written to her school friends about the trip. A woolen sweater, shoes, stockings, shoe horn, apron, flat iron, scissors and gloves are also kept, as is a beautiful alb embroidered by Bernadette for Bishop Forcade of Nevers. Displayed also is the crucifix given her by Pope Pius IX together with her rosary, medals and a badge of the Sacred Heart. The most precious relic of all is, of course, the body of the saint, which visitors approach with deep reverence in the chapel of the motherhouse of the sisters in Nevers.

St. Bernard

BEFORE Bernard was born in 1090, a devout man foretold his great destiny. As a member of the highest nobility of Burgundy, Bernard's education was supervised with particular care. His success in his studies and in virtue were admirable, as was his devotion to the Blessed Mother.

Together with 30 young noblemen, Bernard sought admission into the monastery of Citeaux which had been founded for the purpose of restoring the Rule of St. Benedict in all its rigor. Bernard's unique abilities and his gift of leadership were engaged a mere three years later by St. Stephen, then abbot of Citeaux, who sent him to open a new house at Vallee d'Absinthe (Valley of Bitterness), in the Diocese of Langres. Bernard renamed the place Claire Valle, or Clairvaux, Bright Valley, a name that became inseparable with that of the saint. Here he was joined by his father and his five brothers.

The number of those who placed themselves under the saint's direction was so great that other monasteries in several countries were founded to house them. It is said that he was instrumental in founding, either directly or indirectly, approximately 168 monasteries. So irresistable were Bernard's eloquent appeals in favor of the religious life that Butler tells us, ". . . mothers hid their sons, wives their husbands, lest they came under the sway of that compelling voice and look."[1] With good reason, he was called the Oracle of the Twelfth Century.

At the request of various popes and ecclesiastics, the saint was obliged to travel in attempts to end schisms, settle quarrels between nobles, disputes among clergy, to denounce heresies, to reform disciplines, assist at synods, and to settle matters that disturbed the peace of the Church. He was called upon to compose the rule for the prestigious Order of the Knights Templar, who are thought to have been the custodians of the Holy Shroud for a time. During the last years of his life Bernard was saddened by the failure of a crusade he preached and organized for the defense of the Holy Land, but this failure was caused by the intrigue, greed and treason of certain Christian nobles.

The health of the saint was impaired by the austerities of the abbey and his life of mortification, and were only mitigated under obedience.

---

[1] *The Lives of the Saints*, Rev. Alban Butler, P.J. Kenedy and Sons, New York, 1933, Vol. VIII, p. 232.

He was, nonetheless, troubled by numerous afflictions most of his life. Bernard died in 1153 at age 63, after 40 years spent in the cloister.

A worker of miracles both during and after his life, he was canonized in 1174. He was later named a doctor of the Church in recognition of his numerous writings. He was the first Cistercian monk placed on the calendar of saints and is honored as only the founders of orders are honored, because of the distinction he brought to the Order of Citeaux.

Of the relics of the saint, a vestment worn by him is kept at Clairvaux. Having visited Germany on numerous occasions, his abbot's staff found its way to the German abbey of Ss. Peter and Paul at Dendermonde. The saint's plain staff, originally unadorned and resembling a shepherd's crook, had long ago been enclosed within an artistic staff of precious metal. About the crook, which was left exposed, are baroque designs and a figure of Bernard kneeling before figures of the Blessed Mother and the Child Jesus, a depiction familiar in the saint's iconography.

It is claimed that the words, "O clement, O Pious, O sweet Virgin Mary" were added to the Salve Regina after the saint uttered them spontaneously, and he is held responsible for popularizing the anthem among religious houses and shrines. In 1220 the Cistercian Order is known to have enjoined its daily recitation upon all its members.

The Memorare, a popular prayer of Our Lady, is attributed to St. Bernard of Clairvaux, although this claim is disputed at times.

St. Blaise

ALL ancient martyrologies, as well as the Greek synaxaria, agree that St. Blaise was born in Armenia and was made bishop of the See of Sebaste. Legend tells us that he was also a physician. His episcopal dignity did not prevent him from withdrawing to a cave on Mount Argeus where not only men but animals sought healings.

During the persecution of Lucinius, he was discovered by hunters who were searching for wild beasts for the games in the arena. Argicolaus, the governor, failed in several attempts to make him apostatize. While in prison he cured a child who was in danger of death from choking on a fishbone. This led to the practice of invoking St.

Blaise for maladies of the throat. The use of candles during the blessing of throats is commemorative of the wax tapers given him to dispel the gloom of his prison.

The saint suffered various torments, including the tearing of his flesh with hooks, and iron combs such as were used in processing wool. The saint was finally beheaded in the year 316. In iconography the saint is depicted as a bishop holding a crozier. He is sometimes seen holding lighted candles or the hooks or comb with which he was tormented.

The Abbey of St. Blasius in the Black Forest, as well as numerous other places, claim to possess some of his relics.

St. Catherine Laboure

THE visionary of the Miraculous Medal was born into a large farming family in the peaceful village of Fain-les-Moutiers, France. Catherine was nine years of age when her mother died, and it was then that the future saint chose the Blessed Mother for her mother and protector. Catherine was pious from early childhood, attended daily Mass and fasted twice a week in spite of the fatiguing chores she performed on her father's farm. Having decided to enter the religious life, she declined two marriage proposals. Her father, hoping to discourage his daughter's vocation, sent her to live with a brother who owned a restaurant in Paris. Here she obediently waited on tables. Circumstances eventually permitted her to enter the order of the Sisters of Charity on Rue du Bac in Paris, and it was there that she was favored with several visions.

As a young postulant she frequently beheld Our Lord in front of the Blessed Sacrament during Mass, and on three occasions she saw mystical, symbolic visions of St. Vincent de Paul above the reliquary containing his incorrupt heart, which is enshrined in the chapel of the motherhouse. Undoubtedly the most extraordinary visions were those which concerned Our Blessed Mother.

On July 18, 1830, the eve of the Feast of St. Vincent de Paul, the founder of her order, St. Catherine was awakened during the night by her angel, who appeared as a child of about five years. All radiant with light, he conducted her into the chapel. She was met there by the Blessed Mother, who sat on a chair that was reserved for the director of the sisters. Kneeling before the apparition, Catherine was permitted to rest her folded hands on the knees of the vision who told her, "Come to the foot of this altar. There graces will be showered on you and on all who shall ask for them, rich and poor."

The second apparition occurred on November 27, 1830, while Catherine was making her afternoon meditation. Hearing the rustle of silk which she had recognized from the first apparition, she looked in the direction of the sound and beheld the Blessed Mother standing in the sanctuary near a picture of St. Joseph. The small globe which the apparition held close to her heart slowly disappeared and at once her fingers were covered with rings which streamed rays of light, symbolic of the graces which she bestows on all who ask for them. Slowly there appeared around the Virgin an oval frame on which brilliant letters appeared: "O Mary, conceived without sin, pray for us who have recourse to thee." At the same time a voice said, "Have a medal struck from this model. Persons who wear it will receive great graces, especially if they wear it around the neck; graces will be bestowed abundantly upon those who have confidence." The vision reversed itself and there appeared the Virgin's monogram which is found on the back of the Miraculous Medal.

The third vision was almost identical to the second, except that the Virgin moved to a position above and behind the tabernacle. This place is now occupied by a statue made in the likeness of the vision.

The privileged soul reported these visions only to her superior and her spiritual director, and many difficulties had to be overcome before the medals were made and distributed.

After her profession Catherine was assigned to the Hospice on the Rue de Reuilly where she spent the next 46 years of her life performing the most menial and repugnant tasks for the aged sick and infirm. While all the sisters were aware that one in their midst was the celebrated seer of the Miraculous Medal, the identification was not made known until Catherine was on her death bed. Having often predicted that she would never see the year 1877, she died on December 31, 1876.

Burial was in a crypt of the chapel at 77 Rue de Reuilly where the body remained undisturbed for 56 years. Following the announcement of her beatification the customary recognition of the relics took place. On March 21, 1933, the ecclesiastical and medical delegation witnessed the uncovering of the body. Despite a damp condition in which the body should have disintegrated, it was found perfectly preserved. Two elderly ladies who had known Sister Catherine wept when they recognized the features of their saintly friend. After a careful examination during which preservatives were injected, the body was placed in the motherhouse chapel under the side altar of Our Lady of the Sun, where it still reposes behind a covering of glass. The saint's beautiful blue eyes which had beheld so many visions are open, much to the amazement of those who pray before her altar.

The incorrupt hands of the saint, which had been amputated and replaced on the body by ones made of wax, are kept in a special reliquary which is now enshrined in the novitiate cloister of the motherhouse. The heart of the saint was likewise put into a special reliquary made of crystal and gold which is reverently kept in the chapel at Reuilly where the saint had so often prayed between duties at the hospice. Also shown here is the original tomb in the vault of the chapel where the saint had originally been entombed.

The chapel of the visions is undoubtedly one of the most hallowed in the world, for not only was it visited many times by Our Lord, the Virgin of the Miraculous Medal, and St. Vincent de Paul, it is also enriched by the presence of many precious relics. Near the incorrupt body of St. Catherine is the altar of St. Vincent de Paul, the founder of the order. Here is seen the reliquary containing his heart. On the opposite side of the chapel, above the side altar, is the magnificent reliquary containing a wax figure with the bones of St. Louise de Marillac, the co-foundress of the order. On one side of the main altar stands the blue velvet chair, mentioned elsewhere in this volume, on which the Virgin Mary sat during the first apparition. Visitors to the chapel are permitted to touch or kiss the chair and many leave there slips of paper on which they describe their intentions.

Visitors may also journey to the birthplace of the saint at Fain-les-Moutiers. The picturesque old farm is shown by the custodian, who indicates typical barnyard buildings including a cattle shed and the dovecote where the saint as a child fed and cared for white pigeons. The kitchen is shown as is the bedroom where St. Catherine and the other 10 children in the family were born. The parish church is the site of the saint's baptism and here is shown the baptismal font, the family's pew, the cradle used by the Laboure children and some of the saint's wardrobe. The village has remained practically the same as when the saint walked its streets as a child. The most obvious signs of modern times are telephone poles.

Catherine was canonized on July 27, 1947. The Miraculous Medal, which is based on her visions, has enjoyed a worldwide popularlity.

225

St. Catherine of Siena

I N the Fontebranda section of the medieval city of Siena the houses stand close beside one another and follow the contour of the hillside. Among a row of these buildings is the home of St. Catherine, which is distinguished from the others by a sign above the door that reads: "Sponsae Christi, Katherinae Domus," (this is the house of Catherine the bride of Christ). Here Catherine was born in 1347, the 23rd child of the Benincasa household, the daughter of a dyer of leather and fabrics.

In this house are found her father's workshop, the staircase she often climbed, the kitchen where she helped her mother, and the tiny room where she lived and prayed in solitude for three years before she began her public life at the age of 23 in the service of the Church.

Her early childhood was like those of her siblings, but at the age of six her life was forever changed by a vision that appeared above the Church of St. Dominic. While her brother, Stefano, who was a year or two older, wondered at her conduct during the ecstasy, Catherine saw Our Lord dressed in the robes of a pope, and surrounded by Saints Peter, Paul and John. From this time onward she seemed no longer a child, since her thoughts, conduct and virtues were like those of one superior to her age.

After encountering vigorous opposition from her mother, Catherine succeeded, at the age of 17, in entering the Dominican order as a member of the *Mantellate*, this being an association of laywomen who wore a religious habit and lived in their respective homes, meeting at specified times for community prayer.

After three years spent for the most part in her room engaged in prayer and penance, she began to minister to the sick and poor, and is known to have spent considerable time in the city jails helping the condemned prepare for death. During a fearful plague she ministered to the repulsive sick and buried the dead.

Her life of prayer, penance and works of charity was so exemplary that priests, noblemen, lawyers, theologians and representatives of other professions visited her and left as her followers, attesting to her holiness.

Her influence was so persuasive over sinners that the pope gave permission for three confessors to travel with her to hear the confessions of those she led from a life of sin.

Catherine possibly experienced all the mystical gifts. She is known to have delivered many from diabolical possession, to have performed many miracles of healing, to have levitated frequently during prayer, to have enjoyed an extraordinary intimacy with Our Lord and His Mother, and to have experienced the mystical espousal in which Our Lord gave her a golden ring set with precious jewels. The ring was invisible to all except Catherine, who acknowledged that it was always with her. Her prolonged fasts were divinely transformed into a complete abstinence, and while she subsisted only on the Holy Eucharist, her strength and vitality were spiritually maintained. Catherine also bore on parts of her body the marks of the stigmata, which were visible only to herself, but became visible to others after her death.

Catherine is known to have labored tirelessly for the interests of the Church during a time of schism, and is credited with having persuaded Pope Gregory XI to return the papacy to Rome after it had been exiled in Avignon for 70 years. As a result of her exhaustive travels she brought back to the Holy See many rebellious Italian cities. She corresponded with kings, queens and nobles for the causes of the Church and prayed and pleaded for Church unity.

During her visits to Rome Catherine lived in a house on Via Santa Chiara; which was a mile from the Basilica of St. Peter. Each morning during the last months of her life she journeyed to the Vatican where she spent hours kneeling before Giotto's beautiful mosaic of *la Navicella*, which depicts the ship of Peter tossing about in a storm at sea. This represented to her the Church, tossed about on the storms of schism, divisions, and heresy, many of which she helped to calm or dismiss.

Distressed over the difficulties which afflicted the Church, she offered herself as a victim to God and died in Rome, after a painful illness, on April 29, 1380, being at the time of her death only 33 years of age. The house in which she died on Via Santa Chiara is shown to pilgrims.

We are fortunate in having the story of her life written by her confessor and first biographer, St. Raymond of Capua, who gives ample testimony of her mystical gifts and the extent of her penances and works of charity.

Having died in Rome, the saint was buried there with the main portion of her relics being enshrined in the Church of Santa Maria Sopra Minerva, where they are kept beneath the main altar in a sarcophagus surmounted by a reclining statue of the saint. Major relics have been distributed to a number of Italian and English churches. The most important of these, the head, was taken to Siena in a grand procession followed by St. Raymond of Capua and the saint's mother, Lapa, then an octogenarian, who was clothed in the habit of a Sister of Penance. The relic is kept in the Church of St. Dominic in Siena where, as a child of six, Catherine experienced her first vision and where many of her ecstasies occurred.

Among the many relics kept at the saint's home in Siena are articles she used during her journeys around the city while she cared for the sick and dying: a portion of her walking stick, a lantern and a scent bottle. The visitor can also admire numerous paintings that adorn the home which depict scenes in the life of the saint.

Having been canonized by Pope Pius XII, Catherine was declared a doctor of the Church in 1970 in recognition of her writings, of which the most popular is the *Dialogue of Saint Catherine of Siena*. This is said to have been dictated by the saint during ecstasies.

St. Cecilia

CECILIA was a member of a distinguished Roman family and was given in marriage to Valerianus, a nobleman, despite her desire to remain a virgin. After their wedding, Cecilia was successful in persuading the new groom to respect her vow of virginity and converted him to the Faith. Following his baptism, he was favored with a vision of Cecilia's guardian angel. Valerianus and his brother, Tiburtius, who was also converted by Cecilia, were later martyred for the Faith. Cecilia was arrested for having buried their bodies and was given the choice of sacrificing to heathen gods or being put to death. She steadfastly affirmed her faith and chose to die rather than renounce it. She was confined to the vapor bath of her home to die of suffocation, but when this failed an executioner was ordered to behead her. Due to inexperience or lack of courage, he failed to completely sever her head with the three blows prescribed by law. She lay dying on the pavement of her bath, fully conscious, with her head half severed, until she expired three days later. The position of her fingers, three extended on her right hand and one on the left, was accepted as her final profession of faith in the Holy Trinity. Her death occurred about the year 177.

Christians clothed the body in rich robes of silk and gold and placed it in a cypress coffin in the same position in which she had died. She was first interred in the Catacomb of St. Callistus. In 822 Pope Pascal I had the body removed together with the relics of Valerianus and Tiburtius, and others, to the church dedicated to her memory.

An exhumation of the incorrupt body was made in 1599 and a sculpture made by Stefano Maderno at this time represents the saint in the exact posture of her body. The statue is found immediately in front of the altar under which the body of the saint is kept.

It was long believed that the Basilica of St. Cecilia was built over her family's mansion. Excavations made at the start of this century revealed the remains of a Roman house beneath the nave of the present church. These rooms, as well as a chapel, remain accessible to the visitor. In the basilica, the second chapel on the right is called the Caldarium and is the room where the saint was condemned to be suffocated. The conduits are preserved which contained the water heated in the lower room. The marble slab on the altar is the one on which she was placed during the attempted suffocation and may be the one on which she died.

The Basilica of St. Cecilia witnessed the marriage of St. Frances of Rome, and here two of Frances' children are buried.

Cecilia is often depicted in art with an organ to express what was often attributed to her in panegyrics and poems based on her Acts, that ". . . while the musicians played at her nuptials she sang in her heart to God only." When the Academy of Music was founded in Rome in 1584 she was made patroness of the institute, whereupon her veneration as patroness of church music became universal.

St. Charles Borromeo

A T 22 years of age, when Charles was not yet ordained a priest, he was appointed a cardinal by his uncle Pope Pius IV. The death of his elder brother was a turning point in his life. While he had always practiced virtue, from the time of his bereavement he began to live the life of a saint. He resumed his university studies and was ordained in 1563. As the archbishop of Milan he immediately began the great reform that occupied him until his death. With his inheritance he founded schools, hospitals and seminaries and established many organizations for the rekindling of devotion and the expansion of the Faith. Because of the reforms which were not to everyone's liking, he suffered for a time from slander, vicious criticism and even threats of bodily harm. He completely won the faith and devotion of his people during the plague of 1576 when he cared for the sick, unselfishly giving of his energy and material possessions to relieve their sufferings while many were deserting their sick and fleeing the city. Even though he worked closely with the sick he did not fall victim to the disease and for the next eight years continued to live a holy and austere life.

After his death in 1584 the love of his flock was expressed by constant pilgrimages to his tomb with donations of all manner of precious jewelry and gems for the adornment of his shrine.

The body of the saint is incorrupt, but this is credited to the embalming it received soon after death. The face is covered with a silver mask, while the body is clothed in gem-studded vestments. The saint's jewel-like reliquary is of exquisite beauty, being crafted of geometric pieces of rock crystal set in silver and adorned with numerous miniature angels and religious figures of superior workmanship. The relic is kept in the Cathedral of Milan, Italy.

St. Clare of Montefalco

I N addition to the conserved body of St. Clare, the Augustinian monastery of the saint possesses other relics of exceptional interest: her heart in which are clearly imprinted the symbols of the Redeemer's Passion, and three pellets, which in a unique fashion represent the mystery of the Trinity, a devotion to which the saint was particularly attracted.

Having displayed signs of infused knowledge and an unusual sanctity, Clare was permitted at the age of seven to join a group of recluses. After six years she received permission from the bishop of Spoleto to join her sister, Joan, in a community which was later given the Rule of the Augustinian Order. After the death of her sisters, the saint reluctantly accepted the office of abbess, yet she performed her responsibilities so virtuously and deligently as to merit the admiration of her community.

Her life was distinguished by the performance of miracles, the spirit of prophecy, and a singular understanding of divine mysteries. The saint died in her 40th year on August 17, 1308.

After Clare's death her sisters remembered the words she had once uttered, "If you seek the cross of Christ, take my heart; there you will find the suffering Lord." These words were taken literally and her larger than average heart revealed, upon its extraction, clearly distinguishable symbols of the Lord's Passion. The figures are composed of cardiac tissue and include:

"The crucifix which is about the size of one's thumb. The head of the Crucified inclines toward the right arm. The clearly formed corpus is a pallid white, save for the tiny aperture in the right side which is a livid reddish color. White tissue covers the loins of the Crucified as a loin-cloth. The scourge is formed of a hard whitish nerve, the knobbed ends of which represent the tongues of that cruel instrument of torture. The column is formed of a round white nerve, hard as stone, and entwined by a nerve denoting the cord with which Christ was fastened to the pillar during the scourging. The crown of thorns is of tiny sharp nerves resembling thorns. The three nails are formed of dark fibrous tissue and are exceedingly sharp. The largest of these was attached to the inner wall of the heart by a thread of flesh. The lance is represented by a nerve which has every likeness to the shape of that instrument. The sponge is formed of a single nerve resembling a reed with a tiny cluster of nerve endings resembling the sponge at its tip."[1]

These symbols are believed to have been imprinted on her heart during a vision in which she heard from the lips of the Lord: "I have sought a place in the world where I might plant My cross, and have found no better site than your heart." The iconography of the saint often depicts a figure of the saint holding a crucifix with the end of the vertical beam penetrating her heart.

A large part of the heart is enclosed in a bust of the saint and can be viewed under a sheet of crystal that covers the chest portion of the figure.

The three pellets previously mentioned were found in the gall of the saint at the time of the extraction of her heart. These pellets, about the size of hazel nuts, ". . . were judged by theologians to be symbols of the Trinity, as it was found that any one of them was as heavy as the other two, and at times any one of them equalled the weight of all three together."[2] These pellets can be seen under a circular crystal situated in a jeweled cross.

The incorrupt body of the saint can be seen in her shrine in the Church of the Holy Cross in Montefalco.

Clare's canonization occurred in 1881. During the year 1968 Montefalco and the Augustinian order prayerfully observed the seventh centennial celebration of the saint's birth.

[1]The preceeding is quoted directly from literature supplied to the author by the Sanctuario S. Chiara da Montefalco.
[2]Taken from literature supplied by the shrine.

The Voice of Blessed Clelia Barbieri

S INCE the time of her death in 1870 the voice of Blessed Clelia has been heard innumerable times in the houses of the order she founded. Especially at LeBudrie, Italy, the city of her birth and the location of the first house of her order, her voice is heard accompanying the sisters in their hymns, in religious readings, and in their conversations. It is often heard accompanying the priest during the celebration of Mass and during sermons. Even in the parish churches it is heard lingering among the faithful. The mother superior of the order has stated that, "This prodigious gift stimulates us to do well, increases our faith, is a relief to the trials of life, and gives us a great desire for heaven."

Blessed Clelia was born in 1847 to poor parents engaged in working hemp. Although they were unable to provide her with a formal education she nevertheless grew in the wisdom and grace of God. At the age of 11 she received her First Holy Communion and edified everyone by her fervent religious conduct. By the time she was 21 she had attracted to herself three young ladies who shared a similar desire to participate in the performance of good works. After acquiring a small house near a church in LeBudrie in the province of Bologna, they began living a community life while retaining their secular status. During this time two phenomena were observed. Frequently during work Clelia would become transfigured while exchanging mysterious words with someone the others could not see, but whom they felt to be present, and at times during ecstatic prayer she was seen to levitate.[1] After Clelia's death the devout group developed into a religious order, placed themselves under the protection of St. Francis of Paola, Clelia's favorite saint, and adopted the name *Suore Minime dell'Addolorata* (Little Sisters of Our Lady of Sorrows). Engaged in teaching Christian doctrine, sewing for the poor, aiding the sick and performing every manner of charitable assistance to those in need, the order flourished and proudly claimed Clelia as its foundress.

The saint's final illness was caused by a lung ailment from which she died on July 13, 1870, after seven months of intense sufferings. To console her companions who had assembled around her deathbed, she promised: "Be of good heart because I am going to Paradise, but I will all

[1] *The Power of Goodness, The Life of Blessed Clelia Barbieri*, Cesare Zappulli, St. Paul Editions, The Daughters of St. Paul, Boston, 1980, p. 53.

the time be with you just the same; I will never abandon you."[2] Her promise has been kept in an extraordinary manner, as exhibited by her voice, which was first heard on July 13, 1871, one year after her death. While the sisters were in the chapel,

> "... there was the sound of a high-pitched, harmonious and heavenly voice that accompanied the singing in the choir; at times it sang solo, at others it harmonized with the choir, moving across from right to left; sometimes it passed close by the ears of one or other of the sisters."[3]

The voice has been described as one unlike any of this earth. Always sweet and gentle, it is sometimes sad, and not only is it frequently accompanied by angelic strains, but is itself often transformed into the purest celestial music. Many have claimed that when the voice is very audible, of a high tone and distinct, it signifies happy tidings and approval; when it is deep and mournful it signals suffering or the coming of sad events. Many witnesses of unquestionable integrity, including her original companions, various superiors and sisters of the order, priests and lay workers in the order's hospital, have adquately testified that they have heard the voice. All their testimonies have been carefully kept.[4] Moreover, many witnesses have given sworn testimonies before ecclesiastical tribunals who investigated the prodigy prior to Clelia's solemn beatificiation on October 27, 1968.

As if the sounding of her voice were not enough, the Beata also makes her presence known by "knocks", which were similarly used by St. Pascal Baylon and Bl. Anthony of Stroncone after their deaths.

Among the articles kept by the order is the penitential chain Clelia wore about her body, and a small crucifix. In the chapel of the motherhouse is a silver reliquary containing the bones of the foundress. Here the sisters frequently hear Clelia's heavenly voice that does much to encourage her listeners in the way of spiritual advancement.

St. Colette

THIS saint apparently had difficulty in selecting a religious order whose exercises of virtue were rigorous enough to suit her require-

[2]*La Beata Clelia Barbieri*, Luciano Gherardi, Utoa, Bologna, 1969, p. 35.
[3]Zappulli, *Op. cit.* pp. 61-62.
[4]*Beata Clelia Barbieri, Fondatrice Delle Minime Dell'Addolorata.* Giorgio Cardinal Gusmini, Casa Generalizia, Suore Minime dell'Addolorata, Bologna, 1958, pp. 159-184.

ments. She joined in succession the Beguinage at Amiens, the Benedictine Hospital Sisters at Corbie and the Poor Clares at Moncel, who were then observing the modified rule of Urban IV. Finding all three too relaxed, she became a Franciscan tertiary, took a vow of seclusion and lived for three years in a cell adjoining the Church of Notre Dame in Corbie. After a vision of St. Francis and St. Clare, she undertook the reform of the Franciscan Order, being vested by Benedict XIII who named her superior general of all the convents of the order. The Colettine reform spread quickly throughout France, Spain, Flanders and Savoy, and even influenced the order of the Friars Minor. The saint, a friend of St. Vincent Ferrer, died at Ghent, France, in 1447 and was canonized May 24, 1807.

The saint's relics are enshrined in a golden reliquary, resembling a small church, at the Monastery of St. Claire in Poligny where other small articles are kept, including a wooden bowl that was used by the saint, an autographed letter, her seal and a wax tablet book covered with an ivory cover that depicts the adoration of the Magi.

During a vision of the Redeemer, she received from His hands a small cross with precious stones called by the Poor Clares "The Cross of Heaven." This is kept with great care at the Monastery of St. Claire in Besançon, France.[1]

Cosmas and Damian

COSMAS and Damian were twins and early Christian physicians who performed their services for the poor without payment. It is presumed that this charity brought many to the Christian faith.

Born in Arabia, they practiced their healing ministry in the seaport of Aegea and attained a great reputation.

When the Diocletian persecution began, the prefect had them arrested and ordered them to recant. They remained constant under torture and in a miraculous manner suffered no injury when drowning and burning were attempted. They were finally beheaded with the sword — their three brothers dying as martyrs with them. Their executions took

[1] See the chapter on Crucifixes for details of this cross, and other details of her life.

place on September 27 in the year 287. Their feast day, however, is now celebrated on September 26.

The remains of the two martyrs were for a time buried in the city of Cyrus in Syria. Emperor Justinian I (527-565) was deeply devoted to the saints and not only restored the city of Cyrus in their honor, but also rebuilt and adorned their church at Constantinople after he was cured of a dangerous illness through their intercession.

In Rome, Pope Felix IV erected a church in their honor and embellished it with mosaics that are among the most valuable in the ancient city. The remains of both martyrs are kept in a translucent alabaster tomb under the altar in the lower chapel of the Church of Santi Cosma E Damiano.

The saints are regarded as patrons of physicians, surgeons, druggists and dentists. They are invoked in the Canon of the Mass and in the Litany of the Saints.

St. Dominic

THE founder of the Order of Preachers, otherwise known as the Dominican Order, was born in Old Castile about the year 1170 to parents who undoubtedly belonged to the nobility of Spain. Of his father, Felix Guzman, little is known except that he was in every sense the worthy head of a family of saints. Dominic's mother, Joanna of Aza, was held in the greatest admiration for the nobility of her soul, and was beatified by Leo XII. Dominic's two brothers also benefited from the example of such pious souls: Antonio became a secular priest and spent most of his life ministering to the sick, Manes followed his brother's example as a friar preacher and was beatified by Gregory XVI.

Dominic was ordained a priest after completing his education with distinction. Even before his ordination, however, Don Martin de Bazan, the bishop of Osma, persuaded him to become a member of the cathedral chapter for the purpose of assisting in its reform, an assignment he performed with great success. While on a mission for the church he journeyed through Toulouse and was shocked by the spiritual ruin effected by the Albigensian heresy. It was then that he envisioned an order that would labor in combating error and preaching the lessons of the Gospel.

With his followers Dominic fought valiantly and strenuously against the heresy and opened houses for women where they were safe from the evil influences that abounded. These houses were later recognized as convents of the Second Order of Saint Dominic.

During a visit to Rome Dominic and his bishop were asked by Innocent III to help the Cistercians in converting the Albigensians in France. After the bishop's departure from this endeavor Dominic became head of the mission, but he soon realized that the Cistercians were failing because their sumptuous living was resented by the people who were impressed by the austere living of the heretics. The priests he recruited to help in this venture were those willing to lead lives of poverty and penance. These formed the nucleus of his order. They preached extensively and vigorously and conducted debates with prominent heretics, some of whom they converted.

When one of the Cistercians was assassinated, the crime precipitated the crusade under Simon de Montfort. St. Dominic engaged in the events that followed, but always on the side of mercy, preaching peace and laboring for the restoration of religion and morality. So successful was the crusade at Muret that it was altogether declared miraculous and its success was attributed to the Rosary and the prayers of the saint. In gratitude to God for this decisive victory, the crusaders erected a chapel in the Church of Saint-Jacques, which was dedicated to Our Lady of the Rosary.

While it is universally acclaimed that the Rosary was given to the saint during a vision of the Blessed Mother, it seems that the Rosary was in general use before the time of St. Dominic. Tradition tells us that when the Albigensian heresy was devastating the city of Toulouse, St. Dominic sought the help of the Blessed Mother, who instructed him to preach the Rosary among the people as an antidote to heresy and sin. It is known, however, that the recitation of numbered Paters and Aves was commonly practiced early in the Church's history. We read of the hermits of the desert counting such prayers on little stones, and that later the prayers were counted by others on knotted strings. One reputable source tells us that the practice of meditating on definite mysteries arose long after the saint's death, with the introduction of this system being attributed to a certain Carthusian, Dominic the Prussian.

It is shown that of the thousands of devotional treatises, sermons, chronicles, etc., written by the Friars Preachers between 1220 and 1450, no single verifiable passage has been produced which speaks of the Rosary as being instituted by St. Dominic, nor was the Rosary mentioned by those who testified on his behalf during the examination prior to his canonization. Nor yet is the Rosary depicted in the paintings and sculptures for the two and a half centuries following his death. The devotion was entirely ignored in the numerous frescoes in the Church of St. Dominic where the saint is entombed in Bologna. The saint, however, is credited with increasing devotion to the Rosary during a tragic period in Church history.[1]

Several attempts were made to raise the saint to the episcopate, all of which he successfully declined in favor of working with his group of followers for the propagation of true doctrine and the eradication of heresy.

The saint's order was confirmed December 22, 1216. In the same year Dominic preached in various churches in Rome and before the pope and the papal court, which led to his designation as the pope's theologian. The saint traveled extensively to establish houses of his order and like St. Francis of Assisi, his contemporary, he founded the Second Order for women and a Third Order for laymen.

The life of the saint was distinguished by many miracles, including the failure of flames on three occasions to consume the dissertation he had used against the heretics, the raising to life of one Napoleone Orsini, and the appearance of angels with loaves of bread in the refectory of St. Sixtus, in response to his prayers when there was a lack of food.

In 1221, while in Bologna, the saint became ill and died three weeks later. In signing the Bull of Canonization only 13 years after Dominic's death, Gregory IX declared that he no more doubted the saintliness of St. Dominic than he did that of St. Peter and St. Paul.

The saint's order increased rapidly. Five years after his death there were 90 convents. Fifteen years later there were 30,000 members. Among his followers can be numbered such luminaries as St. Thomas Aquinas, St. Vincent Ferrer, Pope St. Pius V, St. Catherine of Siena, St. Martin de Porres and St. Rose of Lima.

Having died in Bologna, the saint was buried there and it is in the Basilica di S. Domenico that his relics are kept. In 1383 during an exhumation, documents found in the tomb authenticated the bones. The skull of the saint at that time was placed in a separate reliquary. The detailed artwork of this container challenges description.

When a new tomb was being assembled in 1473 only 16 of the 21 statues contracted for were completed before the death of the sculptor. It is claimed that Michelangelo suggested to the new sculptor the type of

[1]The Catholic Encyclopedia, The Encyclopedia Press, Inc., New York, 1912, Volume XIII, pp. 184-187.

statues that would best enhance the shrine and indicated their proper placement.

In 1943, during the height of World War II, it was thought best to remove the bones to a safe refuge, since it was feared that the church and the relics might be damaged. When the marble top of the tomb was removed a rustic wooden box was exposed. The thickness of the wood, its roughness and the type of its metal handles all indicated a box of medieval origins. The bones were then x-rayed and counted. Of the 208 bones in a human body, only 125 bones were found on the ancient red cloth at the bottom of the box. It is surmised that the missing bones were distributed to churches of the order to be used as relics.

The Basilica of Santa Sabina in Rome was given to the Dominicans during the lifetime of the saint. Within the church is a low pillar which marks the spot where St. Dominic is thought to have knelt for his nightly vigils. Atop the pillar is a round black stone. It is said that during one of the nightly vigils this was hurled at the saint by an invisible hand from the upper part of the roof. It grazed his head, tore his hood and buried itself in the ground beside him.

The cell occupied by the saint during his stays at Santa Sabina has been turned into an attractive chapel and is shown to all who request to visit and pray there.

St. Dymphna

NEITHER the name of her heathen father nor that of her Christian mother are recorded, but it is known that Dymphna was the only child of a king and queen who ruled a section of Ireland in the seventh century. Dymphna bore a striking resemblance to her beautiful mother, an attribute that threatened her purity and caused the loss of her life.

After the death of the queen, the inconsolable king, on the verge of mental collapse, consented to the court's entreaties that he marry again. The king's only condition was that the new wife should resemble his first. Since no one in the country could compare except the daughter, she was suggested as the replacement for her deceased mother. The emotional turmoil of the king made this extreme plausible. When the illicit marriage was proposed Dymphna fled the country with her confessor, Father Gerebern, together with a court jester and his wife, and crossed the sea to the coast of Belgium. Traveling inland they settled 25 miles from Antwerp in the village of Gheel near the shrine dedicated to St. Martin of Tours.

The king followed Dymphna and on arriving in the village he became enraged when he was again unsuccessful in his marriage proposal. To break Dymphna's resistance the king had her confessor decapitated. When Dymphna, deprived of the priest's support, still remained steadfast, the father in a fury struck off his daughter's head with his own sword. Dymphna was barely 15.

The maiden was soon regarded as a saint, a martyr of purity and a champion over the wiles of the devil that had brought her father to madness. In due time those afflicted with lunacy sought her intercession and journeyed to her tomb in pilgrimage. On account of the growing number of pilgrims, it was decided to give her body and that of her confessor worthier tombs inside the chapel. In digging for the remains the workmen were surprised to find the bodies in two coffins of white stone, of a kind unknown in the neighborhood of Gheel. This gave rise to the legend that the bodies had been interred by angels, since the bodies had been buried by the villagers in a humble manner and because no one had recollection of an interment in white tombs. On exhuming the remains, a red stone identifying the maiden was found on the breast of the saint.

During the Middle Ages those who visited Gheel to invoke the saint were encouraged to make a novena of nine days at the shrine, while many participated in seven ceremonies called penances. Among other practices they were to attend Mass daily and were to recite prayers that were intended to exorcize the demons who were thought to cause the illness. Until the 18th century the same prayers were said in Gheel for all the sick without distinction between those believed devil-ridden and the mentally ill. During these prayers the red stone found on the remains of St. Dymphna was hung around the necks of the afflicted. The weight of each patient was offered in wheat, which was sometimes substituted by the payment of 32 coins. Depending upon the resources of the most difficult cases, the weight of the patient was offered to the saint either in wheat, wine, silver or gold.[1]

The relics of the saint are kept in a reliquary of precious metal in a church that bears her name in Gheel, near Antwerp, Belgium. The church is believed to be situated over the saint's original burial place.

Today Dymphna is invoked worldwide for restoration of mental stability, as well as religious fervor.

[1]The information in this paragraph is taken from papers supplied by the shrine in Gheel.

St. Elizabeth Ann Seton

ELIZABETH Ann Bayley, the first native-born U.S. citizen to be canonized, was born in New York on August 28, 1774, just two years before the start of the American Revolution. Her father was the city's health officer; her mother was the daughter of the rector of St. Andrew's Episcopal Church on Staten Island.

A devoted communicant of the Episcopal Church, she was married at the age of 20 to William Magee Seton, heir to his family's shipping fortune. Theirs was described as a storybook marriage in which both wealth and influential friends were enjoyed. With Alexander Hamilton as a neighbor, the Setons were hosts in 1797 of a birthday party for George Washington.

During the time that her husband's business and health were failing, they journeyed to Leghorn, Italy, to visit business friends in the hope that the climate would improve his health. Here she was introduced to the Catholic Faith. Being particularly attracted to the doctrine of the Real Presence, she wrote home,

> "How happy would we be if we believed what these dear souls believe: that they possess God in the Sacrament, and that He remains in their churches and is carried to them when they are sick. . . . My God, how happy I would be, even so far away from all so dear, if I could find You in the Church as they do. . . ."

On her return to New York she debated her conversion to the Faith that would turn family and friends against her. Two years after her husband's death in 1803, she made her profession of faith at St. Peter's Church on Barclay Street.

The hostilities, which she had suspected would occur at her conversion, became a reality and forced her to leave in 1808 for Baltimore, where she hoped to gain employment to support her five children.

Soon after her arrival, Archbishop John Carroll invited her to open a school for girls in a small house on Paca Street. The building still stands.

The school proved to be only a part of the larger plan that evolved into the formation of a religious sisterhood to which her two sisters-in-law joined.

At the age of 35 Elizabeth pronounced her first vows of poverty,

240

chastity and obedience in the presence of Archbishop Carroll. This community with its religious vows is regarded as the first religious order founded in America. Because of the school she established, she enjoys the title of foundress of the American parochial school system as we now understand it.

The Rule adopted by the new community was that used by St. Vincent de Paul and St. Louise de Marillac for the order they had established in France in 1634, called the Sisters of Charity. Mother Seton's order, known as the Sisters of Charity of Saint Joseph, was united with the order in France after her death.

From Baltimore a house of the new order was established at Emmitsburg, Maryland, a village ten miles from the battlefield of Gettysburg. At first occupying a log cabin, they were next moved to a building known as the Stone House, which was a primitive dwelling where on winter mornings the community awoke to find themselves covered with snow blown in through the cracks in walls and windows. Here two of her daughters and a dozen of her religious sisters, none over 25 years of age, preceded her in death. Mother Seton, herself, died there in 1821.

Another building on the property, called the White House, was also occupied for a time by Mother Seton and now serves as a museum housing some of the articles she used in life, including her slippers, rosary, a notebook and objects used by the saint and members of the community during the early years in Emmitsburg.

Mother Seton was first buried beside two of her daughters, but her remains were moved in 1846 to the Mortuary Chapel, built with funds provided by her son, which was located in the middle of the graveyard. Ten years later, after saying Mass at her tomb, Cardinal Gibbons announced that he would begin the cause of Mother Seton's canonization — a process that would not end until nearly 100 years later.

A new provincial house for the order was started in Emmitsburg in 1962. Its huge chapel was formally dedicated in 1965 and reflects the relationship of the order with that in France, it being enhanced with stained-glass windows reflecting the acts of mercy performed by the French order — services for which Mother Seton was also noted — and with mosiacs depicting the visions of the Miraculous Medal with which St. Catherine Laboure was favored in Paris.

An area of the chapel had been reserved for the saint's relics. Above the exit door of the chapel is the coat of arms of Pope Paul VI, who proclaimed on September 14, 1975: "Elizabeth Ann Seton is a saint. She is the first daughter of the United States of America to be glorified with this incomparable attribute."

St. Elizabeth of Hungary

WHEN only four years of age, Elizabeth was betrothed by her father, King Andrew II of Hungary, to the hereditary duke of Thuringia, Germany. Ludwig and Elizabeth were married when he was 20 and she 14. During their six years together, two daughters and a son were born. Theirs was a happy and exemplary marriage, but members of the family caused Elizabeth considerable suffering by disapproving of her religious practices and criticizing her generosity to the poor. Her husband, however, defended her actions and encouraged her charitable endeavors.

According to legend, one winter day Elizabeth was carrying bread to the poor when she was approached by her husband, who asked to see the contents of her mantle. Upon opening the garment roses fell instead of bread. It is from pictures depicting this scene that she is most readily identified.

After her husband died on the Crusade of Emperor Frederick II, she was cruelly driven from the castle with her small children, and for a time had to seek shelter in a pig sty. The poor of the city, who had previously benefited from her generosity, refused to shelter her for fear of offending the new ruler, who disliked her. She was at last rescued by her aunt, an abbess, and her uncle, Eckbert, bishop of Bamberg. After a time she and her children were restored to honor.

Elizabeth was a contemporary of St. Francis of Assisi and established a convent for Franciscans in the capital city of Eisenach. Following the death of her husband she took the habit as a member of the Franciscan Third Order, living in her own home, but following a rule designed for laymen.

Elizabeth led an austere and virtuous life, aided orphans and the poor and founded two hospitals where she personally assisted with the care of the sick. She suffered greatly from the severity of her confessor, Conrad of Marburg, who directed her spiritual life for seven years. She died November 19, 1231, at the age of 24 and was canonized four years later on May 1, 1235. She was buried in the chapel of the hospital where miracles of healing were immediately witnessed. During the same year the cornerstone of the Church of St. Elizabeth at Marburg was laid and the following year the body of the saint was moved there.

Pilgrimages to the grave in this church were so numerous they were at times compared to those at the Shrine of St. James at Santiago de Compostela.

The relics were secure until 1539 when the Protestant Philip, landgrave of Hesse, a direct descendent of the saint, visited the church for the purpose of discontinuing the pilgrimages. He had the shrine opened and removed the relics. He placed them in the forage bag of a servant and took them with him to the castle. He also removed the head of the saint, which was kept in the sacristy, together with a crown and a golden chalice given by Emperor Frederick II on the day of the solemn translation 303 years before. In compliance with the command of Emperor Charles V, the relics were restored to the church at Marburg on July 12, 1548, but were not replaced in the magnificent golden shrine. Most were soon dispersed to Hanover, Cologne, Breslau and Berançon. The golden chalice given by Emperor Frederick II is now kept in the Historical Museum at Stockholm. A purse or a robe is in the Benedictine Cloister at Andechs. Several relics are kept in the Marburg University Museum. The head and several bones of the saint lie in a glass case framed with gold in the Convent of St. Elizabeth in Vienna. The golden crown taken by Philip was restored and rests atop the skull of the saint.

What is reputed to be a glass cup used by the saint is at Erfurth; the saint's wedding ring is claimed at Braunfels, where there is also her Book of Hours, a table and a straw chair. A veil is shown at Tongres.

The shrine in which the saint's relics were kept until 1539 is shown at Marburg, where it is considered one of the most wonderful productions of the goldsmith's skill in the Middle Ages. It has also been claimed that ". . . we know not if there be elsewhere so wonderful a work of Christian art of so remote a period." Until 1810 the shrine was encrusted with 824 gems; 117 of the most valuable were removed by order of the Franco-Westphaliangovernment.

Together with St. Louis, king of France, Elizabeth is the patron of the Franciscan Third Order.

St. Frances Xavier Cabrini

FRANCESCA Maria was the last of 13 children born to Agostino and Stella Cabrini, a farming couple of Sant'Angelo Lodigiano, Italy. Born on July 15, 1850, she was accustomed as a child to performing all manner of farm chores and at 13 completed her primary studies under her sister Rosa, the village schoolmistress. Her studies were continued by the Daughters of the Sacred Heart in Arluno, where at age 18 she received her teacher's license with highest honors. She was refused entrance into this order because of her apparent frailty. Instead, she taught at Vidardo, where in 1874 she was persuaded to begin charitable work at an orphanage in Codogno. Here she took a religious habit and made her vows in 1877.

When the bishop was forced to close the orphanage in 1880, she was made prioress of the Institute of Missionary Sisters of the Sacred Heart, an order formed from seven of the orphanage girls. Between 1882 and 1887 seven houses had been opened in northern Italy, with a free school and nursery operating in Rome. Formal approval for the order was received from Rome on March 12, 1888.

Although as a child she had aspired to live the life of a missionary in China (her favorite game was the placement of flowers in paper boats to represent missionaries journeying to the Far East), Divine Providence willed otherwise. Instead of China, Pope Leo XIII and Bishop Scalabrini of Piacenza encouraged her to undertake missionary endeavors in the United States. The pope's wishes were promptly obeyed. Mother Cabrini and six of her sisters sailed to America on March 23, 1889.

In New York, Mother Cabrini devoted her energies to working among Italian immigrants. As a shrewd and astute businesswoman she founded convents, schools, orphanages and hospitals throughout the United States, South America and Europe.

The foundress became a naturalized citizen in 1910 and the following year was elected superior general for life.

Even though revered as the holy foundress of the order she, nevertheless, continued throughout her life to perform all the menial chores necessary for convent life.

Although frail and anemic, she crossed the sea 30 times establishing 67 houses in 38 years.

After suffering from recurring bouts of malaria she had contracted in Rio de Janeiro, where she had established a foundation of her order, she finally succumbed to the disease in Columbus Hospital in Chicago on December 22, 1917.

Pope Pius XI, who knew the foundress well, authorized in 1931 the inquiry for the Process of Beatification. Contrary to reports stating that the body of the saint was found incorrupt, when the Roman commission opened the casket for the official recognition of the relic, the body was found to have been reduced in the normal manner.[1] First buried in West Park, New York, at a place the saint had once designated, her remains were conveyed to New York City in 1933 where they were placed in a simulated figure that was arranged within a crystal coffin beneath the main altar of the chapel of Mother Cabrini High School.

Mother Cabrini was the first United States citizen to attain the honors of the altar. During the canonization ceremony on July 7, 1946, Pope Pius XII praised the accomplishments of the immigrant saint, stating that although her constitution was frail, by acquiescing to the will of God she accomplished what seemed beyond the normal strength of a woman.

St. Francis of Assisi

A S the son of a wealthy cloth merchant, Francis Bernardone had sufficient resources to indulge in the amusements and adventures then in vogue during the latter part of the 12th century. While he engaged freely in these activities, he was conversely disinterested in formal learning or the functions of his father's business. Grace eventually transformed him. With the literal interpretation of the Gospels, Francis began to imitate Jesus in all things and embraced Lady Poverty, going barefoot and wearing rough clothes that caused great distress and embarrassment to his family.

Once when he was praying in the Church of St. Damian, outside the walls of Assisi, he heard a voice coming from the crucifix which said to him three times, "Francis, go and repair My house which you see is falling down." Seeing that the Church of St. Damian was then in poor repair, the saint understood that it was this building and not necessarily the Church in general that should be repaired. Using money from the sale of his father's fabrics to buy materials needed for the repairs, he was subsequently brought to the bishop's court by his enraged father, who not only disinherited him, but also demanded reimbursement for the fabrics Francis took without his permission. It was noted that the father left the court "burning with rage, but with an exceeding sorrow."

After the repairs to St. Damian's Church were completed, the saint

[1]*History of the Precious Remains of St. Frances Xavier Cabrini, Mother Cabrini High School, New York, New York, Paper.*

retired to a deserted chapel belonging to the abbey of Benedictine monks on Monte Subasio, called the Portiuncula or "the little piece," located two miles from Assisi. Named for Our Lady of the Angels, Francis repaired it and established his abode nearby. The Benedictines eventually presented the chapel to Francis on the condition that it continue as the head church of the Franciscan Order.

The first disciples who joined Francis in 1209 comprised the nucleus of the Order of Friars Minor. In 1212 St. Clare of Assisi placed herself under his guidance and brought into being the religious order now called the Poor Clares. Ten years later the Third Order was established for people who wished to follow the ideals of the Franciscans while remaining in the secular world.

During the saint's absence from Assisi in the year 1221, vicars of the order introduced certain innovations that displeased Francis and instigated his resignation from the direction of the order.

During the Christmas season of 1223, while Francis was in residence in Grecchio, he assembled a crib scene and although the making of a crib was probably not unknown at the time, Francis is credited with popularizing the custom.

In 1224 the saint retired to Mount Alvernia, taking with him Brother Leo, his secretary and confessor. On September 17 he received the stigmata, the wounds of the Passion of Christ, the first recorded person in the history of the Church to be so honored. The saint lived only two years after this event, dying on October 3, 1226, at the age of 44 or 45 as he lay on the bare earth to signify his poverty and detachment from all things of the world.

Although he had requested that he be buried in the criminals' cemetery on the Colle d'Inferno, his body was taken in solemn procession to the Church of St. George in Assisi with an emotional pause along the way at the convent of the Poor Clares, who met the entourage and wept at the loss of their spiritual father. The body remained at St. George Church until 1230, two years after his canonization, when it was secretly moved to the great basilica built by Brother Elias. It remained unseen until 1818 when it was relocated deep beneath the high altar in the lower church. His remains now recline in a triple urn atop an altar in a special chapel of the Basilica of St. Francis.

The basilica has, in addition to his remains, several unique relics, including two habits that the saint wore, one of rough grey cloth covered with patches, and a white one made for him during his final illness by St. Clare herself. In the opinion of the priests of the basilica, one of the dearest relics is an autographed blessing of St. Francis written to Brother

Leo, his close companion and confessor. This is displayed in a special reliquary framed with a trailing vine of golden roses.

Standing inside the great church of Santa Maria degli Angeli is the little chapel the saint restored, called the Portiuncula. During a vision, Jesus urged him to request of the pope a plenary indulgence for all who would visit there. The pope readily approved the indulgence, which is called the Portiuncular Indulgence, or the Pardon of Assisi. (See "Portiuncula" elsewhere in this volume for an explanation of the indulgence.) Pope John Paul II mentioned this indulgence in 1982, calling St. Francis a champion of reconciliation.

The order that St. Francis founded encompasses three main branches: the Friars Minor, Friars Minor Capuchin and the Friars Minor Conventual, which together comprise the largest religious institute in the Church.

It has been said that St. Francis has had more books written about him than has any other saint in the history of the Church, a record now challenged by St. Thérèse of the Child Jesus. His popularity is undoubtedly based on his simplicity, his love, respect and intimacy with all God's creations: the birds and animals with which he is often depicted in art. Pope Benedict XV once declared that Francis ". . . was the most perfect image of Christ that ever was."

Numerous popes have extolled the saint's virtues, including Pope John XXIII who did so during a visit to Assisi in 1962 before the Second Vatican Council. The tomb of the saint was likewise visited by Pope John Paul II, who first prayed there in 1978 two weeks after his election. The pope's next visit was in March of 1982 when he closed the celebrations in observance of the 800th anniversary of the saint's birth. And at that time he addressed more than 200 Italian bishops in the Basilica of St. Francis before praying before the tomb of the saint and visiting the Portiuncula.

St. Francis Borgia

D ESCRIBED as one of the handsomest, richest and most honored nobles in Spain, Francis Borgia was the great-grandson of King Ferdinand V of Aragon and a cousin of Emperor Charles V. Known as the Duke of Gandia, Francis was attracted to the religious life even as a child, but his vocation was hindered by his father, who placed him in the imperial court. During his life at court Francis avoided all ambitions, gallantry, luxury and gaming, attended Mass frequently and practiced various penances. Responding to the encouragement of the royal couple, he consented to a marriage with Eleanor de Castro, a Portuguese lady who had been educated with the empress. The marriage produced eight children and brought various titles, honored positions and official duties. In 1546, after 17 years of marriage, Doña Eleanor died. At this time their five young sons were in the imperial service, two girls were married and one was destined to become a Poor Clare.

During his early days as a widower, Francis met a member of the Jesuit order and made a retreat under his direction according to the Spiritual Exercises of St. Ignatius. As a result, Francis was determined to enter a religious order. After properly providing for his children, and with his official titles awarded to his eldest son, Francis set out for Rome in 1550 and was received into the Jesuit order by St. Ignatius himself. After required studies he was ordained a priest, served the order at first in menial tasks, and for a time worked for the order's interests in Portugal.

Regarded as a saint during his lifetime, he was the first to recognize the greatness of the Carmelite nun, Teresa of Avila. His sermons were regularly attended by Cardinal Charles Borromeo and Cardinal Ghislieri, who would become St. Pius V.

Francis fulfilled many offices and was the third successor of Ignatius as general of the Jesuits. For seven years he promoted the work of the order in all parts of the world, founded colleges, enlarged and improved others, and built the Church of Sant'Andrea Al Quirinale in Rome. While general of the order, St. Francis published a new edition of the Rule of the society and drew up regulations and directions for those members who were engaged in special fields of activity. It has been estimated that the society owes to St. Francis Borgia its characteristic form and true perfection.

After sending messages to his children and grandchildren, St. Francis died at midnight of September 30-October 1, 1572, at the age of 62. His canonization was achieved in 1670. His body is enshrined in the principal Jesuit church, Il Gesu, in Rome where the founder of the Jesuits, St. Ignatius, is also entombed.

The first Mass said by Francis Borgia was celebrated in 1551 at Loyola in the family home of St. Ignatius at the same altar where St. Ignatius and his family often prayed. The vestments worn by the saint at this first Mass are carefully kept, as is his death mask.

St. Francis of Paola

A T the tender age of 13, Francis d'Alessio visited the Monastery of S. Marco Argentano and asked for the Franciscan habit. After a votive year among the Friars Minor he made a pilgrimage to Rome, Assisi, Loreto and Monte Cassino. Upon his return to Paola, he retired to a secluded spot and lived as a hermit in a narrow cave, until his hermitage was discovered by hunters who spread the news of his sanctity. Having accepted his first followers in 1435, Francis became, at the age of 19, the founder of a new religious institute, the Order of Minims (Least of Brethren), who lived according to an austere rule that was later approved by Pope Julius II in 1506. With the increase in the number of Religious, Francis built a monastery and church which he dedicated to St. Francis of Assisi. Still standing at Paola is the church which the saint built stone by stone. So numerous were the miracles worked during the construction of this building that various sites are enclosed in the "Zone of Miracles."

Known during his lifetime as a wonder-worker, it was with the encouragement of Pope Sixtus IV that the saint journeyed to France in 1483 where he was called to the bedside of Louis XI, who was then near death. Unwilling at first to leave Italy, the saint remained in France after the death of the king and labored to restore peace between France and Brittany and between France and Spain. These endeavors and the tutoring of the future Charles VIII kept him in France for 25 years until his death at the monastery of Plessis-Les-Tours on Good Friday, April 2, 1507. He was then 91 years of age.

Six years after the saint's death he was beatified by Pope Leo X, who also canonized him in 1519. The saint's body remained marvelously incorrupt for 55 years, until the Huguenots deliberately burned it in 1562. Some of the bones that were saved from destruction were kept by the Cathedral of Tours until they were restored to the Sanctuary of Paola in 1935 on the occasion of the fifth centennial of the order's foundation.

The altar in which the relics are now kept is covered with engraved silver plates embellished with gold, topaz and amethysts. The center of the frontal panel exposes the reliquary, executed in a baroque fashion, that is sculptured of silver and gold. To the left of the altar is a niche which encloses several other important relics. On the top shelf is an imposing bust of the saint which encloses one of his ribs. Made in silver during the 16th century, the figure holds in its right hand a staff with which the saint is usually pictured, while under the left hand is a replica of the city of Paola. The word *Charitas*, which is always included in the saint's iconography, is displayed on the front panel between two attentive angels. Beneath this figure is an ornate glass-sided case containing relics officially recognized by the Church in 1581.[1] These include a capuche, a shirt, a pair of clogs, stockings, a rosary, a pot in which the saint is said to have cooked beans without a fire, an ancient manuscript of the saint's Process of Beatification and a crucifix before which the saint prayed in his hermitage. Also preserved here is the mantle which the saint and a companion used as a boat to cross the Strait of Messina.[2] Because of this miracle and others involving the sea, the saint was declared patron of seafarers by Pope Pius XII in 1943.

Of interest to the visitor of Paola are the oratory and the three original cells that the saint built for his first followers, and the cave in which he lived as a hermit. The Zone of Miracles contains the furnace in which the saint burned lime for the construction of the church and monastery. Of the two miracles worked here one included the saint's entrance into the blazing furnace to repair it when it was on the verge of exploding. The Cucchiarella Spring gushed forth miraculously when St. Francis struck a tufa rock with his stick to produce water to relieve a workman's thirst. Cucchiarella means ladle, and was so named because pious pilgrims scoop up the water with a ladle for drinking and for carrying home. It is prayerfully believed that the waters of the spring contain curative elements. Also in Paola is the house in which the saint was born on March 27, 1416. Transformed into a chapel during the saint's sojourn in France, it miraculously survived destruction by bombing during World War II when all the other buildings in the area were destroyed.[3]

The feast day of the saint, April 2, is observed at Paola with special ceremonies which include the Blessing of the Sea and Seafarers with the saint's mantle, and a procession with the saint's silver bust through the streets of the city.

St. Francis of Paola has inspired men of talent such as Bartolomé Murillo, Diego Velázguez, and Francisco Goya and others who made the saint the subject of now valuable and inspiring paintings. He appears in Victor Hugo's *Torquemada* and is the subject of a sonata by Franz Liszt entitled *St. Francis of Paola Walking on the Waters*.

[1] *Santuario Basilica S. Francesco Paola*, Basilica San Francesco, Paola, p. 24.
[2] *Ibid.* p. 24.
[3] *Ibid.* p. 57.

St. Francis de Sales

FRANCIS was born in 1567 near Anney, France, and received an excellent education at Paris and Padua, but declined his father's worldly ambitions in favor of a priestly vocation. His brilliant preaching, his artful direction of souls and his countless conversions brought him to the attention of Church officials who appointed him bishop of Geneva in 1602.

His saintly friends included St. Vincent de Paul and St. Philip Neri. St. John Bosco, described as the wonder-worker of the 19th century, was so attracted to Francis that the religious order he founded, the Salesians, was named for this saintly bishop. Together with St. Jane Frances de Chantal, Francis founded the Order of the Visitation, which now boasts 185 monasteries throughout the world.

Known for his gentleness and patience, the saint died during his 56th year, the 20th of his episcopate. Attended by numerous miracles, the body of the saint was buried at Annecy, in the first monastery of the Visitation Order where it is still found beside the remains of St. Jane Frances de Chantal.

Having died in 1622, the holy bishop was canonized in 1665 and was declared a doctor of the Church in 1877 in view of his excellent writing of which *Introduction to a Devout Life* and *Treatise on the Love of God* are the most popular.

Following his death and autopsy, the heart of the saint was extracted for placement in a silver coffer that was to be kept at the Church of the Visitation of Lyon, the city where he died. His heart is now kept at the Monastery of the Visitation of Treviso, Italy, and is of particular interest.

As recorded by Father Herbert Thurston, S.J., in the *Physical Phenomena of Mysticism*, the heart was seen to exude a clear oil at intervals throughout the years. In March of 1948, because the crystal in which the heart was kept was not well-sealed, permission was received to wrap the heart in a new piece of linen. The heart, found dry at this time, was then covered with the piece of linen and an outer layer of tissue the same color as the heart. In the spring of 1952 spots of white appeared between the relic and the sides of the crystal container. The superior then ordered another examination of the relic, which occurred the same year on August 27. Although not examined scientifically, the powder was thought to resemble salt. This was considered a natural phenomenon because the seal of the container was not perfect, permitting the penetration of air. But when the tissue was removed from the heart, that which had been placed there in 1948, the linen that surrounded the heart was found imbued with blood. This was carefully kept while the heart was wrapped in a new linen and placed in a hermetically sealed crystal especially made to enclose the heart. The container was then placed within the same reliquary.[1]

A notable examination of the relic was undertaken the following year on August 28, 1953. Present were Professor Menenio Bortolozzi of the Institute of Pathology of the Civil Hospital of Treviso, Professor Vincenzo Mario Palmieri, medical director of the University of Naples together with Superior Ecclesiastical Monsignor Sartori of Treviso. The conservation of the heart was declared to be "Not a common occurrence." A disputed opinion was given by one of the professors who surmised that the blood on the cloth was caused by atmospheric humidity which soaked the external material.[2]

One can only wonder about the amount of humidity necessary to cause such a large blood stain in 1952 when it did not develop in the 300 years before when the level of humidity might well have been higher. It was not explained why those present perceived a pleasant fragrance that lingered about the cloth.

A theory is suggested for this appearance of blood sometime after the year 1948. Following World War II many of the convents and monasteries in Europe were in a sad condition with their Religious suffering various kinds of privations. In an effort to remedy the situation the Church decided to organize various orders into federations and confederations. The Visitation Order was the first to be organized by Rome with the appointment of the order's first mother general. For various reasons the confederation was not entirely accepted, therefore the formation of blood about the heart of St. Francis was accepted as a sign of the founder's dissatisfaction with the arrangement. The confederation was eventually dismissed, although the federation of the order is still functioning for the purpose of offering mutual assistance.

Even though she did not continue to function as head of the order, the one and only mother general of the Visitation Order was Sister Bernard-Marie de Uriarte, who was permitted to retain the title until her death.

[1]From information supplied by the Visitation nuns of Treviso.
[2]Ibid.

St. Germaine Cousin

G ERMAINE was born into poor circumstances in Pibrac, near Toulouse, France. Shortly after her birth she unfortunately lost her devoted mother. Her weak constitution, her withered right arm, and her scrofulous neck with its discharging sores made her an object of revulsion to her stepmother who constantly persecuted her. It is recorded that the father also had little affection for the child, and so it may be rightly assumed, since he permitted her to be ejected from the house when other children were born. She was forced to sleep in the stable upon a heap of twigs beneath a stair. She was begrudgingly fed scraps and was denied the company of the children whom she loved. Even at a tender age she was forced to shepherd the flocks.

The little shepherdess' virtues and sanctity did not go unnoticed by the villagers. Many of them witnessed unusual occurrences, which they considered miraculous. We are told that it was necessary for her to cross a stream, which was often swollen by rain, to reach the village church for her daily attendance at Holy Mass. On one occasion, when the current was particularly strong, the villagers were astonished to see the rushing water separate to provide a dry passageway. The sheep, which she often took with her to church, never strayed from her staff, which she stuck in the ground. And it is known that not once were they threatened by the wolves that inhabited the neighboring forest.

The most celebrated incident involving the little maiden that is often depicted in her iconography occurred one winter day when her stepmother was pursuing her with a stick, loudly accusing her of stealing bread for the poor. Upon being ordered to open her folded apron, there fell out only fragrant flowers of a variety unknown to the region. The witnesses of this event, Pierre Pailles and Jeanne Salaires, gave sworn testimony concerning this miracle, which is reminiscent of a similar marvel recorded of St. Elizabeth of Hungary.

Germaine died one night on her pallet of straw, where her father found her body the next morning. According to tradition, two monks traveling during the night from Toulouse stopped by the ruins of a castle where they heard angelic melodies. They saw a great beam of light rising from a distant building and extending into the sky. Heavenly figures were seen descending into the building and later ascending with another figure. Upon reaching Pibrac the next morning, they inquired if anyone

253

had died during the night and were told of the death of the little shepherdess.

In view of her saintly conduct and the many miracles witnessed by the townsfolk, the body of the maiden was buried in the village church of Pibrac. Germaine was almost forgotten until the year 1644, when a distant relative named Edualde died. Two church workers, Gaillard Barous and Nicholas Case, set about preparing a grave for Edualde adjacent to Germaine's. Upon lifting the flagstone covering the tomb, the workers were amazed to find a beautiful young girl lying in a perfect state of preservation. A tool that one of the men had used to remove the stone had slipped and injured the nose of the corpse, causing it to bleed. The dress and the wreath of flowers upon her head had remained fresh and fragrant. The older villagers identified Germaine, who had died 43 years before, by the withered arm and the wound that the scrofulous condition had left on her neck. The lead casket in which the body was kept for many years is still preserved in the village church.

Because of the many miracles ascribed to her, Church officials were encouraged to seek a formal authorization of her cultus. After unfortunate delays caused by the French Revolution, she was eventually canonized in 1867, 266 years after her death.

The virginal body that remained whole and incorrupt for almost 200 years was barbarously destroyed in 1795 during the French Revolution. Now only some bones are kept in a figure representing the little saint. These are clothed in garments of exquisite lacy fabrics. The figure can be viewed through the Gothic windows of her golden urn. A miniature figure portraying the shepherdess kneeling by some small sheep adorns the top.

St. Helena

ST. Helena is credited with finding the Holy Cross, with collecting the relics of the Passion and with distributing them into secure hands. Such important activities and accomplishments, as well as being honored as the mother of a great emperor, overshadows the fact that she was of humble birth, being the daughter of an innkeeper. Married to a Roman general, Constantius Chlorus, she gave birth to the future Constantine the Great before her husband was made Caesar by Diocletian.

After 22 years of marriage she was divorced by her husband. He had been persuaded to marry Theodora, the stepdaughter of the Emperor Maximianus Herculius. When Helena was widowed 14 years after the divorce, her son Constantine was proclaimed Caesar and, 18 months later, emperor.

It appears that Helena was converted to Christianity when she was 63 years of age. As though to compensate for the years before her conversion, she set out in the year 324 with great zeal and fervor to build churches, to restore and adorn older ones and to find precious relics — in particular the cross on which the Savior died.

She was elevated by her son to the position of empress of the world and mistress of the empire. Still she wore simple clothes, helped the poor and mingled among the humble.

Helena's last days were spent in Palestine venerating the places made sacred by the Lord. With her son beside her she died at the age of 80 about the year 330. According to one report, her remains were taken to Rome. The saint's monumental porphyry mausoleum is kept in the Vatican. Almost six feet high, its reliefs depict Roman cavalry repulsing the Barbarians.

The mausoleum is believed to be empty. Another report claims the relics were taken to Constantinople, where they were laid in the imperial vault of the Church of the Apostles. It is thought that some of the relics were transferred in 849 to the Abbey of Hautvillers in Rheims, according to the report of the monk Altmann in his *Translatio*. Some of the relics are claimed by the Basilica of Santa Maria Aracoeli, where they lie in a splendid 17th-century chapel dedicated to the saint.

Built atop the smallest of the seven hills of Rome, Santa Maria Aracoeli, St. Mary of the Altar of Heaven, stands on the place that once supported the fortress of Rome, and so it symbolizes the triumph of Christianity over the pagan world. Originally built before the fifth century, the little church was progressively enlarged into a magnificent basilica that was entrusted to the Franciscan friars in the 13th century. It seems appropriate that the saint of the fourth century, a convert, should be enshrined in this aged structure that also represents the conversion of Rome to Christianity.

The saint's altar in Santa Maria Aracoeli is surrounded by pillars that support an artistic cupola, while atop the altar stands her statue, dramatically clasping a cross. Beneath this altar is an urn of porphyry, which protects a precious box of the 12th century, which in turn holds some of her remains.

St. Ignatius of Loyola

I GNATIUS was born in the Basque country of Spain in 1491, the last of 13 children. His family belonged to provincial nobility whose members had fought with the kings of Castile since the early 13th century. Ignatius served in the court of a relative during his youth and grew to enjoy gambling, dueling and the exact fulfillment of court rituals. With a chivalrous attitude that was bent on military exploits, he entered the army in 1517. In May of 1521, during a skirmish against the French of Pamplona, he received a serious leg wound that was to leave him with a permanent limp. During his convalescence at his parents' villa at Loyola, he abandoned his worldly life after reading the *Life of Christ* and the lives of the saints. He experienced at this time what he would call the "Discretion of Spirits," a gift whereby he could distinguish between being inspired by God and being led in the wrong direction by other influences. As noted in his *Autobiography*, he was also favored with a vision of the Blessed Mother with the Child Jesus, and this confirmed his reform.

The following year, when he was fully recovered, he bid farewell to his family and pilgrimaged to the Monastery of Montserrat, a famous sanctuary of Our Lady in Catalonia. Here he made a general confession, gave his rich garments to the poor, assumed the clothing of a beggar, and spent a night in prayer before the venerated image of Our Lady. He then journeyed to the nearby Dominican cloister at Manresa, where he spent the next 10 months in a cave subjecting himself to stern trials of self denial and prayer. After receiving mystical graces he began writing the famed *Spiritual Exercises*. Since 1535, when the work was completed, it has served as the basis of countless retreats.

After a visit to the Holy Land, he began at the age of 33 the studies that would result in the reception of degrees from distinguished universities. During his student days his virtuous life caught the attention of several young men, including St. Francis Xavier, who wished to follow his example. To these men Ignatius conveyed his apostolic ideals through his *Spiritual Exercises* and worked with them in hospitals while living a life of poverty. With the motto *"Ad Majorem Dei Gloriam,"*, for the greater glory of God, they identified themselves as members of the Society of Jesus. Ordained priests in 1537, the young men separated to several Italian cities, preaching reform.

In 1540 the order received the approval of Pope Paul III, and St. Francis Xavier journeyed to the Far East as the first Jesuit missionary.

The founding of Jesuit colleges and universities was begun in 1542, and in 1543 the saint organized several institutions for social outcasts.

With the words "Jesus, Jesus" on his lips, Ignatius died in Rome on July 31, 1556. At this time there were already more than 1000 Jesuits in various parts of the world. Today some 30,000 Jesuits work in 103 countries with more than 6,000 in the United States."[1] Two of the missionaries to the United States have been honored by having their statues placed in the Capitol in Washington, D.C.: Père Jacques Marquette, who explored the Mississippi River, and Father Eusebio Kino, who labored in the Mexico-Arizona frontier.

The Church has been enriched by the 31 saints contributed by the Jesuit Order and the 134 other Jesuits who have been beatified.

The body of St. Ignatius lies in a splendid altar in the principal Jesuit church, the Il Gesu in Rome, which was built between 1558 and 1584. In the right transept of this church is found a chapel containing the incorrupt arm of St. Francis Xavier, and in another side chapel are the remains of St. Francis Borgia, an early member of the order. Next to the Gesu are rooms in which St. Ignatius lived and worked during the last 12 years of his life. Here pilgrims may view mementos of the saint and attend Holy Mass.

Dedicated to the saint at Loyola is a magnificent basilica whose cornerstone was laid in 1689. Behind the right wing of the sanctuary, and surrounded by church buildings, is the Santa Casa, the three-storied 14th-century family home of the saint. The pilgrim is invited to tour the rooms and to visit the chamber where the saint was born. The family oratory is conserved, as is the original altarpiece with its statues and paintings.

The most venerated place in this building is the room where Ignatius, at the age of 30, was brought following his serious wounding at the Battle of Pamplona. The place of his conversion is indicated by a statue depicting the saint with a leg bandaged, a book in one hand and the other hand outstretched, while the face is turned heavenward, seemingly at a moment of divine infusion. In addition to the rooms in which Ignatius lived, many articles he used are kept, as well as letters written by him and several of the books he had read. These might have been examined by Pope John Paul II when he visited the saint's birthplace during his celebrated tour of Spain in November 1982. The pope also visited

[1]*Saint Ignatius, A Model for Men with a Mission*, Daniel M. Madden, *Columbia* magazine, November 1979, pp. 12-22.

Navarre, near Loyola, the birthplace of St. Francis Xavier, who was one of the original members and the first missionary of the order founded by St. Ignatius. Thousands crowded a hillside near a medieval castle, where Francis once lived, to hear the pontiff praise missionaries who labor throughout the world.

St. Jean Marie Baptiste Vianney
The Curé of Ars

THE humble 19th-century priest who has endeared himself to Catholics around the world began life in 1786 as the son of a poor farmer in the village of Dardilly, France. Obliged to assist his father in the fields, he was unable to commence his formal education until he was 20 years of age. While an ecclesiastical student he was called for military service and became a delinquent conscript, more or less deliberately, and was obliged for a time to hide to escape Napoleon's police.

Knowing nothing of philosophy and finding it difficult to learn Latin, he twice failed the examinations required before ordination. He was eventually ordained a priest at the age of 30, but was thought to be so imcompetent he was placed for further training in the care of Father Balley, a holy priest in the neighboring village of Ecully. After the death of this good priest, Jean Vianney was transferred to the village of Ars near Lyon, France, where he spent the rest of his life. It was in the conscientious exercise of the functions of the parish priest in this remote French hamlet that the "Curé d'Ars" became known throughout France and the Christian world.

The saint lived an austere life, ate the simplest of foods, wore old clothing and slept on a hard bed. During the last 40 years of his life, his food and sleep were reckoned insufficient, humanly considered, to sustain life. Yet he labored incessantly with humility, gentleness, patience and cheerfulness. It was known that the two hours of sleep he allowed himself each night were frequently interrupted by the devil, who assaulted him with deafening noises, insulting conversation and physical abuse. These diabolical visitations were occasionally witnessed with alarm by the people of the parish, but were casually dismissed by the curé.

The miracles recorded by his biographers are of three classes: the obtaining of money for his charities and food for his orphans; supernatural knowledge of the past and future; and healing of the sick, especially children.

His ability to read the minds and hearts of his penitents caused people to visit him from distant parts. Because of the great number of those who wished to confess to him, he began hearing confessions each day at the unlikely hour of one o'clock in the morning. It has been estimated that, during the last 10 years of his life, he spent from 13 to 18 hours a day in the confessional.

Completely exhausted by apostolic labors and by the additional penances he inflicted on his frail body, he died peacefully on August 4, 1859, at the age of 73. His incorrupt body was exhumed 45 years later on June 17, 1904, because of his impending beatification. His heart was later removed and enclosed in a reliquary that is kept in a separate building called the Shrine of the Curé's Heart.

The magnificent reliquary that contains the body was donated by priests from around the world. It is situated above the altar of the basilica, which was annexed to the old parish church in which the saint labored.

Preserved at Ars are the saint's living quarters, which have been kept exactly as they were on the day of his death. On the walls are the religious pictures that the curé hung himself. These rooms, as well as the old church, can be visited by pilgrims. In both places the articles used by the saint are almost countless. These include: his breviary, a rosary, a blood-stained discipline (knotted rope for self-inflicted punishment), clothing and vestments, kitchen utensils, and a bed once set on fire by a demon.

St. Jean Marie Baptiste Vianney, who as a student had such difficulty being accepted for the priesthood, but who exercised his vocation in such an edifying manner, was canonized in 1925 and was named the patron of parish priests throughout the world.

St. John Berchmans

THE life of this saint closely resembles that of St. Aloysius Gonzaga in many respects, especially in that both were virtuous from early childhood, both were members of the Society of Jesus and both died in

Rome at a young age — Aloysius being 23 and John 22.

Few differences exist in the comparison of their lives. But John was born eight years after the death of Aloysius and, unlike Aloysius, John was not heir to a position in a royal court. Like his counterpart, when a mere nine years of age John delighted in works of piety and religious exercises. He was particularly attracted to the recitation of the Rosary and to serving Holy Mass, a practice which he is said to have performed two and sometimes three times a day.

After meeting certain opposition to his vocation, as did Aloysius, he finally entered the Society of Jesus. He proved an apt student of philosophy and a perfect observer of the Holy Rule. "My penance," he would say, "is to live the common life . . . I will pay the greatest attention to the least inspiration of God." He observed this fidelity in the performance of all his duties until his last illness, as attested by his spiritual directors. At Rome he took sick and died shortly thereafter in the year 1621. That same year Duke Philip of Aerschot presented a petition to Pope Gregory XV for the taking of information with a view to his beatification.

The similarities of the two saints continue with their remains being kept in identical urns beneath altars of almost similar form in the Jesuit Church of Saint Ignatius. The rooms that each occupied during stays in Rome have been converted into chapels which the pilgrims may visit at the church.

Because of John Berchmans' fidelity to serving Holy Mass, he is listed as the patron of Mass servers. He was canonized in 1888. In art the saint is represented holding a crucifix, a book of rules and his rosary.

St. John Bosco

POPE Pius XI once remarked that, "In John Bosco's life the supernatural became the natural and the extraordinary ordinary." Others would call the saint the "wonder-worker of the 19th century."

The saint who merited such remarks was the son of Piedmontese peasants and was born on August 16, 1815 in the diocese of Turin, Italy. When John was merely two years old, his father died. His devout mother, Margaret, was left obliged to labor in the fields of their small farm to support her stepson, Anthony, from her husband's first marriage, and her own sons, Joseph and John.

The saint's lifelong attraction toward helping neglected and deprived youngsters began while John was himself a youth. After perfecting his skills as a ventriloquist, tightrope walker, juggler and acrobat, John would attract his peers about him by displaying his talents and then, after winning their respect, would have them join him in prayer.

His memory, it is said, was as prodigious as Mozart's, and it was this intelligence and the boy's attraction to prayer that prompted a priest of a neighboring village to assist in his education. Among the relics preserved in Turin are the saint's text books and his exercise books of Latin prose and verses.For six years his studies were repeatedly interrupted by the jealousy of his half brother who resented being obliged to work the family farm while John was being trained in gentle arts.

Almost tempted to abandon the religious life after so many delays, John was favored with a mysterious dream in which the Blessed Virgin instructed him to care for her lambs. This was one of many such dreams, the first occurring in 1824 when John was only nine years of age. These visionary dreams occurred at frequent intervals until December 8, 1887, a period of some 63 years. The dreams that were of a prophetical nature were always realized, while those of an instructional nature influenced many of his activities.

In addition to these mysterious dreams and the saint's gift of prophecy, he was known to multiply food on more than one occasion, and could read the thoughts and consciences of those he encountered. He could discern the future vocation of his boys and the length of life of his fellow priests. He also knew exactly what was transpiring in the institutes belonging to his community and was known to levitate during the celebration of Holy Mass.

Sympathetically attracted to abandoned and neglected boys, the saint established schools that would transform these boys into good and industrious citizens. The religious order he founded for this apostolate was placed under the patronage of St. Francis de Sales. Now known as the Salesians of St. John Bosco, the order ranks third in membership among religous societies of the Church. With the help of Mary Mazzarello, the saint organized the Congregation of the Daughters of Mary, Help of Christians, for the care and education of neglected girls.

Nothing the saint attempted, it seems, was completed without difficulties. Expenses for the renovation and construction of buildings were always met, nonetheless, and sometimes by miraculous means. Difficulties were likewise met and overcome when, at the request of the Virgin Mary herself, the saint endeavored to erect a church dedicated to

261

Our Lady, Help of Christians in Turin. A church dedicated to St. John the Evangelist was also built by St. John Bosco in the same city. On the request of Pope Leo XIII he was entrusted with building the Church of the Sacred Heart in Rome.

Somehow between the founding of institutions for his boys, the establishment of his two religious orders, the building of churches and the constant difficulty in raising funds for these endeavors, the saint authored some 130 books and pamphlets. In recognition of this accomplishment he was declared the patron saint of Catholic publishers in 1936, two years after his canonization.

His long catalogue of labors and achievements seems all the more remarkable when one considers the medical ailments to which he was prone: failing eyesight and the eventual blindness of the right eye; weak legs; recurring military fever; headaches; repeated cases of bronchitis; and for the last five years of his life, myelitis, an inflammation of the spinal cord.

The saint died in 1888 at the Salesian house at Valsalice, outside Turin, at the age of 72. January 31, the day following his death, is commemorated each year as his feast day. The room in which he died has been kept as it was at the time of his death. A number of articles used by the saint are kept there, as well as many first-class relics. Included in the collection of relics at Turin is the saint's scapular of Our Lady of Mount Carmel. It was found in perfect condition in the saint's coffin at the first exhumation. The remains were transferred in 1929 to Turin in the Church of Our Lady, Help of Christians. Also in this church are the tombs of two other saints: the co-foundress of the Congregation of the Daughters of Mary, Help of Christians, St. Mary Mazzarello, who was canonized in 1951; and St. Dominic Savio, who died before his 15th birthday in 1857. This young saint, canonized in 1954 and presented to the youth of the world as a model, had been a protegé of St. John Bosco.

St. John Nepomucene Neumann

JOHN Neumann was an immigrant, and like Mother Cabrini who preceded him, he was the first naturalized citizen of his gender in the United States to be canonized.

The saint led a humble, yet a remarkably active life, accomplishing in his 49 years what many have not even approached in a longer life span. His works have profoundly affected the Church in America, with many of his deeds being described as "firsts."

John Neumann's remarkable life began in 1811 in the centuries-old village of Prachatitz in Bohemia (now Czechoslovakia). He was baptized the day of his birth and was given the name John Nepomucene, the patron saint of his homeland. His father was the owner of a stocking mill; his mother is described as being devout.

As a young boy John Neumann was a keen student with a passion for books and learning, but at the age of 20 he was still undecided as to whether he should pursue a career in law, medicine or theology. Acting on his mother's advice, he applied to the Budweis Theological Seminary and was promptly accepted. His academic records at the seminary were excellent, as evidenced by the transcript of his marks that is still preserved. The saint had exceptional skill in mastering languages, and it is said that he could converse in 12 of them.

After hearing urgent appeals for German-speaking priests to assist in ministering to those Germans who had immigrated to the United States, Neumann decided to become a missionary. After completing his studies he was disappointed to learn that, due to illness, the bishop would not immediately ordain his class. His dream of becoming a missionary was so intense that he secured passage on the *Europa*, an American three-master engaged in the transport of immigrants. After an arduous 40-day crossing of the Atlantic, John Neumann landed in New York on April 20, 1836 and was welcomed into the diocese of New York. Ordained within a few weeks, the saint lost no time in setting out for the Niagara frontier, where German immigrants had followed the opening of the Erie Canal. Here the missionary realized his dream of working in rural areas among poor and struggling families, both ministering the sacraments in four churches, teaching the children, and traveling on foot the 900 square miles of his parish. For almost four years the saint worked alone until his brother, Wenceslaus, immigrated and joined him in his work.

John Neumann eventually came into contact with members of the Congregation of the Most Holy Redeemer, the Redemptorists, who impressed the saint with their work among German immigrants. Thinking that he might be more effective as a member of a religious community, rather than remaining a lone missionary-pastor, he asked to be relieved of his responsibilities in New York and joined the order in Pittsburgh, receiving the habit on November 30, 1840. His brother also joined the order that same year and remained a lay brother for the rest of his life.

During the saint's year of novitiate, normally a year of solitude, he was transferred eight times and was active in giving missions in many cities. The saint pronounced his religious vows on January 16, 1842. Since the order had immigrated from Italy only a few years before, John Neumann had the distinction of being the first Redemptorist to be professed in America.

St. John Neumann's initial assignment was as assistant rector of St. James Church in Baltimore, and he was assigned two years later as the superior of the Redemptorist foundation in Pittsburgh. Along with his administrative responsibilities, the saint ministered to 6,000 German Catholics, visited the sick, heard confessions, preached regularly and increased attendance at the parish schools.

Appalled by the religious ignorance of immigrant children, John Neumann wrote two catechisms which saw 38 editions in both German and English. They were to remain popular in America for decades after the author's death. The saint also developed a more complete catechism for adults and authored one of America's first Bible histories.

Experiencing ill health caused by strenuous activities, he was sent to Baltimore to recuperate, but his period of rest was abbreviated when his talents were once again needed by the order. He was appointed vice-provincial of all Redemptorists in the United States, even though he had been a member of the order for only five years. During the 23 months in this position, he appeared in federal court and became a citizen of the United States.

While serving as rector of St. Alphonsus Church in downtown Baltimore, he became the confessor of Archbishop James Patrick Kenrick. He was also the champion of the Oblate Sisters of Providence, a group of black women Religious whose order was threatened with dissolution. The order originally taught slave children and now numbers about 250 members who conduct schools, day nurseries and catechetical centers in a dozen states. The order will soon celebrate the 150th anniversary of its founding.

On Archbishop Kenrick's recommendation, John Neumann was considered for appointment as the fourth bishop of Philadelphia, a diocese that included all of Pennsylvania, as well as parts of New Jersey and Delaware. The saint was sincerely reluctant to accept the assignment, and he appealed to Archbishop Kenrick, the superiors of the order and the Vatican. He was, nevertheless, appointed by Pope Pius IX, "under obedience and without appeal." The saint was subsequently consecrated on March 28, 1852, the day of his 41st birthday. He was to serve Philadelphia less than eight years.

Despite his holiness, his accomplishments and experience, some felt him unimpressive in appearance, manner and speech. He was short, only five feet two inches, a man of humility, self-effacing and soft-spoken with an old-world accent. Even the diocesan paper expressed reservations at his appointment. Nevertheless, the bishop met his duties with vigor.

One of his first interests was to increase the number of children attending parochial school. Within a year the students increased from 500 to 5,000. After two years the enrollment was 9,000. The saint was the first to organize Catholic schools into a unified system under a diocesan board.

The bishop introduced the Forty Hours Devotion that was held at successive churches on a year-round schedule. The devotion had been inaugurated in Rome generations before by St. Philip Neri and had previously been observed from time to time. Owing to its success in Philadelphia, other bishops throughout the United States gradually followed Neumann's lead with the Forty Hours Devotion becoming general throughout the country.

The bishop brought into his diocese 12 religious orders and founded a new congregation, the Sisters of the Third Order of St. Francis, writing a rule for them that was approved by the Vatican.

An astounding accomplishment was realized in his building more than 80 churches, completing eight churches begun by his predecessors, and leaving seven others in the course of preparation.

In the midst of administrative activities he recited all his customary prayers, spent hours in front of the Blessed Sacrament and successfully combined the active with the contemplative life.

The saint's primary wish in life was to work in obscurity, to exercise his priestly functions among the poor and needy, to lead a humble life in the exercise of virtue and penance. To his credit many of these practices were continued despite his episcopal dignity.

Although not feeling well, the saint left his rectory one day on an errand of charity, walking as was his custom, when he collapsed on the front steps of a house. Taken indoors and placed before a fireplace for warmth, he died before help could arrive. The day was January 5, 1860, a few weeks before his 49th birthday.

Burial of the diminutive bishop was not in the cathedral as would be customary. Because he had expressed a wish to be buried among his confreres, he was laid to rest in the lower church of St. Peter the Apostle Church, Fifth Street and Girard Avenue in Philadelphia. His body was exhumed during the process of beatification, relics were taken and the

265

remains placed within a waxen image that is found beneath the altar of the crypt of the same church.

At this church is located the St. John Neumann Center, where many articles used by the saint are kept, including the bishop's episcopal ring — described as being as plain and unpretentious as the man himself — an exquisite monstrance often held by the saint during Forty Hours Devotions, and many personal articles, including reading glasses and books. From this Center booklets, relics and devotional materials are distributed to the thousands of pilgrims who visit there.

Even though Pope Benedict XV considered him worthy of canonization by declaring, "You are all bound to imitate Bishop Neumann," the Sacred Congregation showed serious doubts about his heroism by stating that his life appeared to be, ". . .a series of ordinary, everyday actions performed fearlessly, but not exceptionally." Pope Benedict in 1921 retaliated by declaring, "Work, even the most simple, performed with constant perfection in the midst of inevitable difficulties spells heroism in any servant of God." John Neumann was subsequently beatified on October 13, 1963, during the Second Vatican Council with cardinals and bishops of the world in attendance. He was canonized on June 19, 1977.

The saint received a supreme honor on October 4, 1979 when Pope John Paul II visited the altar of the saint during his historic visit to America.

St. John of the Cross

JUAN de Yepes y Alvarez entered the world in 1542 at Fontiveros, Spain, located some 24 miles northwest of Avila, the birthplace of St. Teresa, with whom he would labor in reforming the Carmelite Order to the observance of the primitive rule. Educated by the Jesuits, he entered the Carmelite Order in 1563 at the age of 20 and later changed his name to Fray John of the Cross.

The saint was a contemplative, theologian and poet, as well as a capable co-founder, reformer and busy administrator. His knowledge of the higher levels of the spiritual life are exemplified in his writings, which include: *The Ascent of Mount Carmel, Dark Night of the Soul,* and *The Spiritual Canticle.* His many poems are verbal rhapsodies of love for God that have been praised by poets through the years. These and other writings have earned for him the title *Mystical Doctor*, and it is a rare book on the subject of prayer that does not quote from one of his works.

The saint was the confessor of the great St. Teresa of Avila and often conferred with her on their experiences in the spiritual life.

At the age of 49 the saint died at Ubeda from a painful illness that first afflicted his legs. At the time of his death in 1591 he had a reputation for great sanctity, a reputation similarly enjoyed by his counterpart, St. Teresa. St. John's body was found incorrupt during a number of exhumations and is now enshrined at Segovia.

The little friar, who was barely five feet in stature, was raised to spiritual heights by his canonization in 1726. Two hundred years later he assumed his rightful position among the Doctors of the Church, being officially designated by Pope Pius XI, who eloquently praised both the saint and his literary works.

One of the most precious relics of the saint is a small drawing made with pen and ink that was inspired by a vision. He gave it to a nun at the Convent of the Incarnation, who fortunately guarded it carefully. It is now kept in a reliquary at the same convent.[1]

St. John Nepomucene (St. John Nepomuk)

R ENOWNED as the Victim of the Seal of Confession, St. John takes his name from his native town of Nepomuk in the province of Bohemia, Czechoslovakia. His family name was really Wolflein, and he was born between the years 1340-1350. Little is said of his parents except that from early childhood they consecrated him to the service of God. He studied at the University of Prague and the University of Padua, earning a doctorate in canon law. He was ordained a priest in 1373. The saint must have been a person of rare abilities since he served the Church in high-ranking positions and successfully avoided bishoprics that were offered him.

Existing documents, ecclesiastical records and contemporaneous accounts of the second half of the 14th century relate in unmistakable fashion that in 1393, John of Nepomuk, then serving as vicar general of

[1]See the chapter on Crosses and Crucifixes for details of this drawing.

the Archdiocese of Prague, was thrown into the Moldau River and drowned on March 20 by command of King Wenceslaus IV of Bohemia. A controversy exists over the true reason the saint was matryred since two incidents are given to explain the king's actions.

A legendary account that resulted in the saint's being considered the Victim of the Seal of Confession is that King Wenceslaus suspected Queen Sophie's infidelity and demanded that the saint reveal to him the contents of the queen's confession. Butler tells us that the queen was a "beautiful and pious woman, who sorely needed the consolations of religion, for she had much to bear from her barbarous husband." He further informs us that Wenceslaus was intensely jealous and harbored unworthy suspicions of his wife, whose conduct was irreproachable. Since the saint steadfastly refused to violate the disclosures of the queen's confession, it is believed that the king, in a rage, sentenced him to death by drowning.

The other reason given for his martyrdom — which historians claim is more likely — is that the king, wishing to establish a new bishopric for one of his favorites, proposed to confiscate the church and revenues of the ancient Benedictine Abbey of Kladrau. The king ordered that, at the death of the elderly Abbot Racek, no new abbot should be elected. This was strenuously opposed by Archbishop Jenstein and St. John, who was his vicar general. Upon the death of the abbot, the monks, in trying to avoid the closing of their monastery, elected a new abbot on the suggestion of the archbishop and John. The appointment of the new abbot was confirmed by the saint without referring to the wishes of the king. When Wenceslaus learned of this, he had the saint, together with the archbishop and the officials of the archdiocese, thrown into prison. After being tortured, all but the saint weakened. After the others were released, John was subjected to other indignities and tortures, including the burning of his sides with hot torches. Half dead, he was secretly dragged at night through the streets, with a wedge of wood in his mouth as a gag to insure quiet. He was thrown from a bridge into the river Moldau. The date was March 20, 1393.

When the body washed ashore the next day and the people learned the circumstances of his death, he was immediately acclaimed a martyr. He was eventually canonized by Pope Benedict XIII.

Some historians have suggested that the king, already furious with the saint's previous refusal to reveal the contents of the queen's confession, could no longer tolerate John's refusal to acquiesce to his more recent order and demanded his death as a means of revenge.

Whether or not the traditional story of John's refusal to violate the seal of confession is accepted, it is a matter of record that, upon opening the tomb of the saint in 1719, it was discovered that all the flesh of his body had been reduced to dust except the tongue. Although brown and slightly dry, it has been kept as a precious relic and can be seen through the crystal covering of its heavily jeweled reliquary. This relic, together with his bones, is kept in St. Vitus Cathedral in Prague. The saint is always depicted in art wearing a cassock, a lace-bordered surplice and a short cape. He is usually seen holding a cross, sometimes a palm, and is often crowned with a halo of stars, this because lights resembling stars appeared during the night of his death at the place where his body was cast into the river. In many works of art the saint is accompanied by angels. In some paintings an angel might hold a key, denoting the seal of confession; another might hold a delicate finger to the lips requesting silence.

St. John Nepomuk is the principal patron of Bohemia, where he is invoked against floods as well as for help in making a good confession.

St. Ladislas

WHILE the establishment of the Hungarian monarchy and the organization of its Church are credited to King St. Stephen I, King St. Ladislas is considered a Christian hero who was as conscientious for the affairs of the Church as was his sainted predecessor. Ruling Hungary some 39 years after the death of St. Stephen, Ladislas restored the laws and discipline Stephen had established, but which were disregarded by the confusions between their respective reigns. Ladislas battled pagans, passed ordinances against heathenism and the decay of ecclesiastical discipline, extended the borders of the country, founded monasteries and churches and left a legacy of peace. He spared no effort to spread the Gospel and governed the religious and civil affairs of his kingdom with a firm hand while still being idolized and loved by his subjects.

It was Ladislas who had St. Stephen's remains removed to a more honorable shrine, and it was Ladislas who founded the Abbey of Szentjobb (Holy Right Hand) for Stephen's incorrupt hand that was discovered during this translation.

Ladislas was honored by the kings of France, England and Spain in being chosen to act as commander-in-chief for the allied crusading armies in their campaign against the Saracens for the recovery of the Holy Land. While preparing for this task he became sick and died. This occurred in 1095, during his 56th year, the 18th of his reign. The saint was buried in the Cathedral of Grosswardein, which he had built. He was canonized in 1192 by Pope Celestine III.

The 14th-century golden reliquary that contains the head of the saint had been kept at Grosswardein, but in 1608 it was acquired by the Cathedral of Győr, where it is still kept. In this cathedral is also found the miraculous painting of the Irish Madonna.

After the saint's death, his heroic deeds formed the theme of many ballads, and he still lives in the sagas and poems of the Hungarian people.

St. Lawrence

U SUALLY depicted in art with a gridiron upon which he suffered and died, St. Lawrence is known to have fallen victim to the persecution of the Roman Emperor Valerian, who in 256 ordered the execution of all bishops, priests and deacons. The imperial edict was immediately enforced in Rome. Pope Sixtus II was apprehended while exiting from a catacomb and was promptly martyred, as were six of the seven deacons of the Roman Church. Three days following the death of Sixtus II, Lawrence was likewise martyred for the Faith. It is absolutely certain that St. Lawrence was a real historical personage and that he was a venerated Roman deacon. Nor is there any doubt as to his martyrdom, the date or place of its occurrence, or the place of burial.

St. Ambrose of Milan (d. 397) was the first to record certain details of the death of St. Lawrence which were gleaned from oral tradition. According to Ambrose, as Sixtus was being led to his death, he consoled the distraught Lawrence with the prediction that he, Lawrence, would soon follow. Since deacons were entrusted with the care of the Church's goods and the distribution of its alms among the poor, Lawrence, as the only remaining deacon, set about distributing the last of the Church's funds to the poor. On learning that sacred vessels were being sold to increase the amount of money given to charity, the prefect of Rome imagined that the Church had hid considerable treasure and he determined to secure it. Lawrence was apprehended and ordered to donate all Church valuables to the emperor for the care of the troops. Three days were allowed Lawrence for the accumulation of the treasure. When the day arrived for the presentation, Lawrence assembled orphans, widows, lepers, the blind and the poor. To the prefect's question, "Where is the treasure?" Lawrence replied, "These are the treasures of the Church."

The prefect's displeasure at seeing such misery and misfortune, combined with his feelings of being mocked, enraged him so that he promptly set about devising a plan whereby Lawrence would be punished by suffering a slow death. The saint was stripped and bound to a gridiron that was placed over hot coals. After suffering a long time over this slow fire, Lawrence is supposed to have said, "Let my body be turned; one side is broiled enough." Several noblemen who witnessed this torment were so moved by the saint's fortitude and piety they were converted at the spot.

The scorched body was removed to the cemetery of Cyriaca in Agro Verano on the Via Tiburtina. The grill believed to be the one on which the saint died is imbedded in the wall of the reliquary chapel of San Lorenzo in Lucina, Rome, a fifth-century church which contains the relics of many early martyrs.

St. Lawrence has been one of the most honored martyrs of the early Church. Having died in the third century, devotion to him reached a peak in the fourth century, with chapels and churches competing for space above or near the place of his burial. In 330 Constantine built an oratory with the altar situated directly over the tomb. This was enlarged and beautified by Pope Pelagius II (579-590). A basilica with three naves was built by Pope Sixtus III (432-440) immediately adjacent to the Constantine structure, but in the 13th century Pope Honorius III made the two buildings into one. The structure is known today as the Basilica of San Lorenzo Fuori Le Mura. Within this church is found the entrance to the catacombs of St. Cyriaca, while behind the main altar is the entrance to the Confessio, where the tomb of St. Lawrence is found. Behind the present silver shrine is a marble slab on which the body of St. Lawrence was placed after his martyrdom. The dark spots on it are believed to be stains made by his blood.

The efforts of various popes to honor the martyr continued with Pope St. Damasus I (366-384), who wrote a panegyric in verse that he had engraved in marble and placed over the tomb. In addition he built a basilica in Rome that was dedicated to the martyr named San Lorenzo in Damaso. It was a favorite of St. Charles Borromeo, St. Bridget of Sweden and St. Francis Xavier.

Standing proudly as confirmation of the saint's popularity were six

271

churches in Rome, all built to honor his memory. In addition to the three previously mentioned, there is San Lorenzo in Fonte, a small church built in 1656 over the site of the prison in which the saint was briefly kept. A magnificent painting by Corona, *The Martyrdom of St. Lawrence*, is over the high altar of San Lorenzo in Miranda. There is also a church built over the place where the saint was martyred, San Lorenzo in Panisperna.

St. Lawrence is named in the Canon of the Mass. His feast day is still observed on August 10, the anniversary of his death.

St. Lucy

A CCORDING to the traditional story, Lucy was born to wealth in Syracuse, Sicily about the year 283. She consecrated her virginity to God and meant to distribute her fortune to the poor, but was refused permission by her mother, Eutychia. During a pilgrimage to Catania, to the shrine of St. Agatha, who had been executed 52 years before, the mother was miraculously cured of an ailment. Lucy seized the opportunity to gain permission to distribute her wealth, but the amount of the inheritance is said to have stirred the greed of a youth to whom Lucy had been unwillingly betrothed. He denounced her to the Governor of Sicily, who was active during the persecution of Diocletian. She was first condemned to a house of immorality, but this could not be enforced since she stood immovable. Fagots were heaped upon her, but again she was unharmed. Finally she was beheaded at the age of 20 in the year 303.

The saint is depicted in art with a palm and with two eyes on a dish. The custom of invoking her for eye disorders derives from the legend that she plucked her eyes when they were admired by a suitor smitten by her beauty. Another legend has it that her eyes were extracted by a tyrant.

Sigebert (1030-1112), a monk of Genbloux, in his *Sermo de Sancta Lucia*, related that her body lay undisturbed in Sicily for 400 years, until the Duke of Spoleto captured the island and transferred the relics to Corfinium in Italy. They were removed by Emperor Otho I about the year 972 to Metz and deposited in the Church of St. Vincent. An arm was sent from here to the monastery of Luitburg in the Diocese of Spires. Some of her relics were found in Constantinople in 1204 and were sent by the Doge of Venice to the monastery of St. Geremia. The relics rested undisturbed in Venice for 777 years, until the seventh of November, 1981, when two thieves forced their way into the church and, while holding three people at gunpoint, broke into the glass casket that contained the remains. Flinging aside the cloths that covered the body, they collected all the bones, tossed them into a sack and hurriedly made off with them. Left behind was the saint's skull and the silver mask that covered it. It has been speculated that the thieves were Sicilians since the isle of Sicily has repeatedly requested the return of the saint's body to the place of her birth and death. To demonstrate this longing for the return, an inscription was placed under the saint's empty tomb at Syracuse: "Lucy, bride of Christ, the people await you."

To the relief and joy of Church officials the relics were recovered one month later in December of 1981.

Venerable Mary of Agreda

M ARY Coronel was born in 1602 to a family described as being noble, but impoverished. She is commonly known for the little town of her birth, Agreda, situated in Old Castile on the borders of Aragon. Her parents were blessed with 11 children, but only four survived infancy — two sons and two daughters. Mary was not yet two years old when she received the use of reason during a supernatural vision, and she was 12 years of age when she disclosed her intentions to become a nun.

One day at prayer a voice told her mother, Catherine, it was the will of God that the Coronel castle be turned into a monastery, and that her husband should join their two sons, who were already members of the Order of St. Francis. The castle was soon remodeled into a suitable convent. Upon the advice of her spiritual director, the mother, together with her two daughters, took the veil on the same day in the presence of the father of the family, then a Franciscan lay brother.

All the extraordinary favors Mary received were preceded by great trials. Much to her embarrassment most of her ecstasies not only occurred during community prayer, but were also accompanied frequently by levitations lasting two or three hours.

When the Venerable was only 25 years old, she was elected abbess

273

and remained in that position all her life. When she reluctantly accepted the position, she demonstrated her reliance on the Mother of God by placing a statue of the Blessed Mother in the abbess' stall of the choir. At the feet of the statue she placed a copy of the rule and the seal of the monastery.

When the old Coronel castle became too small, the Venerable's good judgment and business sense were called upon to oversee the building of a new monastery and church. It was needed to accommodate the many women who aspired to become members of the order and to lead lives of virtue according to the example of the holy abbess.

After Easter in the year 1665 Mary assembled the community and informed them of her impending death. Within the week her illness became critical. With townspeople weeping outside, and with superiors of the order at her bedside, she died at the age of 63, having been a nun for 46 years and abbess for 35 years. Some of the community related that during her last moments they heard a heavenly voice repeat: "Come, come, come." At the last call the Venerable died in a pious and edifying manner. In 1667 her remains were exhumed and were found to be incorrupt.

Since the reputation of her sanctity was widely known, Charles II, King of Spain, requested that Pope Clement X introduce the cause of her beatification. In 1673 she was awarded the title of Venerable.

What has given Mary prominence is not so much the claim to holiness, but her writings, which attracted considerable controversy both before and after her death.

In the same year that Mary of Agreda was elected abbess, history relates that God commanded her to write the autobiography of His Mother. It seems almost unbelievable that she resisted the command of the Lord and the repeated entreaties of the Blessed Mother for 10 years. Nevertheless, we are told that humility prevailed during this time. Finally strengthened by revelations of the highest order, encouraged by heaven and urged on by her spiritual director, Mary began her task in the year 1637.

King Philip IV, on learning that Mother Mary of Jesus, with whom he frequently corresponded, had written a biography of the Virgin Mary, he requested a copy and was reluctantly furnished with one. This copy was submitted to renowned theologians for examination. *The Mystical City of God* received their enthusiastic endorsement.

During the absence of her confessor a substitute priest ordered the burning of Mary's copy. Yet another confessor ordered her to rewrite it. The second manuscript was begun in 1655 and was completed the sixth of May, 1660. Pope Benedict XIV considered the rewriting of the manuscript as miraculous and stated: "It happened not without a miracle, that the same work was rewritten by the servant of God, without any discrepancy from the one which she burned previously." It is assumed here that the second manuscript was compared with the copy given to King Philip IV.

For a time the cause of Mary's beatification and the reading of her book were suspended by papal edict, but the reasons that were outlined were said to have resulted from a poor translation of the work. Individuals of distinction denounced the work for a time, but it eventually won high esteem when Pope Innocent XI issued a brief permitting the publication and reading of the *City of God.* Similar decrees were afterward issued by Popes Alexander XIII, Clement IX and Benedict XIII. Benedict XIV and Clement XIV likewise voiced their approval while Pope Benedict XIII, when he was archbishop of Benevent, used these revelations as material for a series of sermons on the Mother of God. According to decrees, Pope Innocent XI and Clement XI encouraged the reading of the book by all the faithful. Pope Alexander XIII declared that, "The book of Mary of Agreda may be read by everybody with impunity."

No biography of Mary of Agreda is complete without considering a very unusual aspect of her life, but one that has merited the satisfaction of the clergy and ecclesiastics who investigated the matter. It is known that Dr. Carlos E. Castaneda, an illustrious Catholic historian, and Dr. Charles W. Hackett, an eminent Protestant historian, both recorded after careful study of antique documents that Mary of Agreda bilocated to America over 500 times during an 11-year period from 1620 to 1631, a fact also recorded in Mary's diary.

The Indians of New Mexico and surrounding territories who were instructed in the Faith by Mary did not know her name, but called her the *Lady in Blue* because of the mantle she wore.

Mary's confessor, Fray Sebastian Marcilla, to whom she confided the details of her journeys to America, requested of Don Francisco Manzo y Zuniga, archbishop of Mexico, that someone in America find the *Lady in Blue* and give him the details of her visits. The task was entrusted to Fray Alonzo de Benavides, later the auxiliary Bishop of Goa, India and a Franciscan who evangelized the area extending from Texas to the Pacific Ocean. Also curious about the *Lady in Blue* were missionaries themselves who related how groups of Indians, well instructed in the Faith, repeatedly sought them out to be baptized.

When Father Benavides explained the assignment to the general of his order, he was informed that Sister Mary of Jesus in Agreda was the mysterious *Lady in Blue*. It was then, after searching eight years, that he found the *Lady in Blue*, not in America, but in Spain.

The humble Mary was constrained under holy obedience to disclose everything during an interview attended by the provincial of the order, her confessor and Fray Benavides.

Fray Benavides later wrote, "She convinced me absolutely by describing to me all the things in New Mexico as I have seen them myself, as well as by other details which I shall keep within my soul."

Under obedience Sister Mary wrote a letter to the missionaries in America and this, together with her activities there, had a great influence on Fra Junipero Serra and the early missionaries.

That Mary of Agreda actually bilocated to America is beyond dispute and is attested to in the logs of the Spanish conquistadors, the French explorers and in the identical accounts of Indian tribes located at great distances from one another. Bishop Joseph Zimenez Samaniego is known to have read the diary of Mary's own account of her travels, a manuscript which unfortunately was later destroyed.

The Convent of the Conception in Agreda has numerous relics of the Venerable including various statues favored by Mary, altar linens graced with her embroidery, an iron penitential cross, a walking stick, various crucifixes used in her religious exercises, her manuscripts — including a copy of the *City of God* and, of course, her incorrupt body.

St. Maria Goretti

DUE to extreme poverty the Goretti and Serenelli families shared the same house on the Pontine Marshes near Nettuno, Italy. The son of one family became a murderer; the daughter of the other, a saint. Maria Goretti, a devout child of 12, resisted the lustful advances of Alessandro Serenelli and sustained 14 major knife wounds during a struggle. With her virginity preserved, she lay dying in the hospital at Nettuno forgiving and praying for her attacker. Having been wounded on the Feast of the Precious Blood, she died 20 hours later, a model of patience while enduring excruciating pain.

Maria was immediately regarded as a martyr of purity with her beatification occurring 45 years later. Her canonization took place on June 24, during the Holy Year of 1950. Because of the unprecedented crowd attending the ceremony, Pope Pius XII consented to perform the canonization outdoors, the first such ceremony to be held outside St. Peter's. Present were her brothers and sisters and her mother, Assunta, the first mother to witness the canonization of her child.

Alessandro was tried for the murder and received a sentence of 30 years. For some time he remained unrepentant, but he at last experienced conversion during a vision of Maria, who appeared to him in his prison cell. During this vision a garden appeared before him while a young girl with dark golden hair and dressed in white went about gathering lilies. She drew near him with a smile and encouraged him to accept an armful of the blooms. After he accepted them, each flower was transformed into a still, white flame. Maria then disappeared.[1]

Upon his release from prison the now repentant Alessandro first sought forgiveness of the saint's mother and then found employment as a gardener in a Capuchin monastery, where he worked until his death. He also testified to Maria's sanctity during the cause of beatification.

The body of the martyr was buried in the village cemetery, but before the beatification, the bones were enclosed in a waxen image that was transferred to the Sanctuary of Our Lady of Grace, a church in the care of the Passionist priests. During the time of the beatification and canonization, this figure in a glass-sided reliquary was taken to Rome and displayed to countless visitors in the Church of Ss. John and Paul, the same church where St. Paul of the Cross, the founder of the Passionist Order, is enshrined. After a time the relics of Maria Goretti were returned to Nettuno. Visitors there are almost constant, but especially numerous on the anniversary of her death.

In Corinaldo, the village where Maria was born, in the church of St. Francis where she was baptized and confirmed, a white marble shrine, for which St. Pius X generously contributed, was erected in the saint's honor. A bas-relief here depicts Maria prostrate with an arm uplifted in a tremendous refusal. Below, in the crypt of the ancient church of the Addolorata, a bone of this arm is preserved in a tabernacle.

In September 1979, Pope John Paul II traveled the 40 miles from Rome to Nettuno to visit the relics of the saint and to exhort young people to look on Maria Goretti as an example of purity to be emulated in this permissive society. While in Nettuno he visited a 79-year-old Franciscan Missionary nun, Sister Teresa, a sister of the saint.

Maria Goretti, an unschooled child of 12, is the pride of modern Italy and a model for the youth of the world.

[1]*Saint Maria Goretti*, Marie Cecilia Buehrle, Bruce Publishing Co., Milwaukee, 1950, pp. 134-135.

St. Nicholas of Tolentino

A FTER hearing a sermon preached by a hermit of St. Augustine, Nicholas petitioned for entrance into the order and proved to be an outstanding religious. Ordained in 1271 he served various houses of the order for four years before being assigned to the monastery at Tolentino, where he stayed for his remaining 30 years of life. Nicholas' apostolate included daily preaching in the streets, administering the sacraments in homes, hospitals and prisons, spending long hours in the confessional and performing countless miracles to which he would charge the recipients, "Say nothing of this. Give thanks to God, not to me." The faithful were impressed with his persuasive powers and advanced spirituality and placed great trust in his intercession in relieving the sufferings of the souls in purgatory, a confidence that was confirmed many years after his death when he was officially designated the "Patron of the Holy Souls."

In the latter years of his life, when he was enduring a prolonged illness, his superiors, with no success, urged him to partake of more strengthening foods than his customary meager rations. The Blessed Virgin appeared to him one night, instructed him to ask for a small piece of bread, to dip it in water and then to eat it, promising that he would be cured by his obedience. In grateful memory of his immediate restoration to health, Nicholas began blessing similar pieces of bread and distributing them to the sick, a practice that produced numerous favors and marvels of healing. In commemoration of these miracles, the shrine of the saint maintains a worldwide distribution of St. Nicholas Breads that are blessed and which continue to provide favors and graces.

The saint's final illness lasted a year, with his death occurring in 1305 on September 10, the day on which his feast is liturgically commemorated each year.

During the 40th year following his death his incorrupt body was exposed to the faithful. During this exhibition the arms of the saint were removed, thus initiating the strange bleedings that were witnessed and documented for centuries.

The shrine has no documented proof concerning the identity of the amputator, although legend has adopted the report that a German monk, Theodoro, detached the arms, intending to take them as relics to his native country. It is certain, however, that a flow of blood signaled the act and resulted in his apprehension.[1] During a recognition of the relics a century later, the bones of the saint were found, but the amputated arms within the same tomb were found perfectly intact and imbued with blood. These were placed in beautifully crafted silver cases, each resembling a forearm and hand.

Toward the end of the 15th century fresh blood spilled from the arms, an occurrence that was repeated 20 times. The most noteworthy seepage occurred in 1699 when the flow began on May 29 and continued until September 1.[2] The Augustinian monastery and the archives of the bishop of Camerino (Macerata) possess many authoritative documents concerning these discharges.[3]

Relics of the saint's blood that issued from the arms can be found within the basilica known as Sanctuary S. Nicola Da Tolentino, in the 16th-century Chapel of the Holy Arms. In a coffer above the silver altar stands a 15th-century silver chalice containing a quantity of the blood. A gem-studded 17th-century urn displays behind a glass panel the blood-stained linen that is said to be the cloth used to staunch the flow that occurred at the amputation.

The bones of the saint, with the exception of the arms, lay hidden beneath the basilica until their rediscovery in 1926, when they were formally identified and placed in a simulated figure covered with an Augustinian habit. The incorrupt arms, still in their 15th-century silver casings, are found in their normal position beside the figure. The relics can be seen in a crystal reliquary blessed by Pope Pius XI.

St. Patrick

A LTHOUGH born in Dumbarton, Scotland, between the years 380-387, St. Patrick is claimed as the favorite son of Ireland, having labored in the country for most of his life. His father, Calpurnius, belonged to a Roman family of high rank and his mother was a close relative of St. Martin of Tours.

At the age of 16 he was captured by Irish marauders and was sold as

---

[1]*Un Asceta e un Apostolo, S. Nicolo da Tolentino*, P. Domenico Gentili Agostiniano, Editrice Ancora, Milan, 1966, pp. 154-156.
[2]*Ibid.*, p. 137.
[3]From a statement of a representative of the shrine.

a slave to a chieftain named Miluce. From this master who was a Druidical high priest, Patrick became familiar with the practices of the Druids, from whose bondage he was destined to free the Irish people. During his servitude he tended his master's flocks and was anointed by grace. He related in his *Confessio* that while engaged in this service:

> ". . . the love of God and His fear increased in me more and more, and the faith grew in me and the spirit was roused, so that, in a single day, I have said as many as a hundred prayers, and in the night nearly the same, so that whilst in the woods and on the mountain, even before the dawn, I was roused to prayer and I felt no hurt from it, whether there was snow or ice or rain, nor was there any slothfulness in me, such as I see now, because the spirit was then fervent within me."[1]

After six years of servitude he escaped and journeyed to Westport where he boarded a ship to freedom. With a yearning to devote himself to the service of God in the sacred ministry, we find him next in Western Europe under the direction of Bishop Germanus, who had been elected to the See of Auxerre in 418. After Patrick received a proper education, this holy bishop promoted him to the priesthood.

Patrick labored for a time in Britain, but when the missionary Palladius, who had been commissioned to evangelize Ireland, returned unsuccessful due to the fierce opposition of the chieftains, Pope Celestine I, on the recommendation of Bishop Germanus, entrusted Patrick with the mission of gathering the Irish race into the family of Christ. It is believed to be at this time that he received episcopal consecration at the hands of St. Maximum.

The saint's travels about Ireland were extensive. His initial and primary concern was converting chieftains for whom he preached and performed miracles. Under his direction the island was divided into parishes and dioceses and he is said to have consecrated no fewer than 350 bishops. As a result of his labors, churches were erected throughout the country, including those of Downpatrick and Armagh which have been maintained to the present.

In a confrontation with the Druids on the hill of Slane at Tara, he performed a spectacular miracle of fire, and through his prayers dismissed demonic displays with the subsequent conversion of the assembly. On another occasion he destroyed the idol Crom-Cruach with a wave of his crosier. His preaching, travels and his triumph over paganism eventually won the Irish to the Faith, but not without difficulties and opposition. The saint tells us in his *Confessio* that he and

---

[1] *Catholic Enycyclopedia*, op. cit., Vol. XI, p. 554.

his companions were seized 12 times and carried off as captives. On one occasion he was burdened with chains and his death was decreed.

Though credit is given him, scholars consistently claim that there is no historical evidence that the saint ever used a shamrock to explain the doctrine of the Trinity nor that the saint banished snakes from Ireland.[2]

The saint died March 17, 493 (another source claims 461), at Saul (Sabhall) and was buried at Downpatrick where arose the great Cathedral of Down. Here in the church cemetery is an enormous granite slab engraved with the name *Padraig* in Celtic letters. It is believed this stone marks the place of the saint's burial.[3]

In the National Museum of Dublin is a plain handbell once belonging to the saint. This is kept in a covering shaped like a bell that is called a shrine. Made in 1091, this covering is made of brass and is decorated with silver and gold filigree that is inset with crystals and enamels.

In addition to the saint's labors, his extensive travels and his unrelenting efforts to suppress paganism, the saint left two literary works, the *Confessio* and the *Epistola Ad Coroticum*. Both are recognized by all modern writers as of unquestionable genius, as is the beautiful prayer *Lorica of St. Patrick*, St. Patrick's Breast-plate.

St. Pius X

G IUSEPPE Melchiorre Sarto, the future St. Pius X, was born in 1835 at Riese, Italy. His father was a cobbler and village postmaster who died before his son's ordination, but his mother lived to see her son a cardinal.

After finishing his elementary education he was given a scholarship to attend the seminary at Padua, where he finished his classical, philosophical and theological studies with distinction. He was ordained in 1858 and for nine years served as assistant to the pastor of Trombolo. He was then named archpriest of Salzano, where he restored the church and provided for the enlargement of a hospital. His rare administrative ability and prudence were likewise demonstrated when he was made chancellor of the Treviso Diocese in 1875. This office entailed his attention to several offices including those of spiritual director and rector of

[2]*Down Cathedral*, R. W. Kilpatrick, Dean, Nicholson and Bass, Belfast, Northern Ireland, p. 9.
[3]*Ibid.*, p. 9.

the seminary. Throughout his ministry he was known for his habitual generosity to the poor and his interest in religious instruction for adults. Through his efforts it became possible for students of public schools to receive religious instruction.

While the Diocese of Mantua was experiencing severe problems, Pope Leo XIII appointed him bishop. Among his many concerns in this office, which he held from 1884 until 1893, was the formation of the clergy at the seminary, where for several years he himself taught dogmatic and moral theology. The same roman pontiff, Leo XIII, appointed him cardinal and patriarch of Venice.

Upon the death of the pope the future saint journeyed to Rome to take part in the conclave to elect a successor, but despite his pleas of unworthiness he was elected by a vote of 55 out of a possible 60 votes.

His pontificate was noted for his promotion of piety among the faithful and his recommendation of frequent, even daily, reception of Holy Communion. He also recommended that the First Communion of children should not be deferred too long after they had reached the age of discretion. Because of this he became known as the Pope of the Eucharist.

His accomplishments and endeavors were many. He started research into a revised breviary, promoted the use of Gregorian Chant, recodified Canon Law, revised the catechism, founded the Papal Biblical Institute, helped establish the Confraternity of Christian Doctrine and wrote 16 encyclicals. One of these encyclicals, his famous *Pascendi* of 1907, dealt the deathblow for a time to Modernism, which had then threatened the entire edifice of Catholic doctrine.

During his pontificate Pope Pius X remained humble, unaffected and deeply devout. Even during his lifetime he was called the Pope Saint. The advent of World War I put a heavy burden on his heart and hastened his final illness. It is said that on his deathbed he repeatedly cried: "I wish to suffer, to die for the soldiers on the battlefield." His humility was confirmed by the words of his last will: "I was born poor, I have lived poor, and I wish to die poor."

The saint died August 20, 1914, was beatified in 1951 and was canonized in 1954.

Before the pope's beatification his body was exhumed and was found in an incorrupt state, authentic in all respects, with the skin a delicate white. The physician of Pope Pius XII, in order to maintain the condition of the corpse, injected a special preserving chemical which unfortunately turned the body a medium brown. The incorruption, however, has been maintained. The body was placed in a side altar of St. Peter's Basilica where it is visible to the public. The face was covered with a bronze mask and the body was covered with fine vestments.

The feast day of the saint is observed worldwide on August 20.

St. Rita of Cascia

MARGUERITA was married at the tender age of 12 to Paola Ferdinando against her natural inclinations, but in obedience to her elderly parents, who were fearful, so some have recorded, that their deaths would leave her alone in the world. For 18 years the marriage was a veritable martyrdom for Rita because of her husband's quarrelsome nature, but towards the end, Paola's nature was completely changed, due no doubt to Rita's persistent prayers. After the politically motivated assassination of her husband and the untimely death of their two sons, Rita applied for entrance into the convent of the Augustinians in Cascia. She was at first declined entrance, but was eventually accepted after the bolted doors and gates of the monastery were miraculously opened for her one night by her patron saints.

Inspired by a sermon preached by St. James of the Marches, Rita prayed to participate in some way in Our Lord's sufferings and was divinely accorded a thorn wound in her forehead. This festered and produced such an offensive odor that the next 15 years of her life were spent in virtual seclusion.

Three days before her death, at the age of 76, Rita was blessed with a vision of Our Lord and His Mother. At the time of her entrance into heaven her cell was filled with an extraordinary perfume, a light emanated from the wound on her forehead and the bells of the city are said to have been joyously pealed by angels.

During the time the body was displayed in church the miracles reported by the many pilgrims to her bier were so numerous, and the perfume that filled the church was so intense, that the civil and ecclesiastical authorities permitted the body to be placed in a position between the cloister and the church, where the body could be venerated by both pilgrim and cloistered nun. Since it remained in this position for over 150 years and was never properly entombed, the preservation of the body was declared to be truly phenomenal when the remains were examined prior to Rita's beatification on July 16, 1627. At this time the eyes of the relic are reported to have opened unaided. This miraculous occurrence is said to have stopped a riot. The eyes seem to have remained open for some time, as paintings executed during the time indicate.[1] The body at times was also seen to move to one side and after a lapse of some years to have changed position to the other side. The elevation of the entire body to the top of the sarcophagus was also observed, a circumstance which was carefully recorded by eyewitnesses whose testimonies are still preserved in the archives of the Archdiocese of Spoleto.[2] Such movements of the body have not been noted for some time.

When Rita was canonized in 1900, the devotion to the saint had already spread beyond Italy into Europe and across the seas. In 1946 a basilica was built in her honor in Cascia. Located in this impressive sanctuary is the golden shrine that houses the saint's miraculously preserved body.

Frequently noticed at the shrine is the heavenly sweetness, which in past ages was recognized by the most reputable persons, who also gave sworn testimonies to its presence about the body. Although it is not continuous, the perfume is observed on the occasion of some miracles.[3]

The convent of the saint has several interesting relics which figured importantly in Rita's life. Of interest is the cell where her first decorated sarcophagus is kept, and the oratory where she received the thorn of the Crucified. Also kept are her wedding ring and other small mementos. Still growing in the courtyard is one of the most unusual relics: the 500-year-old vine which owes its existence to an incident in the saint's early religious life. To test her obedience her superior selected a piece of dry wood and ordered Rita to plant it and water it each day. The stick sprouted into a healthy grapevine that still bears fruit. Each year the harvest is distributed among high-ranking ecclesiastics, while the leaves are dried, made into a powder, and sent to the sick around the world.[4]

The bees of St. Rita are another curiosity. As an infant, tiny white bees were once seen swarming about Rita's mouth. This unusual incident is always mentioned in Rita's biographies and is usually given a miraculous connotation. Bees still play a part in the saint's history. About 200 years after her death in 1457, a strange variety of bees began living in a 15th-century wall of the monastery and have lived there continu-

[1] *Saint Rita*, Willey De Spens, Hanover House, Garden City, New York, 1960, pp. 140-141.
[2] *A Life of the Saint of the Impossible*, Rev. M. J. Corcoran, O.S.A., Benziger Bros., New York, 1919, pp. 155-161.
[3] Taken from a statement made by the Sisters of Cascia.
[4] *The Life of Saint Rita of Cascia*, Fr. Atanasio Angelini, O.S.A., Poligrafico Alterocca, Terni, Italy, pp. 146-147.

ously ever since. They remain in hibernation for 10 months of the year and emerge during Holy Week. They are never seen to leave the convent enclosure, and after a few weeks of activity about the gardens and rooms of the convent, they return to the ancient wall after the Feast of St. Rita, May 22, and seal themselves into holes they make themselves. Contrary to some opinions, the members of the order and the sisters of the convent of Cascia do not consider the bees' presence or behavior to be of a miraculous nature. It is regarded as a purely natural feature which, by an unusual coincidence, occurs in the walls of their convent.

St. Rita has taken her rightful position among the great saints who served in turn as wives, mothers, widows and nuns providentially given to us for our edification. The saint is overwhelmingly and affectionately regarded by her many satisfied devotees around the world as the "Guardian Saint of Desperate and Impossible Cases."

St. Sebastian

SEBASTIAN joined the Praetorian Guard during the reign of Diocletian and was instrumental in helping several martyrs remain constant in the Faith. He was condemned to death in A.D. 286 when his own faith was discovered. He was tied to a tree on the Palatine Hill where Mauretanian archers pierced him with arrows. He was left for dead, but when a pious lady named Irene came to bury the body, she found him still breathing and took him to her home to nurse him to health. On recovering, Sebastian confronted Diocletian near his palace and was again imprisoned. After being clubbed to death his body was thrown into the common sewer, where it was retrieved by a woman named Lucina. She buried it in the catacombs on the Appian Way, in the same vault where the bodies of St. Peter and St. Paul had laid for a time during a period of unrest.

One of the seven chief churches of Rome was built over his grave in A.D. 367. The present church, San Sebastiano, was completed in 1611 by Cardinal Scipio Borghese. The cardinal removed the remains from the crypt to the present chapel, which is directly over the original tomb.

Part of the saint's relics were taken in the year 826 to St. Medard at Soissons, but the greater part remain in San Sebastiano. The head of the saint is retained in the church of Santi Quattro Incoronati, The Four Crowned Martyrs.

St. Sharbel Makhlouf

T HE perfectly preserved body of this holy monk remained one of the most amazing phenomena in modern Christian times for 67 years, its lifelike condition and its sweat of oil and blood remaining for that time a source of wonder to men of medicine who examined it.

The holy monk was born in 1828 in Biqa-Kafra in the high mountains of Northern Lebanon and was given the name of Joseph by his humble farming parents. As the youngest of five children he displayed from early childhood a strong attraction to prayer and solitude. Despite the displeasure of his family he left home at the age of 23 to join the Lebanese Maronite Order. He was sent to the Monastery of St. Maroun where he pronounced his vows in 1853 after two years of novitiate. His assumed name, Sharbel, was that of a martyr who died in A.D.121. Having received a thorough theological education in a seminary of the order, he was ordained a priest on July 23, 1859 and was reassigned to the Monastery of St. Maroun where he spent 16 years in the practice of monastic virtues. In 1875 he received permission from his superiors to retire a short distance from the monastery to the hermitage of Ss. Peter and Paul, which was used by priests during days of quiet retreat. In this secluded sanctuary he spent the remaining 23 years of his life practicing severe mortifications.

It is recorded by his companions that he wore both a hair shirt and a chain belt. His bed was composed of oak leaves covered with a palliasse; his pillow was merely a piece of wood rolled up in the end of a soutane. His prie-dieu was a cluster of sticks covered in the same way by a piece of a soutane.[1]

The saint's devotion to the Holy Eucharist was exemplary. His daily Mass was celebrated at about 11:00 each morning so that the morning hours could be spent in preparation for the service and the rest of the day in thanksgiving. He is known to have performed several miracles during his life. He once saved his brothers from a poisonous snake by ordering it to vanish; he recited his Divine Office by the light of a lamp which a brother purposely filled with water instead of oil; he cured a madman by reciting a prayer while imposing his hands upon him;

---

[1]*A Miraculous Star in the East, Charbel Makhlouf,* Paul Daher, Lebanese Maronite Monastery of Annaya-Djebeil, Lebanon, 1952, p. 62.

and once, on the orders of his superiors, he saved their farming lands from a scourge of grasshoppers by sprinkling the fields with holy water.

In 1898, on December 16, while at the Elevation of the Host during Mass, he suffered an apoplectic stroke from which he never recovered. Eight days later, on Christmas Eve, at the age of 70, the saint died, having been a priest for 39 years. According to monastic tradition, the body was not embalmed, but was dressed in a simple cassock and was placed in the monastery chapel for 24 hours. The body was then conveyed to the monks' burial chamber in the presence of his confreres and village folk who had braved the snow and cold to witness the interment.

The burial chamber consisted of a large subterranean room located partially beneath the high altar of the chapel and extending eastward to an area beneath the monastery garden. Those who descended into this chamber found the ground covered with rainwater that converted the floor into a veritable swamp. In view of this situation the body was not laid on the ground as was customary, but was placed on two planks which did not prevent the water and mud from encroaching upon and subsequently submerging it. The entrance to the vault was closed with a great stone.

The villagers who lived in houses facing the monastery saw a great light over the tomb the night following the burial, a phenomenon that recurred for 45 nights. This apparition of light, together with the enthusiasm of the faithful, encouraged the ecclesiastical authorities to open the tomb and transfer the remains to a grave more accessible to the villagers who wished to pray beside it.

The tomb was subsequently opened on April 15, 1899 in the presence of the community and 10 witnesses who had been present at the burial four months earlier. They were unanimous in testifying that the water had undermined the burial ground, turning the tomb into a quagmire, and that the monk's body was actually floating on the mud. When the body was cleaned it was found perfectly incorrupt, the muscles supple, with the hair of his head and beard intact. At this time it was also noticed that a serum mixed with blood seeped from the pores. They placed the body in a wooden coffin that was glassed on top, and carried it into a small monastic oratory. From then on, because of the great amount of blood seeping from the body, the clothing of the saint was changed twice weekly. News of the phenomenon prompted ever increasing numbers of visitors who for 27 years were permitted to view and touch the body.

Among the men of medicine who examined the body was Dr. Elias Elonaissi who declared on November 16, 1921:

"I observed that the pores emitted a matter like sweat; a strange and inexplicable thing according to the laws of nature, for this body that has been dead for so many years. I have renewed the same examination many times, at different periods; the phenomenon has always been the same."[2]

Another physician, Dr. George Choukrallah, examined the body a total of 24 times during 17 years and declared:

"I have always been astonished at its state of preservation and especially this reddish liquid exuded by it... My personal opinion based on study and experience, is that this body is preserved by a supernatural power."[3]

The phenomenon is more astounding when one considers that in 1918, following a simple autopsy, the body was exposed on the terrace during the heat of summer for three months without drying the source of the fluid.[4]

When the authorities of the order petitioned Rome for the beatification, a solemn reburial was conducted. After being dressed in sacerdotal vestments and the monastic hood the body was placed in a new coffin of wood covered with zinc. Various documents were composed by physicians, a notary and superiors of the order, and were placed in a zinc tube which was placed beside the body before the coffin was sealed with the episcopal crest. Burial was in a new tomb specially prepared in the wall of an oratory.

During February of the Holy Year 1950, pilgrims in the chapel noticed that a watery fluid streamed from a corner of the tomb and coursed its way onto the floor of the chapel. The fluid was traced to a corner of the casket where the liquid was seen dripping through a small crack. Twenty-three years after being placed in this tomb, the body was again examined in the presence of numerous authorities and was found completely free of any trace of corruption and was perfectly flexible and life-like. The sweat of liquid and blood continued to exude from the body, and the garments were found stained with blood, the white content of the fluid having collected on the body in an almost solidified condition. Part of the chasuble had rotted and the zinc tube containing the official documents was covered with corrosion. The remains were later entombed in the same location.

The holy monk was beatified December 6, 1965 and was canonized by Pope Paul VI on October 9, 1977, a day on which several miraculous

[2]*A Cedar of Lebanon*, Paul Daher, O.L.M., The Philosophical Library, New York, 1957, p. 100.
[3]*Ibid.*, p. 102.
[4]*Ibid.*, p. 102.

cures took place at the new saint's shrine. Since the 1950 examination and especially since the beatification and canonization the number of pilgrims to the shrine has been so great as to be inestimable.

For 67 years the remains of the saint remained perfectly preserved and exuded a blood fluid described by all accounts as being supernaturally sustained, but the body was found at the time of the beatification in 1965 to have complied with the laws of nature. Only bones were found and these of an inexplicable reddish color.[5] The fluid, of course, had ceased, but enough had been gathered before the beatification to furnish a supply from which small quantities are still distributed. Small pieces of cloth from his garments and those that were saturated in the fluid are likewise distributed.

Still in existence is the poor stone house of the saint's birth, his hermit's cell, the altar on which he offered his last Mass, and many small articles such as his chalice, crucifix, crude table utensils and bowls.

The most important relics, of course, are the bones of his body, which for an unknown reason still maintain their reddish tint.

St. Simon Stock

THE facts relating to the early life of the visionary of the scapular are uncertain, but it is believed St. Simon Stock was born in England in the county of Kent about the year 1165. Tradition has it that at an early age he left his family to live the life of a hermit and made his home in the hollow of a tree. The actual date of his entrance into the order of Our Lady of Mount Carmel is likewise uncertain, but it is known that his sanctity and wisdom, his prudence and vigor were known to voting members of the order who named him the sixth prior general of the Carmelite Order during a general chapter at Aylesford, England in 1247. If hagiographers are correct, St. Simon was at the time about 82 years of age. Despite his years the saint did much for the benefit of the order and is deservedly recognized as one of the order's most celebrated generals. He is credited with establishing houses of the order in the university cities of Cambridge, Oxford, Paris and Bologna, thereby aiding in the growth of the order and the training of its younger members.

[5]Taken from information contained in a letter to the author from Francis M. Zayek, bishop of St. Maron diocese.

During the chapter at Aylesford the rule was apparently modified from the strictly hermitical one observed in the Holy Land, to one that best suited those who had settled in Europe and were intent on preaching, teaching and working in the ministry. The rule's revision was approved by Pope Innocent IV. While effecting great successes for the order the new rule, nevertheless, provoked areas of dissention both within and without the order. Some Carmelites claimed that the changes were too drastic and not in keeping with the prohetic spirit observed for so long on Mount Carmel and in the Holy Land, being quite discontent and vocal in their opposition. The success and growth of the order provoked so much jealousy among other religious orders that the saint was obliged to appeal directly to the pope for the order's protection. This was obtained in 1252 in the form of a decree that threatened censure to those who would harm members of the Carmelite Order.

During this time of stress and trial the saint was further burdened by age and the duties of his office. He continually invoked the Blessed Virgin with a prayer he had authored, the *Flos Carmeli*. After numerous recitations of this appeal, the Blessed Virgin appeared to him holding in her hands the scapular of the order. Handing it to the saint, the Virgin said: "This shall be a privilege for you and for all Carmelites, that whoever dies clothed in this shall not suffer eternal fire; rather, he shall be saved."

The scapular consisted of a long length of fabric hanging over the shoulders and falling to the front and back of the Religious. This garment had already been worn by members of the order for many years before the vision, and was used primarily during manual labor as an apron to keep the clothing neat and clean. With the formal presentation of this garment to members of an order dedicated to her, the symbolism could be accepted as twofold. Since the garment was worn during labor, the wearer of the scapular could be recognized as being in the service of Mary and the Church. Since it was worn to protect the Religious, the garment could be accepted as a sign of heavenly protection. The vision is thought to have occurred on July 16, 1251.

Because of the vision in which heaven in a marvelous way confirmed the Carmelite Order and their endeavors, the order's prestige increased and the wearing of the scapular became widespread. Numerous pontiffs have continually affirmed and endorsed the devotion while some have enhanced it with privileges and indulgences.

St. Simon Stock was making a visitation to the Carmelite foundation at Bordeaux, France when he became ill and died on May 16, 1265. Burial was in the Cathedral of Bordeaux, but a year later the remains were returned to the room of the monastery where he died. Numerous miracles were reported after prayers were said in this room, which had been converted into a chapel.

Eleven years after his death the Holy See permitted the Carmelites of Bordeaux to celebrate Holy Mass in his honor, a privilege later extended to the entire Carmelite Order. The main portion of the saint's relics rest at Bordeaux, where he died, but in July 1951 the skull of the saint was removed to Aylesford, where it is reverently enshrined.

St. Stephen of Hungary

THE father of St. Stephen, Duke Geza, was the ruler of Hungary from 970-997. He was converted to the Christian Faith through the influence of his Polish-born wife, Adelaide. In the year 985, together with his son who was then 10 years of age, Geza was baptized; his son, Vaik, adopted at that time the name of Stephen in honor of the first martyr. A large number of Geza's retainers and a considerable number of his people were likewise baptized, although a proportion of the newly converted exercised the Faith only in externals and retained the private practice of their heathen customs. It was not until the reign of Stephen that the true conversion of the country is said to have occurred.

Stephen was 20 at the time of his marriage to Gisela, a sister of Duke Henry, the future St. Henry II of Bavaria. Two years later, in 997, with the assumption of power, Stephen extended an invitation to priests, Christian nobles and knights to settle in Hungary to aid in the conversion and instruction of the people. In due time a revolt was spawned by two factions: those who feared that the favors Stephen showed these strangers would harshly affect national influence, and by those people who were so obstinately attached to superstitions as to take up arms in defense of pagan customs. After this uprising was suppressed, ecclesiastics from Germany, France and Italy arrived to aid in the spread of the Faith. For these St. Stephen built churches, monasteries and other pious foundations, and completed the building of Pannonhalma which was begun by his father. Also known as Martinsberg, in honor of St. Martin of Tours (d. 397), who was born and reared in the locality, Pannonhalma served for centuries as the motherhouse of the Hungarian Benedictine Congregation.

At the urging of his nobles, he petitioned the papacy for the title of king that he might with majesty and authority accomplish other deeds for the Church and the good of the people. This was granted by Pope Sylvester II who provided the crown for Stephen's coronation that occurred on August 17, 1001. Thus endowed with royal dignity and the pope's benediction, Stephen divided the land into dioceses and archdioceses, and built churches, religious houses and even hospices for pilgrims at Rome, Ravenna and Constantinople, as well as a monastery in Jerusalem. His edicts concerning Church tithes, and ordinances regarding the support of the clergy, attendance at Mass, observances of feasts and Church fasts were confirmed by the pope.

During the last years of his life, Stephen was troubled by sickness, family difficulties and pagan movements among a small portion of the population. His cherished hope of having his only son, Emeric, succeed him to the throne was destroyed when the prince lost his life on a bear hunt in 1031. The saint was subsequently troubled by quarrels among members of his family concerning the right of succession with some even participating in a conspiracy against his life.

His death occurred on the Feast of the Assumption, August 15, 1038, when the king was 63 years of age. Burial was beside his son in the church at Stuhlweissenburg that he had built in honor of the Mother of God, where the kings of Hungary were afterward both crowned and buried.

Because of the miracles that attended his tomb, Pope St. Gregory VII, at the request of King St. Ladislas, decreed in the 45th year after the saint's death that the relics be removed to the splendid chapel that bore his name in the church of Our Lady of Buda (now known as the Cathedral of St. Stephen in Budapest). Occurring as it did on August 20, this date of the translation was observed in Hungary for many years as the main feast day of St. Stephen, being celebrated as both a national and religious festival.

In recognition of the personal attention he gave to the care of the poor, the subsistence he provided for orphans and widows, the virtues he practiced in the fair and charitable administration of his office and because of his love for the Church, he was canonized in 1083, the year of the transferrence of his relics to Budapest.

There are two outstanding relics of St. Stephen: the crown that was used at his coronation and his incorrupt right hand. Pilgrims to the shrine of the saint are reminded that the incorrupt hand, enshrined in a golden reliquary, is the hand that signed orders for the building of numerous houses of piety and is the same hand that dispensed charity to the humble. The incorrupt right hand was discovered when the body was exhumed during the year of his canonization, for the removal of the relics to the shrine in Budapest. To preserve this relic St. Ladislas, one of the saint's successors, founded the Abbey of Szentjobb (Holy Right Hand), but it was not destined to remain in peace. During the Turkish domination that lasted for 150 years, the relic was removed elsewhere. On the orders of the Catholic Habsburg ruler, Queen Maria Theresa, who ruled Hungary from 1740 until 1780, the relic was returned to Buda where it was entrusted to the Provost of St. Sigismund's Chapel in the royal palace. At this time the queen ordered a coin medal to be struck in memory of the relic's return to Hungary. For this relic the Hungarian bishops in 1882 provided a new and highly artistic reliquary. In 1944 the relic was removed to Austria during the Russian invasion, but was returned to Hungary soon after, and was presented to Primate Mindszenty who received it amid the tremendous enthusiasm of the faithful.

The crown of St. Stephen consists of two parts. The upper part was presented to the saint by Pope Sylvester II; the lower section is believed to have been the crown of a successor, King Geza I, who ruled Hungary from 1074 until 1077. Now joined together, both parts have costly jewels and enameled plaques of Christ, the apostles, two Byzantine emperors and various saints.

Considered a national treasure of Hungary, the crown was entrusted for safekeeping to the United States during the Second World War. It was eventually returned to Hungary on January 6, 1978 and was placed in the hands of government officials by Secretary of State Cyrus Vance, who acted for the United States Government. Regarded as a symbol of Hungarian political and religious freedom, the return of the crown was made over the protest of the Hungarian people, who had wanted it returned when the country was free of communist domination and suppression.

The Cathedral of St. Stephen, where his relics are enshrined in Budapest, was the titular church of the famed Jozsef Cardinal Mindszenty, who outspokenly opposed the communist occupation of Hungary and who was subsequently sentenced to life imprisonment by the communist Hungarian government, living in refuge in the U.S. Embassy in Budapest from 1956 until 1971.

St. Theophile

CANADA seems an unlikely place to find the relics of a Roman martyr, yet it is in that country that the relics of St. Theophile are reverently enshrined at the Trappistine Abbey of Our Lady of the Assumption, located in the forest near the French-Canadian village of Rogersville, New Brunswick.

Documents of authenticity from the Congregation of Sacred Relics identify the relics as being the bones of a boy of about 10 years. He was martyred during the persecution of Diocletian, who ruled between 284-304. According to the documents, the body was removed in the early 19th century from the cemetery of St. Cyriacus at Campo Verano where St. Lawrence was first buried. The relics were given by the Vatican to the Trappist Dom Augustin de Lestrange in 1826 and were entrusted to the Trappistine nuns at Vaise, France. Included with the relics were an ampul of the martyr's blood and the documents of authenticity. The relics remained with the nuns until 1903 when anticlerical laws went into effect. At this time the nuns felt the need to move to New Brunswick where they could preserve their way of life, but it was considered unwise at the time to convey the relics with them to Canada. The relics were therefore entrusted to the care of a devout family in Lyon. In May of 1934 the relics were returned to the Trappist order and soon found their way to New Brunswick, where they were restored to the Trappistine nuns.

The details of the martyr's life are nonexistent, but since the skull and neck bear the marks of his martyrdom, and because he was buried in sacred ground and his blood was collected, as was that of the brave and devout martyrs of his time, it is believed he steadfastly defended his faith and won the crown of martyrdom by an exemplary death.

The relics of St. Theophile are kept in a waxen figure of a Roman boy that is exposed to view in a glass-sided case with the ampul of blood at his feet. On close scrutiny, part of the skull can be seen where the wax was deliberately omitted.

About a thousand visitors a year are counted at the shrine with most arriving during the summer months, when the chapel is visited by those who pilgrimage to the notable shrines of Canada.

St. Teresa of Avila

T HE first woman to be named a Doctor of the Church was born on March 28, 1515 in Avila, Spain. Although pious as a child her fervor languished during her adolescence due to her fascination with the romantic literature of her day. She was attracted to the religious life after her devotion was rekindled following a serious illness. She joined the Order of Carmel in Avila and pronounced her vows in 1534.

At the time of her entrance, the observance of the mitigated rule permitted socializing in the parlor and the satisfaction of curiosities and comforts. The saint lived 27 years under this relaxed rule until she experienced her "conversion" while reading the Confessions of St. Augustine. Finding the convenient atmosphere of her convent in opposition to the spirit of prayer which she felt Our Lord had intended for the Caremelite Order, she began reforming its laxities in 1562 at the cost of countless persecutions and difficulties, eventually establishing 17 monasteries of the Primitive Observance for her nuns. She was encouraged in this endeavor by her advisor, St. John of the Cross, who extended the reform to the friars of the order.

Under the Primitive Observance she attained the heights of mysticism and enjoyed countless visions. There seems to be no phenomenon peculiar to the mystical state which she did not experience, yet she remained a shrewd businesswoman, administrator, writer, spiritual counselor and foundress. In the golden age of Catholic Spain she was widely acknowledged as one of the most outstanding persons of her day.

Teresa was a reluctant writer, engaging in this task under obedience. Her *Autobiography*, *The Way of Perfection* and the *Interior Castle* are widely known. Three hundred years after her death the value of her writings was acknowledged by the world-renowned University of Salamanca when they conferred upon her the title of Doctor of Divinity, an honor never bestowed on any other woman. Another honor was bestowed on her on September 27, 1970 by Pope Paul VI when he officially annexed her name to the list of 30 distinguished Doctors of the Church, the first woman to join such an illustrious group.

Never a healthy woman, the saint died of her many afflictions on October 4, 1582 while on a visit to her convent at Alba de Tormes. On her deathbed she found support in humbly recalling that she was dying "a daughter of the Church." The delightful fragrance that frequently enveloped the saint during her lifetime was so intense at the time of her death that the door and window of her cell had to be opened to prevent dizziness.

The saint's body was found incorrupt during various exhumations, the last occurring in 1914 when the same fragrance of flowers was detected. Various relics were removed from the body during the years to satisfy the houses of her order, but her foundation at Alba de Tormes is privileged to have her remains enshrined in a splendid reliquary above the main altar of their church. Here, too, is kept the pierced heart, which is of special interest.

While the saint was at the Convent of the Incarnation in Avila, the same convent in which she first entered religious life, she experienced a remarkable vision that is recorded in her *Autobiography*:

> "I saw an angel close by me on my left side, in bodily form. He was not large, but small of stature and most beautiful — his face burning as if he were one of the highest angels who seem to be all of fire. I saw in his hand a long spear of gold, and at the iron's point there seemed to be a little fire. He appeared to me to be thrusting it at times into my heart and to pierce my very entrails; when he drew it out, he seemed to draw them out also, and to leave me all on fire with a great love of God."

The wounded heart was meticulously examined in 1872 by three physicians of the University of Salamanca, who studied the perforation made by the dart. They unanimously agreed that the preservation of the organ could not be credited to any natural or chemical means.

The pierced heart is kept in a unique reliquary at Alba de Tormes, but at the Incarnation, the very cell where the saint had this experience is now a chapel with a magnificent baroque altarpiece and polychromatic wooden statues.

Articles used by the saint are carefully kept at her various foundations, with many being displayed for the edification of visitors. Reverently kept at St. Joseph's in Avila is a bed used by the saint as well as some books, a jug, a drum and castinets that she played at Christmas. A walking cane used on journeys, a rosary, a belt and a sandal are kept by the Carmelite Fathers at Avila, while the Carmelite Sisters at the Incarnation have embroidery pieces made by Teresa and kitchen utensils she was accustomed to using. A white robe is kept at Seville, and at Vallodolid an autographed copy of the Way of Perfection and several letters are preserved.

Of the many persons of honor and distinction who visited the tomb of the saint, none can exceed the importance of the visit in November 1982 by Pope John Paul II who went to Alba de Tormes to close the year-long celebration of the 400th anniversary of the saint's death. The pope also visited the Convent of the Incarnation where the saint lived. During his visit to Avila he praised the 16th-century nun as being one of the most remarkable women in the history of Christianity, also declaring that her life of poverty and meditation was an example for Christian women around the world.

St. Thérèse of Lisieux

HAVING chosen her lengthy name in religion, Thérèse of the Child Jesus and of the Holy Face, the saint from Lisieux is known the world over by this and by a more simple title, The Little Flower, a metaphor she frequently applied to herself.

Born to devout parents on January 2, 1873, Thérèse was the last of nine children. Of these only five daughters survived, all of whom joined the religious life. One of the sisters was a Visitation nun, while the four others were members of the same Discalced Carmelite community.

Even as a child Thérèse was attracted to prayer, as she mentions in her autobiography: "From the age of three I have never refused our good God anything. . . . I have never given Him aught but love, and it is with love He will repay." She advanced rapidly in the spiritual life and entered Carmel when only 15 years of age. Hers was a life of hidden sacrifice endured with a smile. Her exercises of heroic virtue were willingly performed for priests and the salvation of souls. Her autobiography, entitled *The Story of a Soul*, proved exceedingly popular in a remarkably short time, endearing her to souls around the world.

Towards the end of her life the saint suffered both spiritual and physical torments, with tuberculosis claiming her life on September 30, 1897. Having reached an advanced stage of spirituality by means of her way of spiritual childhood, a way of confidence and self-surrender, she died at age 24 repeating: "O . . . I love Him. My God . . . I love Thee. . . ." She was canonized a mere 28 years later.

Thérèse is honored with a dual distinction, having been named Secondary Patroness of France Equal to St. Joan of Arc, and because of her interest in the missions she was designated the Principal Patroness Equal to St. Francis Xavier of All Missionaries and Missions of the World.

Many interesting relics are preserved. The statue of the Virgin Mary that came to life and smiled at her during an adolescent illness is kept at the monastery in Lisieux, as are her Carmelite habit, veil, mantle and flower wreath. Of interest is a cascade of hair that was shorn upon her entrance into the convent and was kept by her father as a keepsake. Also preserved are her copy books, a pair of wooden shoes and many other articles all indicating a simple, humble life.

The saint's sister, Pauline, gave to the National Shrine of the Little Flower in Chicago, Illinois, a number of interesting relics and souvenirs that are admired by countless visitors. The most noteworthy collection of relics outside of France is contained in a golden branch of five roses, each flower holding a major relic of the saint. This is kept in a casket of crystal and gold. Also kept in a reliquary is a lovely crucifix made from the wood of a rose bush from which the saint gathered flowers to place before the statue of the Christ Child. The rush-bottomed, ladder-back chair Thérèse used in her cell, two small reliquaries she hung on its walls, a lily made from a lock of her hair, a toy tambourine from her childhood, a map of the United States drawn and annotated by the saint at the age of 12 — all are reverently kept to the admiration and edification of visitors.

From an obscure convent in the north of France the fame of the Little Flower has spread like a fragrance throughout the world, inspiring millions to prayer and prompting Pope St. Pius X to declare her the "greatest saint of modern times."

St. Valentine

SIXTEEN men named Valentine are listed in the Vatican's official encyclopedia of saints, the *Bibliotheca Sanctorum*. The one associated with the practice of sending sentimental cards on February 14 was a holy priest of Rome who assisted the martyrs during the persecution of Claudius II until he himself fell victim. After his apprehension he was sent by the emperor to the prefect of Rome, who failed in his efforts to have Valentine renounce his faith. He was beaten with clubs and was afterward beheaded on February 14, A.D. 269. The martyr was buried near the Via Flaminia, two miles from Rome.

The custom of exchanging notes of affection on this saint's feast day, which we find recorded in literature as early as the time of Chaucer, seems based on the observation that birds began to pair on February 14, the saint's feast day.

The greater part of the saint's relics are found in the chapel of St. Zeno in the Church of Santa Prassede in Rome to which they were moved during the 13th century. A notable relic is found in the church of San Sebastiano, Rome.

St. Veronica Giuliani

WHEN Veronica was four years of age, her dying mother entrusted each of her five children to a sacred wound of Christ. Veronica, the youngest, was assigned the wound in the side. This action of the dying mother might well have been of a prophetic nature because her daughter's interest in the Passion developed into an intense devotion to the sufferings of Our Lord.

When Veronica came of age her father weakened under her insistent pleadings and permitted her to enter the Capuchin Monastery at Città di Castello where the primitive rule of St. Clare was observed. Here she was favored with revelations, ecstasies and many visions of the suffering Christ. In one vision she accepted the chalice of Our Lord's sufferings and soon recognized some of the sufferings in her own body and soul. On Good Friday, 1697, she received the impression of the five sacred wounds.

To guard against fraud, the bishop of the diocese, at the direction of the Holy See, thoroughly tested the phenomenon. She was for a time forbidden to receive Holy Communion, was kept under constant supervision, and was shut off from the rest of the community. Her hands were placed in special gloves fastened with the bishop's signet, and various medical treatments were tested without success. In the sworn testimony submitted for her beatification, her confessor and her fellow religious stated that the stigmatic wounds opened and bled at command, and that they closed and healed in a short time while the bishop waited. Her obedience, patience, and humble demeanor proved the genuineness of the mystical experiences to the eventual satisfaction of her skeptical associates and contemporaries.

The mystical ring was given her from the hand of Christ in a vision on April 11, 1694. As witnesses testified, the ring encircled her finger and supported a raised stone as large as a pea, but of a reddish color. Although not ordinarily visible, it was seen and examined on several occasions.

St. Veronica Giuliani has been likened to St. Teresa of Avila, having been a woman of great common sense and administrative ability, in addition to having been endowed with many supernatural favors. Her judgments must have been highly respected since she served the community as novice mistress for a period of 34 years, and held the office of abbess for 11 years. In her diary of 10 volumes, written at the command of her confessor, she left an invaluable record which was used during the process of her beatification and which has proved to be of great interest to hagiographers. Her total works include 44 volumes comprising one of the most intriguing accounts of mystical phenomena.

Toward the end of her life she was afflicted with apoplexy and died of the complications of the disease on July 9, 1727. She was canonized in 1839.

The body of the saint remained incorrupt for many years until it was destroyed during an inundation of the Tiber River. Her bones now repose in a composite figure of the saint. The heart of the saint, which was extracted soon after her death, bore for many years distinct symbols of the Passion which corresponded exactly to drawings made by the saint shortly before she died. This is kept in a special reliquary and is said by physicians to be well preserved, although in recent years the figures have become less defined.

A museum within the convent of the saint contains many of her relics and mementos, but pilgrims are permitted access to it only when accompanied by the convent's confessor since the order is one of strict enclosure.

Veronica's cell, her bed and various reliquaries have been carefully maintained. Indicated in the infirmary is the area she occupied during her last illness. A favorite crucifix is likewise shown, but of great interest is a death mask which clearly indicates the features of the saint.

St. Vincent Ferrer

THIS celebrated Dominican preacher was born to parents whose families had been ennobled for valor during the conquest of Valencia.

Born in that city on January 23, 1350, he was the fourth child, and while destined to serve his Church in marvelous ways his brother, Boniface Ferrer, was also called to Church activities, serving as general of the Carthusians at the Grande Chartreuse and as a representative of the pope during diplomatic missions.

Vincent was educated at Valencia and because of a keen intellect he completed his studies at the age of 14. The Dominicans accepted him into the order in 1367 and before he was 21 he began teaching philosophy. While retained by Cardinal Pedro de Luna, a papal legate, who was later to be antipope Benedict XIII, he was chosen confessor to Queen Yolanda of Aragon whom he served for four years.

During a life-threatening fever St. Francis and St. Dominic appeared to him, effected his miraculous cure and encouraged him to set out to preach penance and words of salvation. Supported by this vision and with the blessing of the pope he began the missionary journeys that would occupy the next 20 years of his life. His wanderings took him through Spain, Switzerland, France and Italy, where he singled out from among his listeners St. Margaret of Savoy and St. Bernardine of Siena, who would help in evangelizing Italy.

It is reported that he was followed by an army of penitents and that while speaking only Limousin, the language of Valencia, he was understood by many nationalities. His contemporary biographers maintain that he was endowed with the gift of tongues, an opinion supported by Nicholas Clemangis, a doctor of the University of Paris who was a witness to the marvel.

Miracles of healing punctuated his preachings, and his converts were numerous. His first biographer, Peter Razzano, estimates that 25,000 Jews were won to the Faith and that the number of converts among the Moors numbered in the thousands.

The saint steadfastly refused all honors and ecclesiastical promotions and continued to lead an austere life. The floor served as his bed and while his travels were rigorous he observed a perpetual fast, traveled on foot and wore the poorest of clothing.

His judgment was well respected as evidenced by his being called to decide which of six claimants was to be king of Aragon. At this same time, 1378-1417, the Great Western Schism divided the Church into two and then three papal obediences, with three popes claiming a right to the papal throne. The Council of Constance met in 1414 with the intention of having all three resign so that another could be elected. Only one refused to resign, Benedict XIII, a longtime friend of the saint. When asked to intercede in the matter and being unable to persuade his friend,

301

he declared that since Benedict was hindering union that was vital to the Church, the faithful were justified in withdrawing their allegiance. His pronouncement set in motion a unification of purpose with an election soon following. The saint is, therefore, credited with being directly responsible for ending the Great Schism.

Vincent became sick at Vannes, Brittany, in northern France and died on April 5, 1419. His canonization occurred in 1455 with his feast set for the anniversary of his death, April 5, a feast day still observed in the liturgy.

The house of his birth is still preserved in Valencia while the house of his death is likewise a place of interest in Vannes.

The relics of the saint are kept in the Cathedral of Vannes as is an ornate reliquary bust. A missionary cross was given by the saint to Saint Colette of the Monastery of Poor Clares, Besançon where it is still kept in an honored place above the altar in their chapel. It was St. Colette who prophesied that he would die within two years, not in his native Spain, but in France.

Bibliography

BOOKS FROM FOREIGN SOURCES

AUSTRIA
Hl. Johannes Von Nepomuk, 250 Jahre, Dommuseum zu Salzburg, Salzburg, 1979.

BELGIUM
De Abdij Van Dendermonde, Algemene Spaar-En Lijfrentekas, Brusselsestraat, Dendermonde.
St. Pieters En Paulusabdij, Dendermonde, Leaflet.

CZECHOSLOVAKIA
The Holy Infant of Prague, Kostel Prazského Jesulátka, Prague.

ENGLAND
Corathiel, Elizabethe, *Catholic Fireside*, Catholic Fireside Ltd., London, England, Vol. CL, March 26, 1959.

FRANCE
Berland, Dom J.M., *Saint-Benoit sur Loire*, Nouvelles Editions Latines, Paris, France.
The Cathedral of St. Lazarus at Autun, (Paper).
Curé of Ars, A Pilgrim's Guide, The Basilica of Ars, Editions Xavier Mappus, Lyon.
Delaporte, Yves, *Le Voile De Notre Dame*, Maison Des Clercs Dix-Huit, Cloître Notre-Dame, Chartres, 1927.
_____ *Les 3 Notre-Dame de la Cathedrale de Chartres*, E. Houvet, Chartres, 1955.
Fourault, Fr. *The Month of the Holy Face*, Oratory of the Holy Face, Tours, 1891.
LaCroix, Pierre Thomas, *Saint Vincent Ferrier*, Vannes, 1954.
La. Ste Tunique de A.S. en l'Eglise d'Argenteuil, (Paper).
Le Cloître de l'Abbaye, Faverney, (Paper).
L'Eglise-Forteresse des Saintes-Maries de la Mer, (Paper).
Le Miracle de Faverney, l'Abbatiale de Faverney, M. Lescuyer & Fils, Lyon, 1957.
Les Gitans aux Saintes-Maries de la Mer, (Paper).

Notre-Dame de Chartres, Revue Trimestrielle, Pèlerinage Notre-Dame, Chartres, Paris, Mars 1971 and Septembre 1976.
Ravier, S.J., André, *Bernadette, the Saint of Poverty and of Light*, Nouvelle Librairie de France, Besançon, 1974.
_____ *The Body of Saint Bernadette*, Convent of Saint Gildard.
_____ *Sainte Collette de Corbie*, Monastere de Ste Claire, Poligny, 1976.
Sainte Germaine-Pibrac, Pibrac Basilique, Pibrac, 1958.
Translation des Reliques de Saint Francois de Sales et de Sainte Jeanne-Françoise de Chantal, Guide-Manuel du Pelerin a Annecy, Annecy, 1911.

GERMANY
Bauer, Hermann, *St. Elisabeth Und Die Elisabethkirche zu Marburg*, Buchdruckerei Hermann Bauer Verlag, Marburg-Lahn, 1964.
Abtei St. Walburgh, *St. Walburg Eichstätt Kloster-Und-Pfarrkirche*, Druck: Funr-Druck, Eichstatt, 1967.
Leben und Wirken, *Heilige Walburga*, Abtei St. Walburg, Eichstätt, 1979.
Schulten, Walter, *Der Schrein Der Heiligen Drei Konige*, Luthe-Druck, Köln.
_____ *Cologne Cathedral*, Greven Verlag, Köln, 1977.
St. Walburg Eichstätt Kloster und Pfarrkirche, Abtei St. Walburg, Eichstätt-Bayern, 1967.
St. Walburga V, et Abb. O.S.B., Abtei St. Walburg, Eichstätt-Bayern, 1935.

IRELAND
Down Cathedral, The Cathedral of the Holy and Undivided Trinity, Down, Downpatrick.

ITALY
The Abbey of Monte Cassino, The Abbey.

Alfieri, Nereo, Edmondo Forlani, Floriano Grimaldi, *Contributi Archeologici Per La Storia Della Santa Casa Di Loreto*, Archivio Storico E Biblioteca Della Santa Casa, Loreto, 1977.

Angelini, Father Atanasio, *Life of Saint Rita of Cascia*, Poligrafico Alterocca, Terni, Italy.

Basilica of St. Nicholas in Tolentino, Santuario S. Nicola, Tolentino.

Bedini, S.O.Cist., D. Balduino, *Le Reliquie Sessoriane Della Passione Del Signore*, 1956.

Bollettino Di S. Nicola, Padri Domenicani, Basilica Di S. Nicola, Bari, 1951 and 1967.

Bottari, Stefano, *L'Arca Di S. Domenico in Bologna*, Casa Editrice Prof. Riccardo Patron, Bologna, 1964.

Calvino, Raffaele, *S. Luigi Gonzaga nella Basilica del Gesu Vecchio*, Napoli, 1969.

Calvo, Francesco, *Church of St. Ignatius-Rome*, Officine Grafiche Poligrafici il Resto del Carlino, Bologna.

Cioni, Raffaello, *S. Veronica Giuliani*, Libreria Editrice Fiorentina, Citta di Castello, 1951.

—— *S. Veronica Giuliani*, Monastero Delle Cappuccine, Citta di Castello, 1965.

D'Anghiari, O.F.M. Cap., Rev. Angelo Maria, *The Authenticity of the Holy House*, Congregazione Universale della Santa Casa, Loreto, 1967.

Drenkelfort, S.V.D., P. Heinrich, *The Basilica of the Holy Cross in Jerusalem*, Rome.

Elenco Delle Sacre Reliquie Nella Patriarcale Basilica Liberiana (Paper).

Gamboso, O.F.M. Conv., V. *St. Anthony of Padua*, EMP Messaggero Editions, Padova, Italy.

Gentili, Domenico, *Un Asceta E Un Apostolo S. Nicola Da Tolentino*, Editrice Ancora, Milano, 1966.

Gherardi, Luciano, *La. B. Clelia Barbieri*, Utoa, Bologna, 1969.

Gioacchino, Pelagatti, *Il S. Cingolo Mariano*, Santuario Madonna del Sacro Cingolo, Prato, 1937.

Gli Spedali Riuniti Di S. Chiara Nel VII Centenario Della Fondazione, Pisa, 1957.

Grimaldi, Siro, Uno Scienziato Adora, Cantagalli, Siena, 1956.

Gusmini, Card. Giorgio, *Beata Clelia Barbieri*, Edizioni Paoline, Bologna, 1968.

Il Miracolo Eucaristico Permanente Di Siena, by a cura dei Frati Minori Conventuali del Santuario Eucaristico di Siena, Siena, 1962.

Il Miracolo Permanente Di Siena, Santuario delle SS. Particole, Basilica S. Francesco, Siena.

Il Sacro Speco E Il Monastero Di Santa Scolastica, by a cura dei Benedettini di Subiaco, 1975.

Il Tesoro Eucaristico, Periodico Spiritualita Eucaristica, Siena, Gennaio-Febbraio, 1979.

Il Tesoro Eucaristico Nei Documenti Dell'Autorita Ecclesiastica, a cura dei Frati Minori Conventuali, Santuario delle SS. Particole, Siena, 1969.

Imperato, D. Giuseppe, *Un Testimone S. Pantaleone*, Ravello, 1970.

La. Basilica Di S. Giustina in Padova Arte E Storia, The Basilica di S. Giustina, Padova, 1970.

La Sacra Culla, Basilica St. Mary Major, Rome, (Paper).

La Tradizione Lauretana, Congregazione Universale Della Santa Casa, Loreto, 1977.

La Voce Del Pastore, Bollettino della Parrocchia di S. Andrea Ap. Amalfi, Oct. 1973, Feb. 1979, March 1979.

L'Osservatore Romano, Citta Del Vaticano, Anno CXI, Settembre 1971.

Mac Gowan, Kenneth, *The House of Loreto*, Congregazione Universale S. Casa, Loreto, 1976.

Matthiae, G., *San Pietro in Vincoli*, Edizioni Roma, Marietta, Rome, 1969.

Messaggero di S. Antonio, Basilica del Santo, Padova, Italy. Numerous issues.

Mortari, da Luisa, *Chiesa Santuario Di S. Maria Maddalena*, S. Maria Maddalena, Roma, 1969.

Mullen, O.F.M. Conv., Fr. Roland, *Miracle of Siena*, Siena, 1966.

Palmieri, Gian Giuseppe, *La Ricognizione Radiologica A Feretro Chiuso Dei Resti Di San Domenico*, Pontificia Academia Scientiarum, Anno VII, Vol. VII, N. 24, 1943.

Patavino, D. Jacobo Cavacio, *His-
toriarum Coenobii D. Justinae
Patavinae Libriex*, Monasterium Sanc-
tae Justinae, Patavii, 1696.

*Pellegrinaggio Spirituale Ossia Guida Del
Monastero Di S. Veronica Giuliani*,
Clarissa Cappuccina in Citta di
Castello, Citta Di Castello, 1927.

Politi, Mons. Antonio, *Ortona*, Editrice
Itinerari Lanciano, Ortona, 1974.

Prevedello, G. *Il Capo Di S. Luca Evange-
lista Di Padova E L'Imperatore Carlo
IV Re Di Boemia*, Abbazia Di S.
Giustina, Padova.

Ridolfini, Cecilia Pericoli, *St. Paul's Outside the Walls*, Il Resto del Carlino,
Bologna, 1977.

Romanelli, Emanuele, *Santa Maria in
Aracoeli*, Roma.

Rossetti, Felice M., *Una Delle Piu Grandi
Meraviglie*, Edizioni Periccioli, Siena,
1965.

Salotti, Msgr. Carlo, *La Beata Anna
Maria Taigi, Madre Di Famiglia*,
Libreria Editrice Religiosa, Francesco
Ferrari, Rome, 1922.

Salus Populi Romani, Basilica of St. Mary
Major, Rome, (Paper).

Salvatore, Prov. Lo Piccolo Don, *Pompei
Citta'Mariana*, Edito E Stampato dalla
Plurigraf, Narni-Terni, 1974.

Sammaciccia, Bruno, *The Eucharistic
Miracle of Lanciano, Italy*, Sanctuary
of the Eucharistic Miracle, Lanciano,
1977.

Santuario Basilica S. Francesco Paola, Basilica San Francesco, Paola.

*Santuario San Gerardo Maiella-Guida
Del Pellegrino*, Santuario San Gerardo
Maiella, Materdomini.

*Sanctuary of Our Mother of Good Coun-
sel*, Sanctuario Madonna del Buon
Consiglio, Genazzano.

Sanctuary of the Eucharistic Miracle,
Santuario Del Miracolo Eucaristico
Lanciano.

Scognamiglio, O.P., P. Pio, *La Manna Di
S. Nicola, Nella Storia, Nell'Arte,
Nella Scienza*, S.T.E.B., Societa Tipo-
grafica Editrice Barese, Bari, 1925.

*Solenni Celebrazzioni Per La Reposizione
Delle Sacre Ossa Di S. Nicola*,
Bolletino Di S. Nicola, Numero Spe-
ciale, Bari, 1957.

St. Patricia, Virgin, Patroness of Naples,
Monastery of S. Gregorio Armeno,
Naples, 1954.

St. Paul's Outside the Walls, Basilica St.
Paul's Outside the Walls, Rome.

Tansey, Anne, *Chalice of Art and Mystery*, Messaggero di S. Antonio, Basilica Del Santo, Padova, Italy, February
1981.

Tescari, Sante, *Il Tempio Di S. Giustina
V. E.M. In Padova*, Tempio di St.
Giustina, Padova, 1853.

Urbani, O.F.M. Cap., Fr. Fabian, *The
Shrine of the Holy House*, Loreto,
Vol. 6, No. 4, 1973.

Vanti, S.O.S. Cam., P. Mario, *St.
Camillus the Saint of the Red Cross*,
published by the Order of St.
Camillus, Rome, 1950.

—— *San Camillo*, Basilica S. Maria Maddalena, Rome, 1960.

Villa, P. Giuseppe, *Un Uomo Che Sapeva
Amare*, S. Giuliano, Verona, 1977.

LEBANON

Blessed Sharbel, The Hermit of Lebanon,
Monastery of Annaya, Lebanon.

Daher, Paul, *A Miraculous Star in the
East, Charbel Makhlouf*, Lebanese
Maronite Monastery of Annaya,
Beirut, Lebanon.

—— Charbel, *Un Homme Ivre De Dieu*,
Monastere S. Maron D'Annaya, Jbail,
Liban, 1965.

PORTUGAL

Mowatt, Archpriest John H., *The Holy
and Miraculous Icon of Our Lady of
Kazan*, Byzantine Center Domus
Pacis, Fatima, Portugal.

SICILY

The Weeping Madonna, Sanctuary of
Our Lady of Tears of Syracuse, 20th
anniversary issue 1953-1973, and the
silver jubilee issue 1953-1978.

Musumeci, Dr. Ottavio, *The Madonna
Wept In Syracuse*, Santuario Madonna Delle Lacrime, Siracusa, 1954.

SPAIN

Beltran, Antonio, *El Santo Caliz*, Catedral
de Valencia, Valencia, 1960.

Boix, Maur M., *What is Montserrat, A
Mountain, A Sanctuary, A Monastery, A Spiritual Community*, Publicacions De L'Abadia De Montserrat,
Barcelona, 1976.

Bruguera, Dom Justino, *Montserrat*, Editorial Planeta, Barcelona, 1964.

deLeon, S.J., J.M. Gomez, *The Sanctuary of Loyola*, Santuario de Loyola, Azpeitia.

Salo, Juan Gasca, *Preve Noticia del Pilar*, La Parroquia de Nuestra Senora del Pilar, Zaragoza, 1977.

_____ *Ritual del Peregrino Nuestra Senora del Pilar*, Zaragoza, (Paper).

Santuario De Loyola, (Pamphlet).

A Visit to the Relic Chapels of the First Monastery of the Discalced Carmelite Nuns Founded by St. Teresa of Jesus, the Carmelitas Descalzas de S. Jose, Avila.

Selected Bibliography

Abbott, S.J., Walter M., general editor, *The Documents of Vatican II*, Guild Press, America Press, Association Press. An Angelus Book, 1966.

Adams, Henry, *Mont-Saint-Michel and Chartres*, Houghton Mifflin Co., Boston, 1963.

Aradi, Zsolt, *Shrines to Our Lady Around the World*, Farrar, Straus & Young, New York, 1954.

_____ *The Book of Miracles*, Farrar, Straus & Cudahy, New York, 1956.

Art Treasures in France, McGraw-Hill, New York, 1969.

Art Treasures in Italy, McGraw-Hill Book Go., New York, 1969.

Attwater, Donald, *A Catholic Dictionary*, The Macmillan Co., New York, 1958.

Auffray, S.D.B., A., *Saint John Bosco*, Salesian House, Tirupattur, South India, 1930.

Barbet, M.D., Pierre, *A Doctor at Calvary*, Image Books, Doubleday & Co., Inc., Garden City, New York, 1953.

Bougaud, Monseigneur, Bishop of Laval, *St. Chantal and the Foundation of the Visitation*, Benziger Bros., New York, 1895.

Brewer, LL.D., E. Cobham, *A Dictionary of Miracles*, Cassell & Co. Inc., New York, 1884.

Bruno De J. M., O.D.C., *Three Mystics*, Sheed & Ward, New York, 1949.

_____ *St. John of the Cross*, Sheed & Ward, London, 1936.

Buehrle, Marie Cecilia, *Saint Maria Goretti*, Bruce Publishing Co., Milwaukee, 1950.

Bussard, Fr. Paul, publisher, *Our Lady of Chartres in France*, Catholic Digest, Inc., St. Paul, Minn., 1959.

_____ *Our Lady of the Miraculous Medal in France*, Catholic Digest, Inc., St. Paul, Minn., 1959

_____ *Our Lady of Lourdes in France*, Catholic Digest, Inc., St. Paul, Minn., 1958.

Butler; Thurston; Attwater; *The Lives of the Saints*, P.J. Kenedy & Sons, New York, 1936, 12 Volumes.

Camillus De Lellis the Hospital Saint, Benziger Bros., New York, 1917.

Carrico, James A., *Life of Venerable Mary of Agreda*, Crestline Book Company, San Bernardino, Calif., 1959.

Cartwright, Rt. Rev. John K., *The Catholic Shrines of Europe*, McGraw-Hill Co., New York, 1954.

Cassidy, Joseph L., *Mexico, Land of Mary's Wonders*, St. Anthony Guild Press, Paterson, N.J., 1958.

The Catholic Encyclopedia, The Encyclopedia Press, Inc., New York, 1912.

The Catholic Register, Toronto, Canada, July 12, 1980.

Charboneau, O.S.M., Damian Mary, *Saint Peregrine Laziosi, O.S.M., The Cancer Saint*, National Shrine of St. Peregrine, O.S.M., Chicago, 1954.

Clarion Herald, Archdiocese of New Orleans, Vol. 6, No. 6, April 4, 1968.

Clasen, O.F.M., Sophronius, *St. Anthony, Doctor of the Gospel*, Franciscan Herald Press, Chicago, Ill. 1960.

Columbia magazine, Vol. LX No. 5, May 1980, and Vol. LIX No. 6, June 1979, New Haven, Conn.

Corcoran, O.S.A., Rev. M.J., *A Life of the Saint of the Impossible*, Benziger Bros., New York, 1919.
—— *Our Own St. Rita*, Benziger Brothers, New York, 1919.
Coyne, William D., *Our Lady of Knock*, Catholic Book Publishing Co., New York, 1948.
Cristiani, Msgr. Leon, *Saint Francis of Assisi*, Daughters of St. Paul, 1975.
Cruz, Joan Carroll, *The Incorruptibles*, Tan Books & Publishers, Inc., Rockford, Ill., 1977.
Daher, O.L.M., Paul, *A Cedar of Lebanon*, The Philosophical Library, New York, 1957.
De Montalembert, Count, *The Life of Saint Elizabeth*, P.J. Kenedy & Sons, New York.
De Rivieres, F. Philipin, *Holy Places: Their Sanctity and Authenticity*, London, 1874.
De Spens, Willey, *St. Rita*, Hanover House, Garden City, New York, 1960.
Devotion to the Infant Jesus of Prague, Benedictine Convent of Perpetual Adoration, Clyde, Mo., 1968
Divine Love, The Apostolate of Christian Action, Fresno, Calif., Vol. 21 No. 3-4, 1978.
Dolan, O.Carm., Albert H., *Where the Little Flower Seems Nearest*, The Carmelite Press, Chicago, Ill., 1928.
Dooley, S.V.D., Rev. L.M., *That Motherly Mother of Guadalupe*, St. Paul Editions, Boston, Mass., 1962.
Dorcy, O.P., Sr. Mary Jean, *Shrines of Our Lady*, Sheed and Ward, New York, 1956.
Dowse, Ivor R., *The Pilgrim Shrines of England*, The Faith Press, London, 1963.
Duby, Georges, *The Europe of the Cathedrals, 1140-1280*, Skira, Geneva, Switzerland, 1966.
Ebon, Martin, *Saint Nicholas: Life and Legend*, Harper & Row, New York, 1975.
Englebert, Omer, *The Lives of the Saints*, Collier Books, New York, 1964.
Emmerich, Anne Catherine, *The Dolorous Passion of Our Lord Jesus Christ*, Burns & Oates, London, 1955.
Flowering of the Middle Ages, McGraw-Hill Book Co., New York, 1966.

Gainor, O.P., Rev. Leo C., *St. Jude Thaddeus, His Life and His Work*, Catechetical Guild Educational Society, St. Paul, Minn., 1956.
Gheon, Henri, *St. Vincent Ferrer*, Sheed & Ward, New York, 1939.
Glories of Czestochowa and Jasna Gora, Millennium Edition, Our Lady of Czestochowa Foundation, Massachussets, 1966.
Govern, C.SS.R., Raymond F., *Saint John Neumann, C.SS.R.*, Redemptorist Fathers, St. Petersburg, 1980.
Grant, Ian, *The Testimony of Blood*, Burns & Oates, London, 1929.
Gueranger, Rev. Prosper, *Life of Saint Cecilia*, Peter F. Cunningham, Philadelphia.
Gunta, L., *Saint Peter's Vatican City*, Artistic-Religious Guide, Rome, 1954.
Haffert, John M., editor, *Soul Magazine*, Ave Maria Institute, Washington, N.J., 1978, Vol. 29 No. 4.
Harvey, John *The Cathedrals of Spain*, Bt. Batsford, Ltd., London, 1957.
History of the Precious Remains of Saint Frances Xavier Cabrini, Mother Cabrini High School, New York, (Paper).
Hoagland, M.D., Arthur N., *Miracle at Santarem*, (Paper).
Hoever, S.O. Cist., Rev. Hugo H., *Saint Bernard, The Oracle of the 12th Century*, Catholic Book Publishing Co., New York, 1952.
Holisher, Desider, *The Eternal City, Rome of the Popes*, Frederick Ungar Publishing Co., New York, 1943.
Hollis, Christopher, and Ronald Brownrigg, *Holy Places*, Frederick A. Praeger, Pub., New York, 1969.
Holy Miracle of Santarem, (Paper).
Horgan, Paul, *Rome Eternal*, Farrar, Straus and Cudahy, New York, 1959.
Horizon Book of Great Cathedrals, American Heritage Pub. Co., New York, 1968.
John Neumann, C.SS.R., The Immigrant Shepherd, St. Anthony Guild, Paterson, N.J., 1973.
Keyes, Frances Parkinson, *St. Anne, Grandmother of Our Saviour*, Julian Messner, Inc., New York, 1955.
—— *The Grace of Guadalupe*, Julian Messner, Inc., New York, 1941.

Larned, Walter Cranston, *Churches and Castles of Mediaeval France*, Charles Scribner's Sons, New York, 1906.

Lees-Milne, James, *St. Peter's: The Story of St. Peter's Basilica in Rome*, Little, Brown & Co., Boston, 1967.

Life and Revelations of Saint Gertrude, The Newman Press, Westminster, Md., 1949.

Life, Virtues and Miracles of St. Gerard Majella, A Lay Brother of the Congregation of the Most Holy Redeemer, Mission Church, Boston, Mass., 1907.

Madden, Daniel M., *A Religious Guide to Europe*, Macmillan, New York.

—— *Saint Ignatius: A Model for Men with a Mission*, *Columbia* magazine, Vol. LIX, Nov. 1979, New Haven, Conn.

Manton, C.SS.R., Rev. Joseph, *Bishop John Nepomucene Neumann, C.SS.R., D.D., Fourth Bishop of Philadelphia*, The Catechetical Guild, Huntington, Ind., 1960.

Manual of Devotions, National Shrine of Our Lady of Prompt Succor, Ursuline Convent, New Orleans, 1963.

Mary of Agreda, *The City of God*, The Theopolitan, Chicago, Ill., 1913.

Maus, Pearl, *The World's Great Madonnas*, Harper & Row, New York, 1947.

Mirsky, Jeannette, *Houses of God*, The Viking Press, New York, 1965.

New Catholic Encyclopedia, Catholic University of America, McGraw-Hill Co., New York, 1967.

Our Lady Patroness of the Americas, Franciscan Marytown Press, Kenosha, Wis., 1974.

Rahm, S.J., Harold, *Am I Not Here?*, AMI Press, Washington, N.J., 1963.

Schmoger, C.SS.R., Carl E., *The Life of Anne Catherine Emmerich*, Tan Books & Publishers, Inc., Rockford, Ill., 1976, Vol. II.

Schuster, O.S.B., His Eminence Ildephonse, *St. Benedict and His Times*, B. Herder Book Co., St. Louis, Mo., 1951.

Seton Shrine Chapel, Daughters of Charity, St. Joseph's Provincial House, Emmitsburg, Md.

Sharp, Mary, *A Guide to the Churches of Rome*, Chilton Books, Philadelphia and New York, 1966.

Singleton, Esther, *Famous Cathedrals as Seen and Described by Great Writers*, Dodd, Mead & Co., New York, 1909.

Society of Saint Mary Magdalene, Newton Lower Falls (leaflet).

Society of Saint Mary Magdalene, Dighton, Mass. (leaflet).

Soul Magazine, Blue Army of Our Lady, Washington, N.J., July-August 1975 and May-June 1978.

St. Anne De Beaupre in Canada, Catholic Digest, Inc., St. Paul, Minn., 1957.

St. Catherine Laboure, The Association of the Miraculous Medal, Perryville, Mo., 1948.

Stevenson, Kenneth E., and Gary R. Habermas, *Verdict on the Shroud*, Servant Books, Ann Arbor, Mich., 1981.

St. James of Compostela in Spain, Catholic Digest, Inc., St. Paul, Minn., 1958.

Stoddard, Whitney S. *Monastery and Cathedral in France*, Wesleyan Univ. Press, Middletown, Conn., 1966.

Taralon, Jean, *Treasures of the Churches of France*, George Braziller, Inc., New York, 1966.

Thornton, Francis Beauchesne, *Catholic Shrines in the United States and Canada*, Wilfred Funk, Inc., New York, 1954.

Thurston, S.J., Herbert, *The Physical Phenomena of Mysticism*, Henry Regnery Co., Chicago, 1952.

Toynbee, Jocelyn and John Ward Perkins, *Shrine of St. Peter and the Vatican Excavations*, Pantheon Books, New York, 1957.

Wilcox, Robert K., *Shroud*, Macmillan Publishing Co., Inc., New York, 1977.

Wilson, Ian, *The Shroud of Turin, The Burial Cloth of Jesus Christ?*, Doubleday & Co., Garden City, N.Y., 1978.

Wilson, Robert H., *St. John Neumann, Fourth Bishop of Philadelphia*, Institutional Services, Inc., Archdiocese of Philadelphia, Philadelphia, 1977.

Zappulli, Cesare, *The Power of Goodness, The Life of Blessed Clelia Barbieri*, St. Paul Editions, The Daughters of St. Paul, Boston, 1980.

Zayek, S.T.D., Bishop Francis M., *A New Star of the East*, Diocese of St. Maron, New York, 1977.

Zinkin, Taya, *India*, Walker & Co., New York, 1965.